Take-Home Leveled Readers

On-level

Science

Editorial Offices: Glenview, Illinois • Parsippany, New Jersey • New York, New York
Sales Ofices: Needham, Massachusetts • Duluth, Georgia • Glenview, Illinois
Coppell, Texas • Sacramento, California • Mesa, Arizona

PEARSON
Scott Foresman

sfsuccessnet.com

Table of Contents

To the Teacher

Scott Foresman provides three Leveled Readers for every chapter of *Scott Foresman Science*, Grades 1–6: a *Below-Level Leveled Reader*, an *On-Level Leveled Reader*, and an *Advanced Leveled Reader*.

All three readers teach the same science concepts, same vocabulary, address the same target reading skill and contain the same graphic organizer as the corresponding student edition chapter, just at three different reading levels—providing access to important science content for all students. The On-level and Advanced readers also use additional examples to enrich the chapter and extend ideas

This book contains reproducible copies of the On-Level Leveled Readers for Grade 5. These are designed for you to reproduce and send home with your students as appropriate. Encourage students to share these books with parents or family members in order to practice reading skills and reinforce science content.

Online versions of these and other readers are also available through the Scott Foresman Leveled Reader Database.

Grouping Living Things

by Patricia Walsh

Genre	Comprehension Skill	Text Features	Science Content
Nonfiction	Compare and Contrast	• Labels • Captions • Charts • Glossary	Classifying Organisms

Scott Foresman Science 5.1

PEARSON
Scott Foresman
scottforesman.com

DK

ISBN 0-328-13917-3

9 780328 139170

90000

What did you learn?

1. What are the benefits of a scientific classification system?

2. Which is the largest group in the classification of organisms? Which is the smallest, or most specific, group?

3. Why do scientists use Latin to name organisms?

4. **Writing** in Science The classification system originally had only two kingdoms: plant and animal. Write to explain how and why the system has changed and how it might continue to change in the future. Include details from the book to support your answer.

5. **Compare and Contrast** How are the animal kingdom and the plant kingdom alike and different?

Picture Credits
Every effort has been made to secure permission and provide appropriate credit for photographic material.
The publisher deeply regrets any omission and pledges to correct errors called to its attention in subsequent editions.

Photo locators denoted as follows: Top (T), Center (C), Bottom (B), Left (L), Right (R), Background (Bkgd).

Opener: Paul Nicklen/NGS Image Collection; 4 (T) ©Kennan Ward/Corbis;
5 (TCR, CAR, CAR1, CR, CBR, BCR) ©Darren Bennett/Animals Animals/Earth Scenes, (TL, CLA, CL) ©Darrell Gulin/Corbis;
6 (T) ©T. Beveridge/Visuals Unlimited, (CL) ©Stanley Flegler/Visuals Unlimited, (CL) Corbis, (CL) ©Michael Fogden/
Animals Animals/Earth Scenes, (BC) ©D. Robert & Lorri Franz/Corbis; 7 (T) ©Jerry Young/DK Images;
14 Paul Nicklen/NGS Image Collection; 19 (TL) ©American Museum of Natural History/DK Images;
22 Doug Wechsler /Nature Picture Library.

Unless otherwise acknowledged, all photographs are the copyright © of Dorling Kindersley, a division of Pearson.

ISBN: 0-328-13917-3

Glossary

class	the level of classification below phylum
classify	to use a system to put things into groups
invertebrates	animals without backbones
kingdom	highest and most general group of organisms in the classification system
phylum	second level of classification below kingdom
species	lowest level of classification that names a particular kind of plant or animal
vertebrates	animals with backbones

Grouping Living Things

by Patricia Walsh

PEARSON
Scott Foresman

DK

What is a classification system?

Let's say you've just returned from grocery shopping. You bring the shopping bags into the kitchen. Now, where do all these things go? Let's put the frozen food away first. Frozen vegetables go into the freezer. Eggs, milk, and cheese go into the refrigerator. Canned foods go on the top shelf of the cabinet. Boxes of cereal go on the bottom shelf. Bread goes in the breadbox. Toothpaste belongs in the bathroom. Where will you put the fruit and vegetables? They might go into the refrigerator or maybe in a bowl on the kitchen table.

kestrel

clown fish

golden beetle

iguana

Everything is all ordered, right? Not so fast! Scientists continue to discover new organisms all the time. Sometimes they debate where the new organisms should go in the classification system. Is it a plant? Is it an animal? Is it something else? Today's scientists are still trying to put the world in order. To do this, they sometimes add to or even change the classification system. Classifying organisms helps us better understand our planet and know more about the living things in our world.

Now, let's see if you can recall the classification system of organisms. Did you remember that the different levels are kingdom, phylum, class, order, family, genus, and species? Here's a sentence that might help you: **K**ing **P**hillip **C**ome **O**ut **F**or **G**oodness' **S**ake. The first letter of each word is the same as the first letter of the level in the classification system.

You have just sorted the groceries. You used a classification system. Your system tells you that frozen food goes into the freezer and canned goods go on a shelf. Your classification system helps avoid confusion. Once everything is in its place, everyone in your family will know where to find it. Classifying happens in science too. All organisms, or living things, are put into groups. Why do scientists **classify** organisms? They want to make sense of our living world. They also want to be sure that all scientists use the same name for each organism, so they always know exactly what they're talking about.

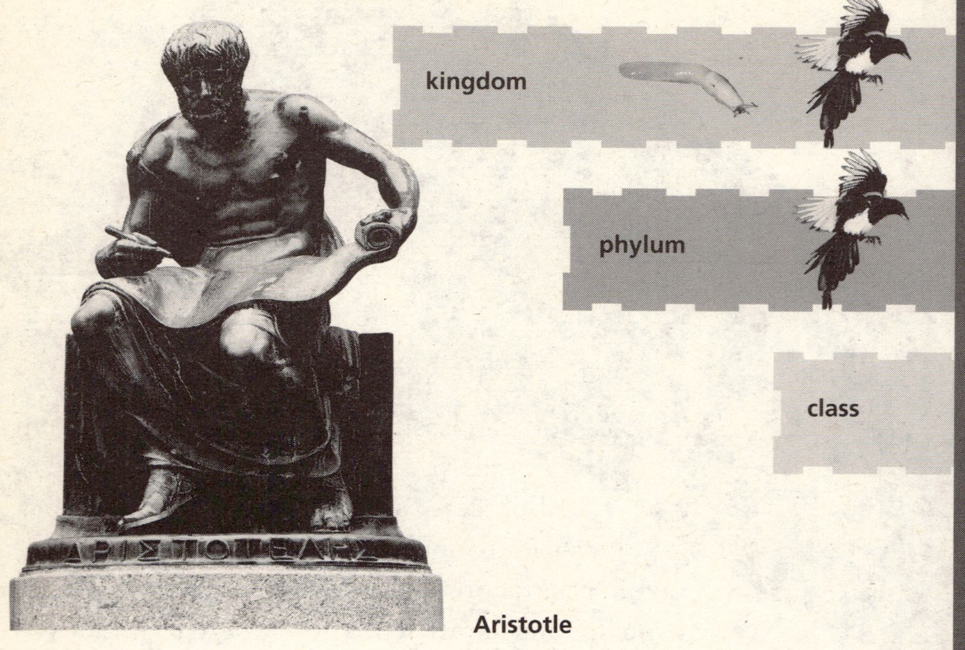

Aristotle

History of The Classification System

More than two thousand years ago, a man named Aristotle came up with one of the first classifying systems. He looked at organisms and decided whether they were plants or animals. It was the first step in ordering living things.

About five hundred years ago, scientists started using Latin as the language for naming organisms. They chose Latin because it was a language that scientists from many different countries knew. Modern scientists still use it for the same reason.

Archaebacteria

Archaebacteria may just be the toughest things on Earth! They can survive in places that would kill any other organism. These tiny single-celled life forms do well in boiling springs where the water is full of acid. Some of them live deep in the ocean, around vents where very hot water shoots out of the Earth. This environment has no light or oxygen, and is under great pressure from the weight of the water above. The archaebacteria survive there by turning chemicals in the water into energy.

Archaebacteria living around deep sea vents provide food for other animals.

Eubacteria

Have you been sick lately? Eubacteria may be to blame! These single-celled organisms can cause illnesses like strep throat. Most eubacteria are helpful to people, though. Some of them produce vitamins. Some even help people make yogurt! Eubacteria come in many different shapes, such as spheres or spirals.

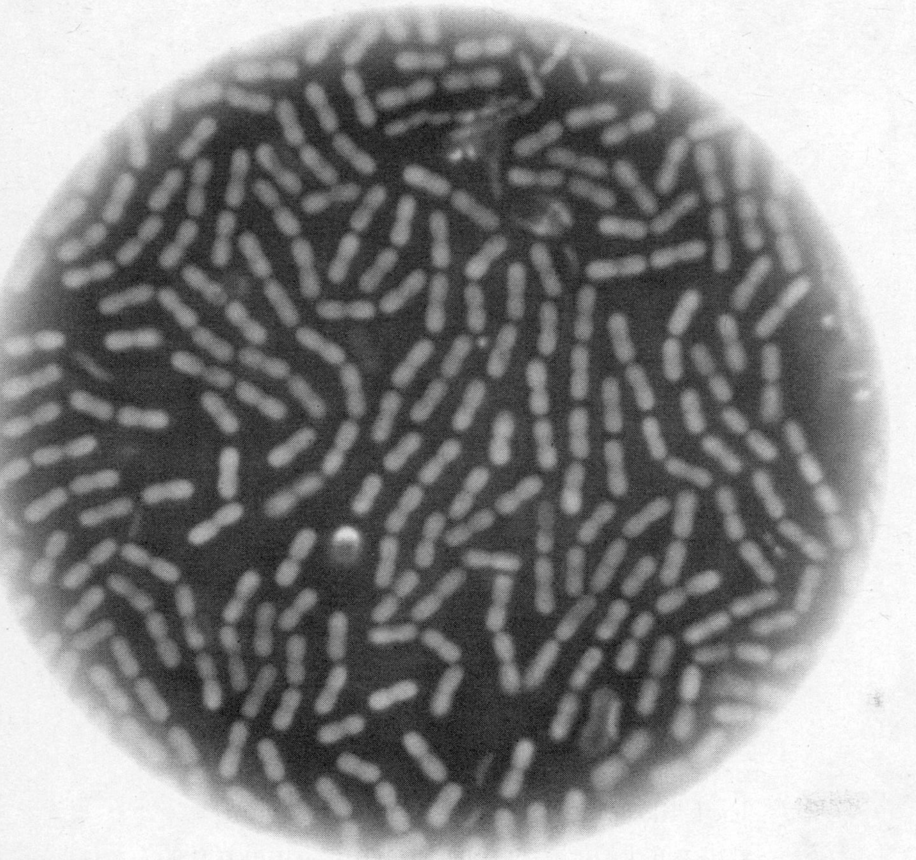

bacteria

Through the years, scientists kept working at ordering and naming organisms. The classification system used by many scientists today has seven levels. **Kingdom** is the highest level. It is the most general group of organisms. **Species** is the lowest level. It is the most specific group of organisms.

Kingdom

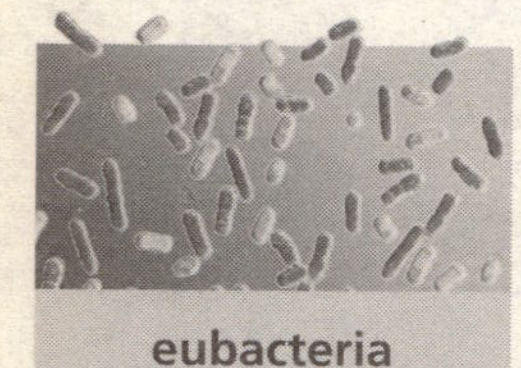

archaebacteria

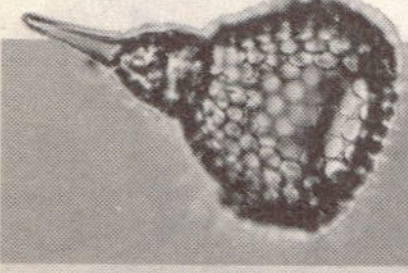

eubacteria

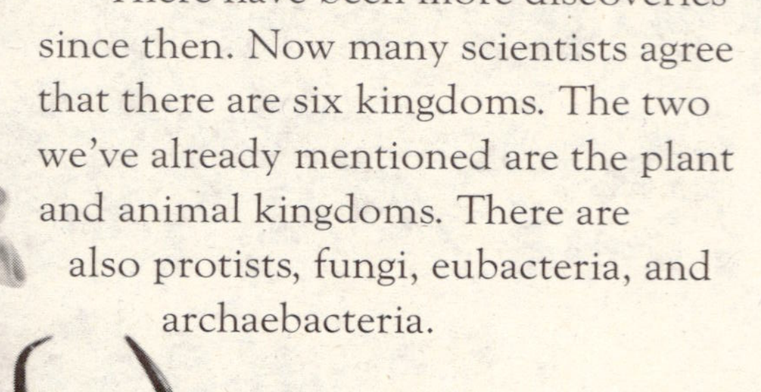

protist

fungi

plant

There are six kingdoms in the living world. Remember Aristotle? He classified everything into the huge kingdoms of plants and animals. This two-kingdom system worked pretty well until the microscope was invented. Then scientists discovered tiny, single-celled organisms that were neither plants nor animals. In the nineteenth century, a German scientist came up with a third kingdom for these living things. He called them protists.

There have been more discoveries since then. Now many scientists agree that there are six kingdoms. The two we've already mentioned are the plant and animal kingdoms. There are also protists, fungi, eubacteria, and archaebacteria.

animal

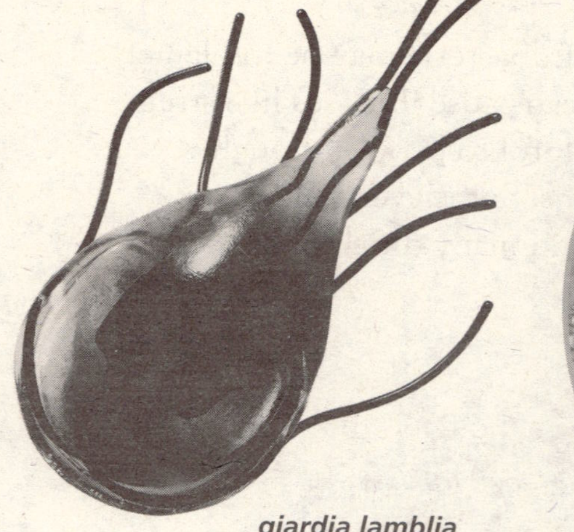

giardia lamblia

green alga

Protists

Protists are tiny life forms. Many are just a single cell. Some, like algae, live in colonies of cells. Others live inside the digestive systems of animals. Cows and termites could not survive without the protists that help them digest their food.

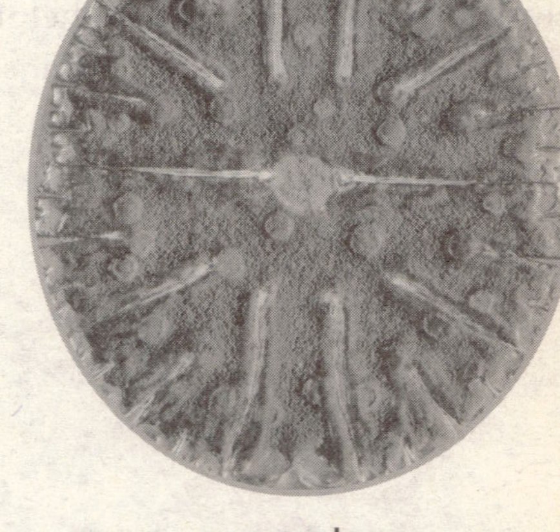

Fungi

You have probably seen fungi before. In fact, you've probably eaten some! These organisms include mushrooms and yeast. Many fungi look like plants, but they are not. Plants can make their own food, while fungi must absorb it from the material they grow on.

Other Kingdoms

If someone asks you to list some life forms, you'll probably start with things such as cats, dogs, monkeys, and elephants. You might also include flowers and trees. But plants and animals are really only part of the picture when talking about living things. Many scientists group life into four other kingdoms besides plants and animals. The organisms that fall into these kingdoms have some things in common with plants and animals. They all need food, water, habitats, and a way to get rid of waste. Many also need oxygen or carbon dioxide.

Phylum and Class

Level two is called **phylum.** In the animal kingdom you'll find the phylum chordata with the subphylum of **vertebrates,** or animals with a backbone. Then there are the many phyla of **invertebrates,** or animals without a backbone. The mollusk phylum contains snails and slugs. The annelid phylum contains certain kinds of worms.

Class is the level under phylum. The five classes in the vertebrate subphylum are mammals, reptiles, birds, amphibians, and fish. What about all those invertebrates such as spiders and insects and lobsters? Well, they are each a class in the largest phylum called arthropods.

Order

There are four more levels to go in the classification system. The next one is order. These groups are based on their differences. For example, birds are a class, but the class is divided into orders of birds that perch, birds that are woodpeckers, and birds that are penguins. They are all birds, but each order is different from the others.

The conifer phylum includes pine trees, fir trees, and spruce trees. The needles you find on these trees are actually special leaves. Conifers are vascular like ferns, but they are different because they produce cones. The cones hold the seeds that will become new conifer trees.

Flowering plants are also vascular like ferns and conifers. As the name tells you, it is the only one of these four phyla that produces flowers. The flowers become seeds and the seeds grow into new flowering plants.

The Plant Kingdom

Does the organism you are studying use sunlight, water, and carbon dioxide to make sugar for food? If yes, then it's in the plant kingdom. Four phyla of plants that you may have seen are mosses, ferns, conifers, and flowering plants.

Mosses, which can be found on trees and along streams, have tiny leaf-like structures. They do not have flowers or seeds. Ferns grow in woodlands. They are often kept as houseplants. Ferns are vascular, which means that tubes carry food and water to the different parts of the plant. Mosses are different from ferns in that they are not vascular. Neither mosses nor ferns produce seeds. Instead, they reproduce through tiny bodies called spores.

ferns

Family, Genus, and Species

The last three levels are family, genus, and species. In a family, all the members look alike in important ways and have similar characteristics. Members of one family might all have webbed feet or long necks. Genus is a smaller group within the family. Species is the lowest and most specific level.

Felis domestica

Felis cougar

Felis leo

Scientific Names

It is the last two levels, genus and species, that give each animal and plant its scientific name. Here's how the naming system works. *Felis*, the Latin word for cat, is the genus that includes big and small cats. *Felis* plus the species name tell us that the house cat is *Felis domestica*. The cougar is *Felis cougar*. The lion is *Felis leo*.

The Animal Kingdom

How does each organism get put into its correct group? A scientist looks at a plant or an animal very carefully and compares it with others. The scientist wants to find out how the plant or animal is like other species and how it is different. Scientists study an organism's life cycle to find out more about it. A life cycle is a pattern of birth, growth, reproduction, and death.

Is the organism made up of more than one cell? Does it get energy by eating other organisms? Does it move on its own? If yes, then it's in the animal kingdom. Does the animal have a backbone? Yes, so it's in the subphylum of vertebrates. Does the animal breathe air with lungs and make milk for its young? Does the animal have hair or fur? Are its young born looking very much like the parent animals? Then it's in the class called mammals.

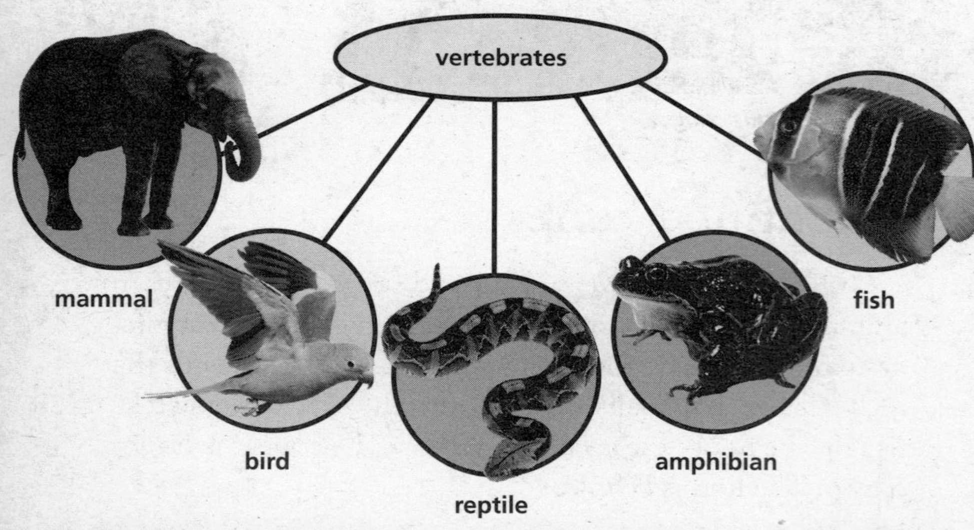

Using a Dichotomous Key

A dichotomous key is a series of questions you can answer to figure out just what kind of organism you are looking at. There are different keys for different kinds of life forms. For example, some keys are for identifying arthropods, while others are for mammals.

The key below is for arthropods. As you answer each question on the key, you follow the correct arrow to the next question. Keep answering questions till you come to the name of the animal you are looking at. For example, the first question asks how many legs the animal has. The animal shown has eight legs, so you'll follow the arrow that says "eight." Now the key asks if the animal has claws. This animal does not have claws, so you follow the arrow to "no." This box tells you that the animal is a spider.

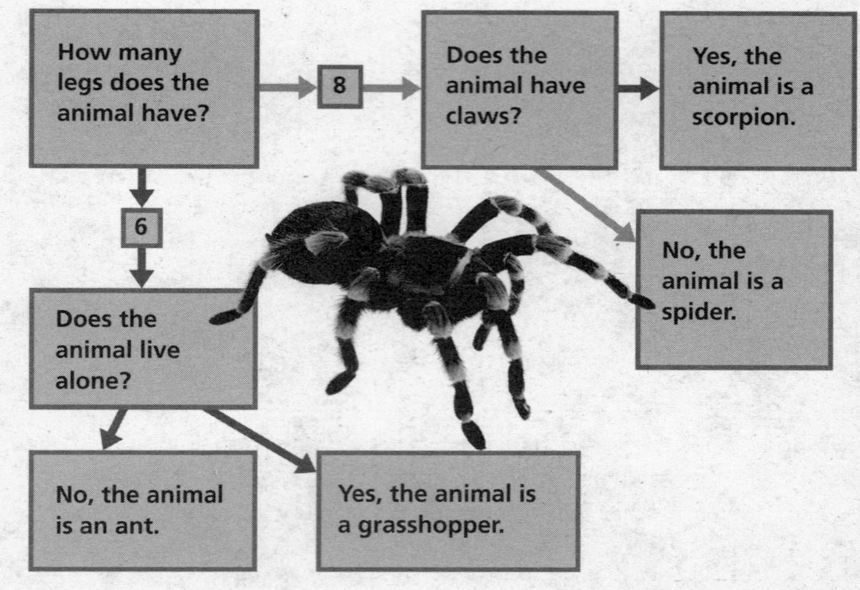

The phylum Cnidaria contains jellyfish and coral. Jellyfish have very strange life cycles. They hatch from eggs and swim around for a few days or weeks. Then they attach to the ocean floor. At this stage they are called polyps. The polyp grows and bits of it fall off, forming new jellyfish.

You have probably seen a few arthropods lately. They are in the air, in our houses, and even at seafood restaurants! Arthropods are the largest phylum of animals on Earth. This phylum includes insects, spiders, and lobsters. *Arthropod* means "jointed feet." Many arthropods go through big changes during their life cycles. These changes are called metamorphosis. One example of metamorphosis is when a caterpillar turns into a butterfly.

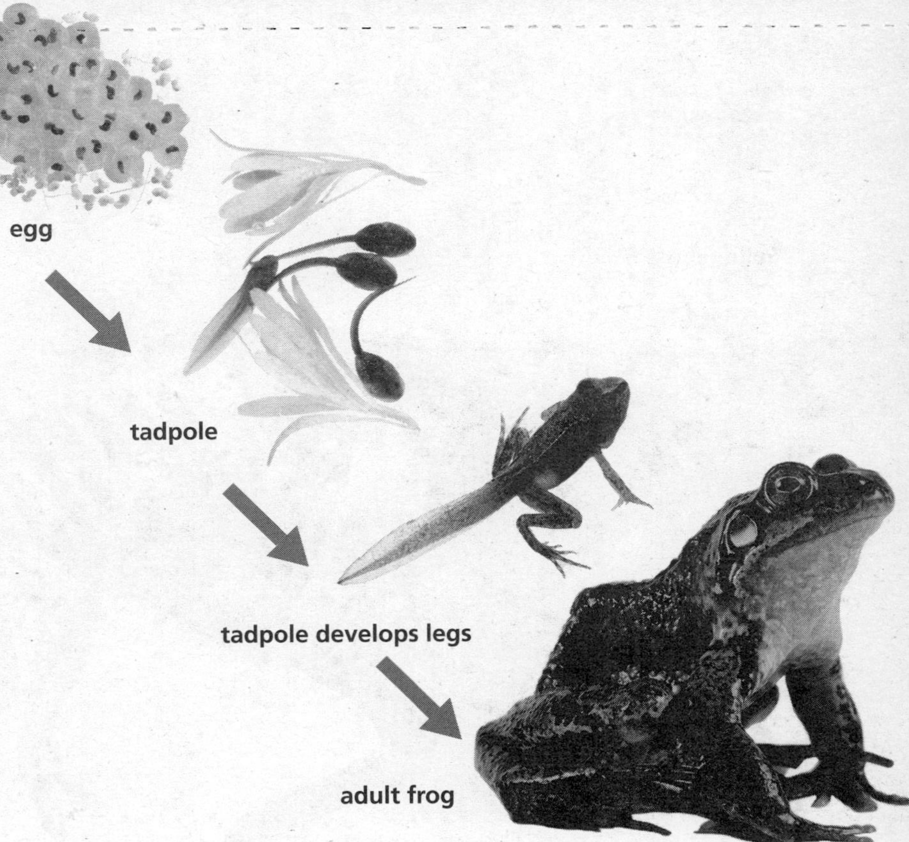

Not all animals are mammals. What if the animal has lungs for breathing air like a mammal, but it doesn't have fur or hair? Instead it has dry skin with scales. It is cold-blooded and its young hatch from eggs. An animal like this belongs to the reptile class.

What if the animal has feathers and its young hatch from eggs? This animal is a bird.

What if you have a cold-blooded animal that looks a lot like a reptile, but its moist, soft skin absorbs water and oxygen? Its young do not look like the parents, and they go through a big change called metamorphosis. This animal must belong to the amphibian class.

Gallimimus

What if the animal you are studying has no backbone? It must be from one of the many phyla of invertebrates. In the phylum of mollusks you'll find animals with soft bodies, and often with hard shells for protection. The phylum of mollusks includes the classes of snails, slugs, clams, and octopuses.

Worms are divided into many different groups. Flatworms, roundworms, and segmented worms each have their own phylum. Worms come in all shapes and sizes. Some worms are so small they can only be seen with a microscope. Others can be longer than a car!

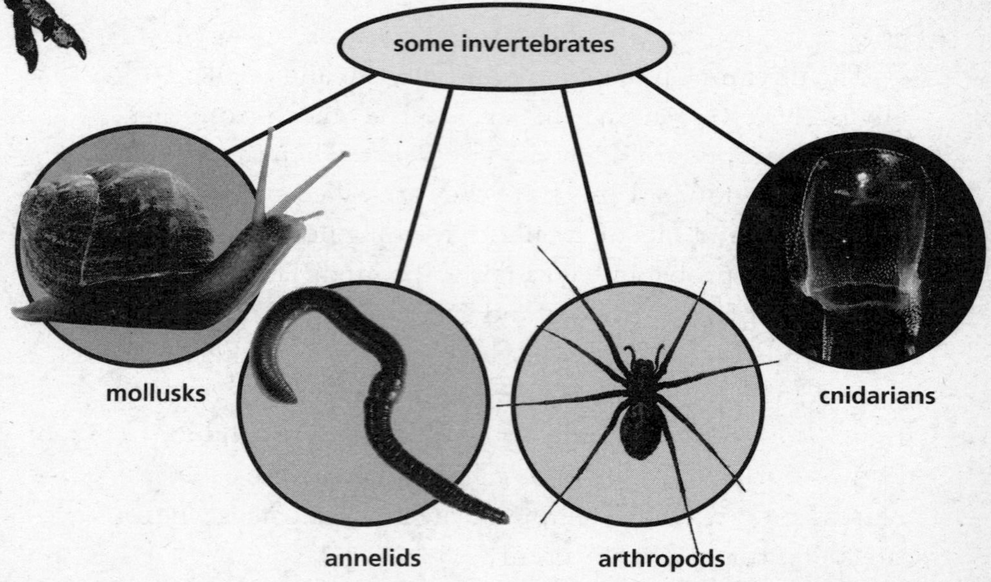

The discovery of dinosaur fossils raises many questions for scientists. These animals of long ago looked like lizards of today, which belong to the reptile class. Dinosaurs had backbones, which makes them vertebrates. They also had scales and walked on four legs. But some dinosaurs had feathers and bones like birds. Sometimes fossil finds create more questions than answers.

Cells, Tissues, Organs, Systems

by Donna Latham

Genre	Comprehension Skill	Text Features	Science Content
Nonfiction	Draw Conclusions	• Labels • Call Outs • Diagrams • Glossary	Cells to Systems

Scott Foresman Science 5.2

What did you learn?

1. Why are cells known as "life's building blocks"?

2. Give an example of how a cell's shape helps it to perform a specific job.

3. What kinds of tissues come together to form your skin?

4. **Writing** in Science Organ systems work together to do your body's complex jobs. Write to explain how several systems work together to help you move. Include details from the book to support your answer.

5. **Draw Conclusions** Without the skeleton, what would your body be like?

Picture Credits
Every effort has been made to secure permission and provide appropriate credit for photographic material. The publisher deeply regrets any omission and pledges to correct errors called to its attention in subsequent editions.

Photo locators denoted as follows: Top (T), Center (C), Bottom (B), Left (L), Right (R), Background (Bkgd).

Opener: Dr. Dennis Kunkel/Visuals Unlimited; 3 Dr. Dennis Kunkel/Visuals Unlimited; 6 Science Photo Library/Photo Researchers, Inc.; 7 (BL) Science Photo Library/Photo Researchers, Inc., (TR) Dr. Dennis Kunkel/Visuals Unlimited; 8 (C) Custom Medical Stock Photo, (BL) Lester V. Bergman/Corbis; 9 (TC) Dr. Dennis Kunkel /Visuals Unlimited; 12 Leonello Calvetti.

Scott Foresman/Dorling Kindersley would also like to thank: 14 (CA) Geoff Brightling/ESPL/DK Images.

Unless otherwise acknowledged, all photographs are the copyright © of Dorling Kindersley, a division of Pearson.

ISBN: 0-328-13920-3

Glossary

cell membrane	a material that surrounds a cell and holds it together
cell wall	in a plant cell, the tough wall that surrounds a cell membrane
chloroplast	the part of a plant where photosynthesis takes place
cytoplasm	all the material in a cell between the nucleus and the cell membrane
nucleus	the part of a cell that contains chromosomes
organ	grouping of different kinds of tissues combined in a single structure
organ system	a group of organs working together
tissue	a group of the same kind of cells working together at the same job
vacuole	a cell part that breaks down and stores material

Cells, Tissues, Organs, Systems

by Donna Latham

Teamwork:
On the Field
And Inside the Body

Leo and Jack might not realize it, but there are many living things at work in their bodies.

As the boys run across the soccer field, the large bones and muscles in their legs work to help them move. Their brains send messages to their muscles to tell them how to move. Blood carries oxygen to their muscles so the muscles can do their job.

As members of a soccer team, Leo and Jack work hard on the field. Inside their bodies, teams are working too. All this teamwork begins with the cell. The smallest parts of all living things, cells are life's building blocks. That means every living thing is made up of cells.

Like your cells, tissues, and organs, Leo and Jack are part of a team. You have learned how the cells in the body form tissues. You have learned that tissues form organs, and organs form systems. You are carrying an amazing and complicated team inside you!

You've learned that the skeletal system works with the muscle system to move the body. But it's important to the circulatory system too. Did you know that many of your bones make the red and white blood cells in your body? These cells are made in bone marrow. Marrow is a soft, reddish substance that is found inside large bones.

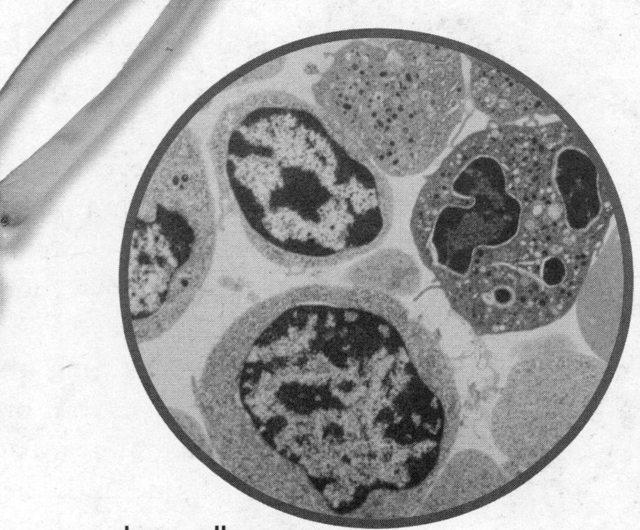

bone cells

Look at this photo of bone cells. Between the bone cells in your body is a hard material. It has calcium in it. Calcium is what makes bones hard. Other parts of your body, like muscles, need calcium to do their jobs. Bones store calcium until it is needed.

Inside The Cell

Inside a single drop of blood are millions of tiny red blood cells. If one drop has millions, imagine the number of cells in the 2.5 quarts of blood flowing through your body!

What are cells?

All cells are alive, like you. And like you, cells in most living things must do certain things to survive. They take in food and clear out wastes. They use materials in food to grow and to repair injuries.

On the soccer field, Leo alerts Jack when an opponent is closing in. Jack then blocks a kick. Like good team members, cells communicate and work with other cells. That way, they are able to sense a change in their environment. Next, they can react to it.

What happens when you feel low on energy? Is it hard to run, read, or concentrate? Cells are the same way. They need energy to do their jobs—growing, moving, and dividing. Most cells get energy by combining oxygen and food, a process called respiration.

What are the parts of cells?

Cells are protected by the **cell membrane,** which acts like the walls of a building. The cell membrane surrounds a cell, holding it together and helping it keep its shape. The cell membrane lets some materials, such as sugar and oxygen, come into the cell. It also allows waste to leave.

At the center of the cell is the nucleus. The **nucleus** contains chromosomes, which are made up of the chemical called DNA. The chromosomes are very important messengers. They carry the instructions that tell the cell to do its job. Chromosomes also have little sections called genes. Genes contain information for making new cells. Genes are passed on to the next generation. This process is called heredity.

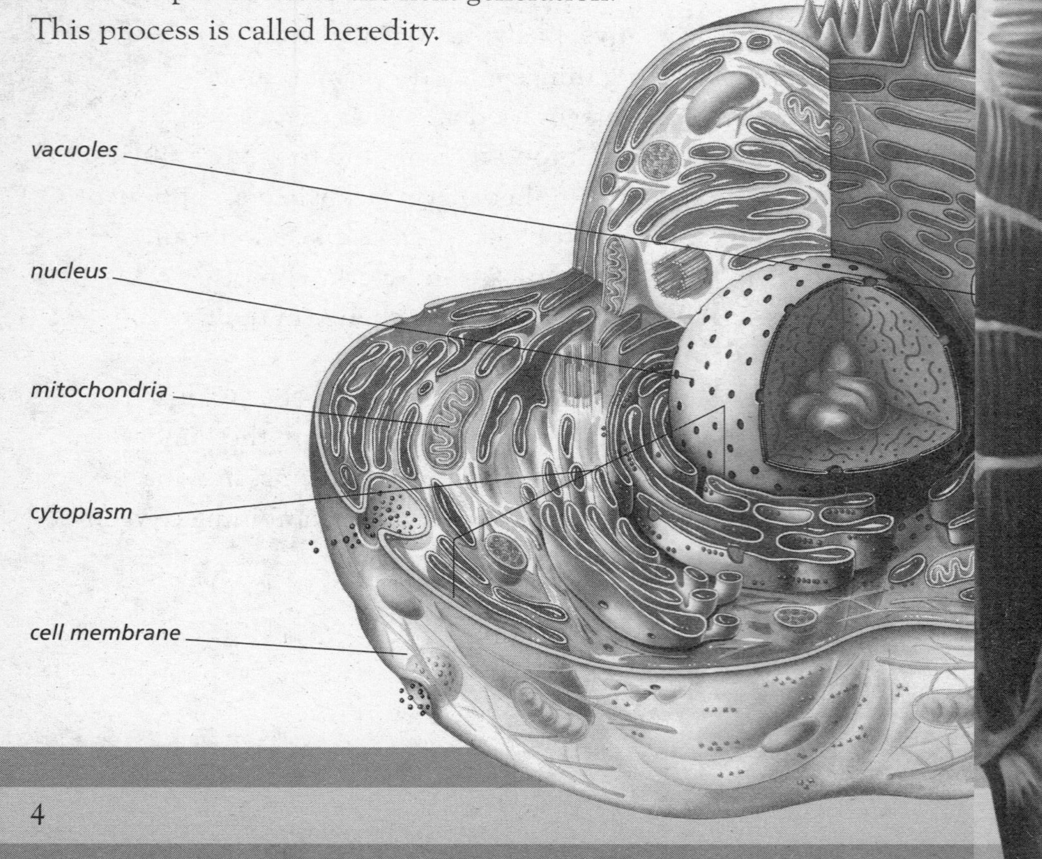

How do organ systems work together?

Sometimes different organ systems work together. For example, your muscle and skeletal systems team up to do the important job of moving your body.

Without bones to pull on, your muscles would have a hard time moving your body. Muscles usually work in sets of two to move bones. That's because muscles can only pull. They do not push. One muscle can pull a bone in one direction, but you need an opposite muscle to pull the bone back.

Your nervous system plays a role in movement too. It sends electrical signals that control the way your muscles move your bones.

Muscles aren't only connected to bones. Smooth muscles are found in your organs. For example, cardiac muscles are found in the heart. They are some of the strongest muscles in your body.

Organs Work Together

Your organs also work together in teams. A group of organs working together is called an **organ system.**

Bones Form a System

Each of your bones is an organ. The skeletal system is made up of about two hundred bones. It supports your body and protects your most important organs. For example, your skull protects your brain, and your ribs protect your heart.

Muscles Form A System Too

The body has nearly seven hundred muscles. Each muscle is made up of fibers that are able to tighten. When a muscle tightens, it pulls on the tissue it is attached to—and that causes your body to move.

Between the nucleus and the cell membrane is the **cytoplasm.** Cytoplasm is made up of a jelly-like fluid with tiny structures in it. Some of the structures are called mitochondria. They mix food and oxygen to produce the cell's power. This process is called respiration. **Vacuoles** break down and store food and waste, almost like tiny stomachs.

Plant Cells

Plant cells have some parts that animal cells do not. A **cell wall** surrounds the cell membrane. Strong and firm, it gives the cell extra protection. **Chloroplasts** give plants their green color. They use energy from sunlight to turn water and carbon dioxide into oxygen and sugar.

Cells Work Together

You're ready to pour some orange juice. What do you reach for in the cabinet? You probably choose a cup or a glass. But when you want to eat cereal, you grab a bowl and spoon instead. Each item in the cabinet is shaped and structured in a certain way. Each has a special job. Cells have their own shapes, structures, and jobs too. There are about two hundred different kinds of cells in your body.

Branching Cells

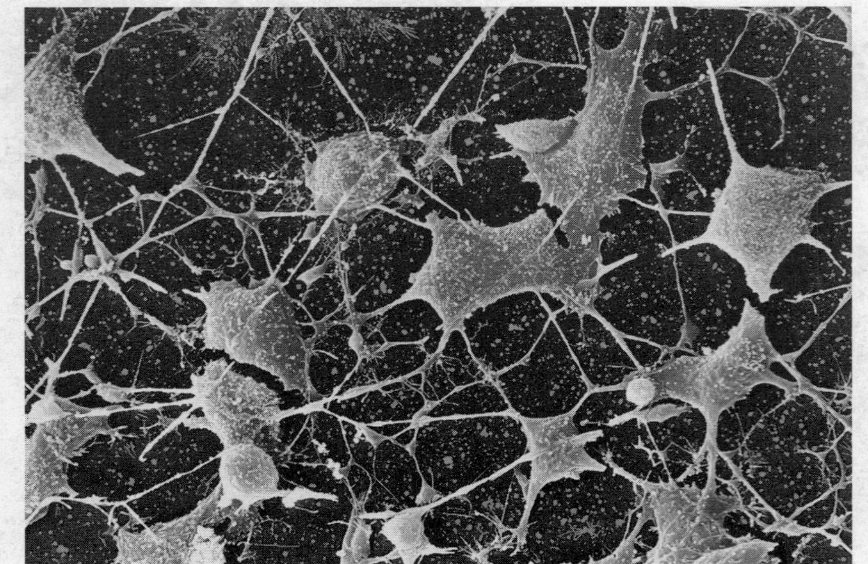

Nerve cells conduct signals between the body and the brain. These cells have branching shapes. Some of them are very long, which makes them perfect for sending messages.

Skin Cell Tissue

When you poured that glass of orange juice earlier, you left your fingerprints on the glass. The top layers of skin cells make the ridges on fingerprints.

Hair Follicle

Hair is a tissue. It protects your skin and keeps warm air next to your body. In the cells at the bottom of follicles, hair grows. As with skin, new cells push away older ones as they grow, making your hair longer.

Sweat Gland Pore

Sweat glands help control your body's temperature. Sweat leaves your body through pores, or small openings. As sweat evaporates your skin is cooled.

Muscle Tissue

What happens to your skin when you feel chilly? Muscle tissues pull the hair in your skin and cause it to stand up straight. This helps the hair to trap a layer of air near your skin, which helps keep you warm. You've probably noticed your skin doing this, and you even have a name for it. Goosebumps!

Tissues in the Skin

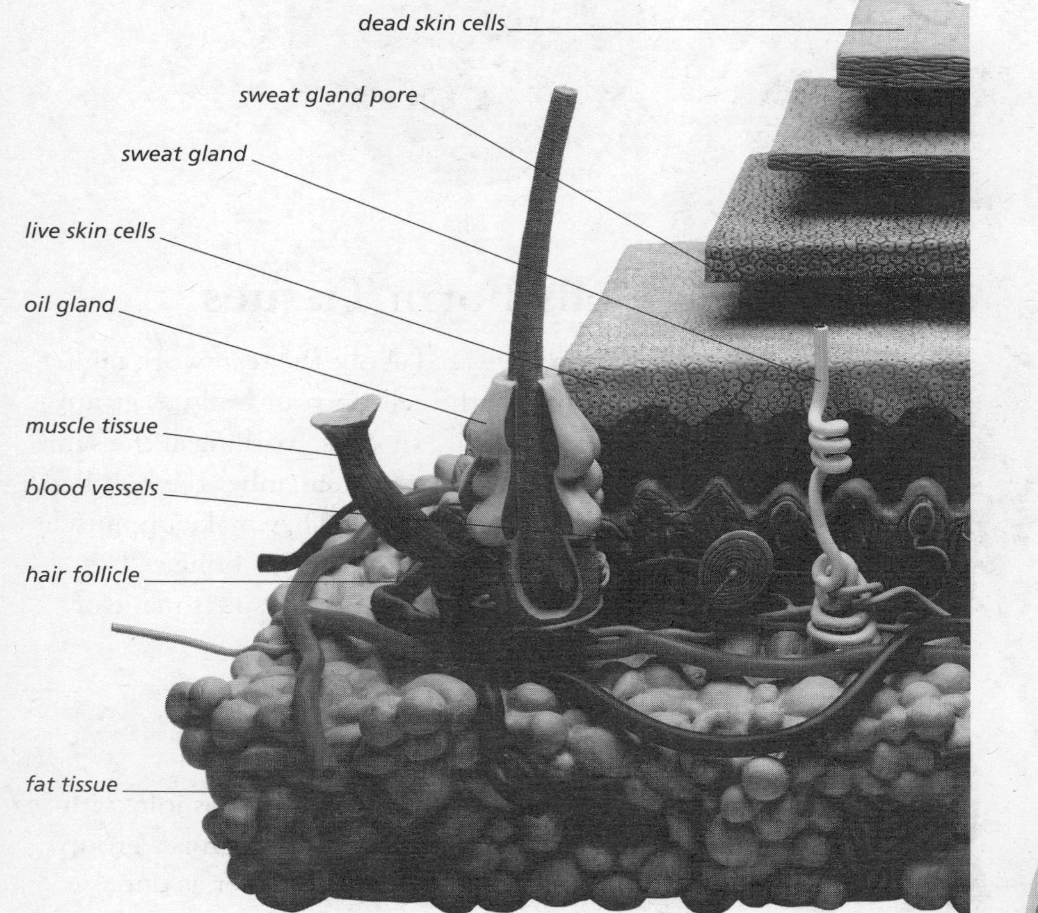

Your body's largest organ, the skin, has many jobs to do. Its many layers work to keep out germs, keep in water, and control body temperature. Take a look at the different tissues your skin uses to do these jobs.

Round Cells

Red blood cells are round. Their smooth, disk shape helps them move easily through the blood vessels as they do their jobs. They carry oxygen to all the cells in your body. Red blood cells are a bit thinner in the middle than they are at the edges. This shape is perfect for scooping up and carrying oxygen.

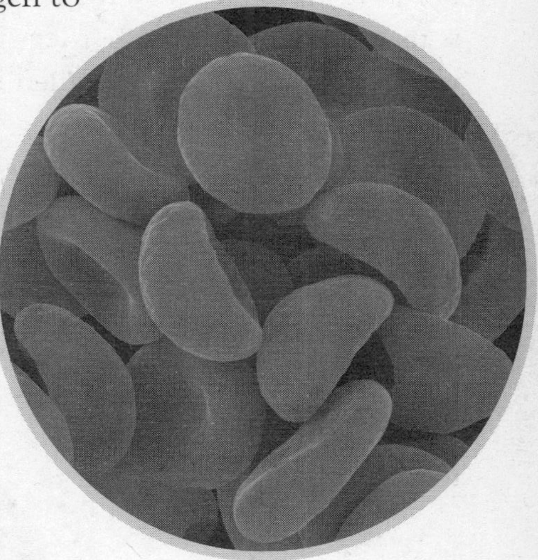

Flat Cells

Your skin is made up of flat cells. You also have flat cells on the surfaces of your mouth and stomach. Flat cells are shaped to cover a surface by joining together. They form overlapping stacks. With many layers of these flat cells, your skin is both tough and flexible. That's perfect for its job of protecting your insides!

Special Cell Structures

The shape of cells isn't the only thing that helps them do their jobs. The structure helps too. For example, this girl is using the muscles in her legs to kick the ball. Muscle cells work together in groups called bundles. On their own, muscle cells are not too strong. But in a bundle, they are able to do a lot of work, such as making the girl's leg move.

Hair-like structures called cilia have special jobs in the body. Found in the nose, the ears, and the lungs, these little brooms sweep dirt and germs away. In the lungs, they help to clear airways.

cilia

muscle cell

skin cell

Cells Form Tissues

You have read about the teamwork taking place among the cells in your body. A group of the same kind of cells, working at the same job, is called a **tissue.** Remember the bundled muscles in the girl's leg? They make up muscle tissue. Bone tissue is made up of bone cells. Can you figure out what nerve tissue is made of? That's right, nerve cells!

Tissues Form Organs

But the teamwork doesn't stop there. Tissues join with other kinds of tissues to form **organs.** An organ is a group of different kinds of tissues that work together as one structure to do a major job in your body. Can you think of some examples of organs? Your heart, liver, kidneys, and eyes are all organs. The largest organ in your body is your skin. When you are an adult, you will probably have about 20 square feet (1.9 square meters) of skin!

Systems of the Human Body

by Raymond Wong

Genre	Comprehension Skill	Text Features	Science Content
Nonfiction	Sequence	• Captions • Labels • Diagrams • Glossary	Human Body Systems

Scott Foresman Science 5.3

PEARSON

Scott Foresman

scottforesman.com

ISBN 0-328-13923-8

90000

9 780328 139231

What did you learn?

1. How is your body's circulatory system like a car's fuel system?

2. What are the sacs with thin walls that are at the end of the bronchioles called?

3. If you hold your breath, what gas builds up in your blood?

4. **Writing** in Science The kidneys take out wastes from the blood. They also take out things the body needs, which must be put back. Write to describe what the kidneys take out of the blood and what helpful things they put back into the blood. Include details from the book to support your answer.

5. **Sequence** What is the order in which blood moves through the heart?

Picture Credits
Every effort has been made to secure permission and provide appropriate credit for photographic material.
The publisher deeply regrets any omission and pledges to correct errors called to its attention in subsequent editions.

Photo locators denoted as follows: Top (T), Center (C), Bottom (B), Left (L), Right (R), Background (Bkgd).

6 National Cancer Institute/Photo Researchers, Inc.; 9 Dennis Kunkel/Phototake;
14 Innerspace Imaging/Photo Researchers, Inc.

Scott Foresman/Dorling Kindersley would also like to thank Denoyer-Geppert International/DK Images for use of photos on the Opener and pages 1 (C), 3 (TL, CL, CA, CRA), 8 (CB), 10, 13 (CB), 15 (CB), 16 (CLB), 19 (C), 20, 22 (CB), 23 (CA).

Unless otherwise acknowledged, all photographs are the copyright © of Dorling Kindersley, a division of Pearson.

ISBN: 0-328-13923-8

Glossary

air sacs	tiny, air-filled pouches in the lungs where oxygen enters the blood and carbon dioxide leaves the blood
artery	a blood vessel that carries blood away from the heart to the rest of the body
bronchioles	tubes that branch from the bronchi
capillary	the smallest kind of blood vessel
esophagus	a tube that moves food from your mouth to your stomach
mucus	a thick, sticky liquid that traps dust and germs that may be in the air
trachea	a tube that carries air from the larynx to the lungs
valve	a flap that keeps blood flowing in one direction
vein	a blood vessel that takes blood back to the heart

Systems of the Human Body

by Raymond Wong

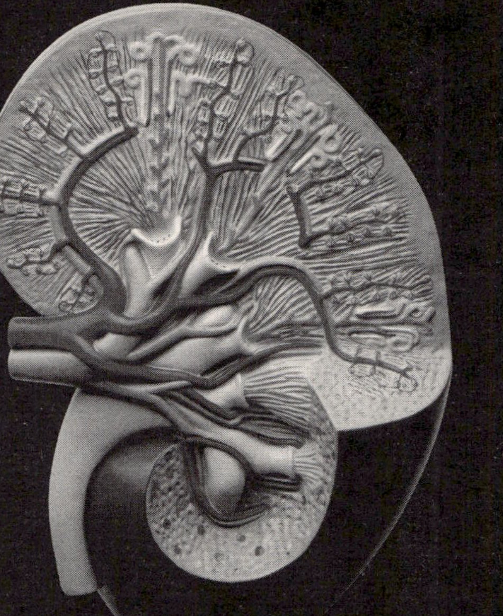

PEARSON
Scott Foresman

DK

What are the systems of the human body?

A car is a very complicated machine, with many different systems in it. A system is a group of parts that work together to do a job. A car has a system to move fuel to the engine. It also has a system to keep the engine cool. Another system removes the waste the engine creates. All these systems must work together so the car can function.

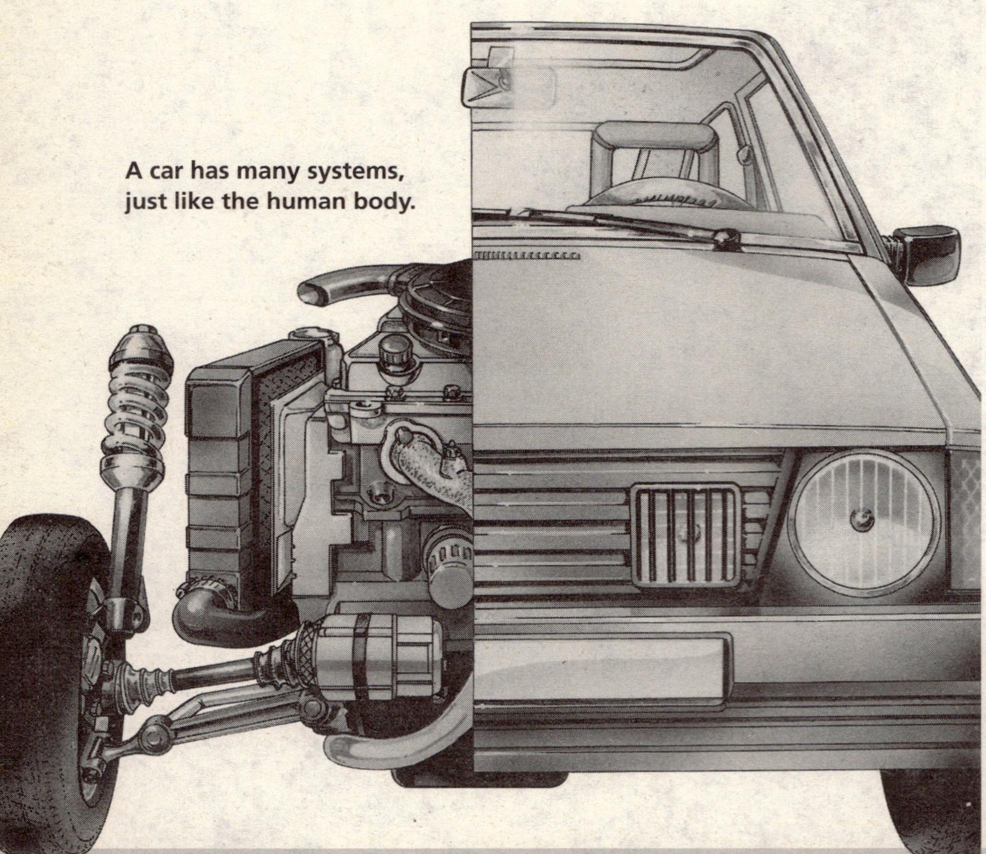

A car has many systems, just like the human body.

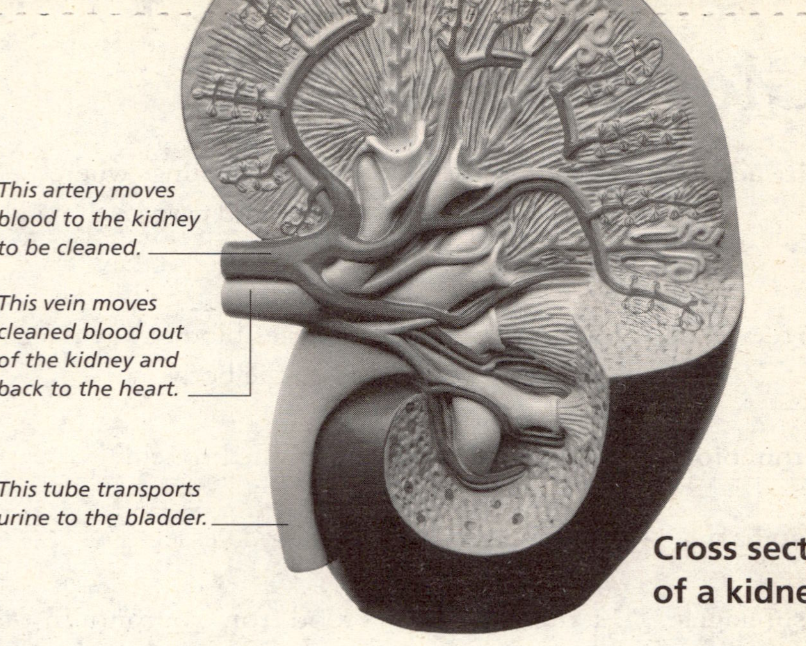

Cross section of a kidney

The kidneys also remove some water along with wastes. The water and wastes make up urine. The urine moves from the kidneys to the urinary bladder. The bladder holds the urine until it leaves the body. A tight round muscle at the bottom of the bladder holds the urine inside.

The kidneys are not the only organs that remove the cells' wastes. The lungs get rid of carbon dioxide, and sweat glands remove waste from cells in sweat.

Your body is very complicated, and it has important needs that must be met. Food and oxygen need to get to every one of your trillions of cells. Each one of these cells also produces waste and carbon dioxide, which must be taken away and moved out of the body. To meet these needs, you have different systems that often work together. There's a lot going on inside of you, but your systems handle it with no trouble at all!

What is the urinary system?

The cells in your body make waste and pass it into the blood. This waste can be poisonous. If your body did not get rid of wastes, it could not live for long. People and other living things have systems that remove waste from the blood. Your body does this mostly through the urinary system.

The kidneys are a pair of organs found in the lower back, on either side of the backbone. They have the same shape and dark-red color as kidney beans. The kidneys have the important job of removing waste from the blood.

When the wastes are taken out, some things that the body needs are taken out also. These things include salt, calcium, and other chemicals. The kidneys put back just the right amounts of these things to keep your body healthy.

Parts of the urinary system

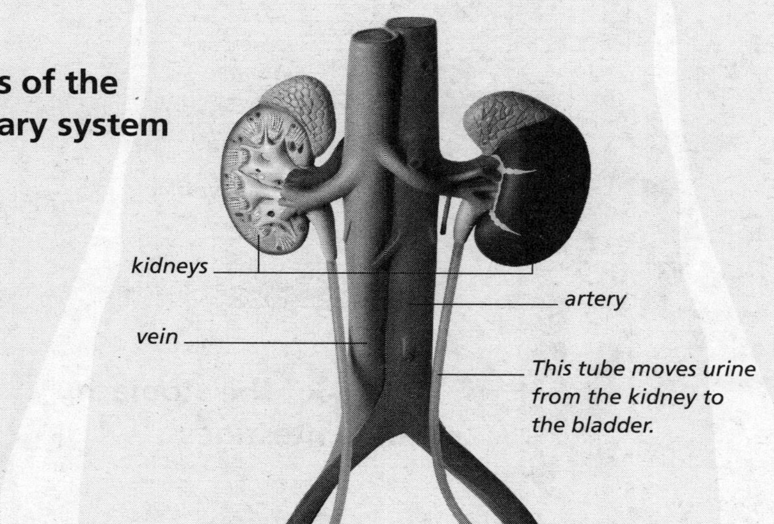

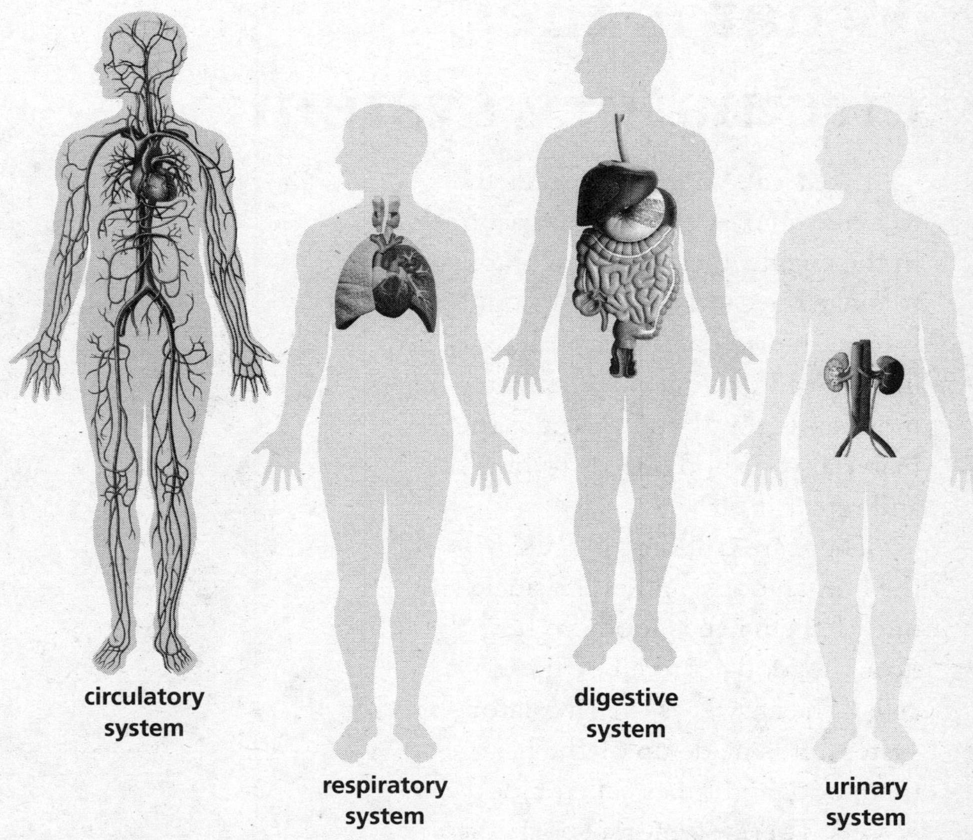

Your body also has many different systems. In this book, you will learn about four of your body's systems— the circulatory, respiratory, digestive, and urinary systems. Each of these systems has a very important job to do and works with other systems to keep you healthy!

What is the circulatory system?

Like a car, your body needs fuel to make it go. A car's fuel is gasoline. In the engine, it combines with oxygen to make the car move. Your body's fuel is food. It also combines with oxygen, in your cells, giving you energy to move and grow. Food provides the material your body needs to build and repair itself.

There are trillions of cells in the human body, and every single one of them needs food. So how does the food get to all of these cells? The answer is the circulatory system. It is made up of the heart, the blood, and tubes called blood vessels. This system transports the food and oxygen your cells need. It also takes away wastes.

Food is your body's fuel, so make sure you eat healthful food!

Food that cannot be digested moves into a tube called the large intestine. The large intestine is wider than the small intestine. Its lower part is called the colon. Helpful bacteria are found in the large intestine. These bacteria make vitamins and keep harmful outside bacteria from getting in. The large intestine removes water and salts from the waste. Then muscles push the waste out of the body.

Parts of the stomach and intestines

Stomach and Intestines

A tight, round muscle is at the bottom of the esophagus. When you swallow, this muscle opens to let food into your stomach. The muscle then closes to keep food from going back into the esophagus.

The stomach is behind the lower left ribs. It can stretch to hold all the food from a meal. To help digest food, the stomach makes fluids. Strong muscles in the stomach's walls squeeze together to mix the fluids and food into a soupy paste.

The stomach then squeezes the food into a narrow, winding tube called the small intestine. Its muscles move the food along. The liver and pancreas are organs that send chemicals to the small intestine to break down food. When digestion is finished, the food moves into your blood.

Villi are tiny, finger-shaped parts on the inside walls of the small intestine. Villi give the body more chances to absorb food since they are filled with tiny blood vessels.

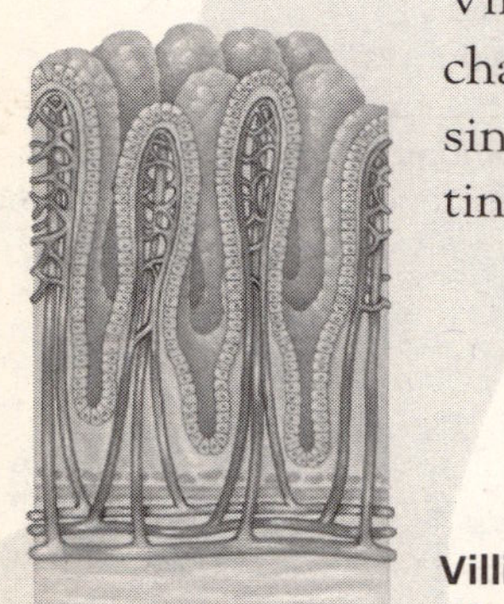

Villi contain a network of tiny capillaries.

Functions of the Blood

Did you know that your blood is made of several different parts? Each part has a specific name and function. Plasma makes up most of your blood. It is a liquid that is yellow in color. Your blood gets its red color from red blood cells. Plasma, red blood cells, white blood cells, and platelets are all parts of your blood.

Plasma moves food from your digestive system to each of your cells. It also brings water to your cells and takes away their wastes. Sometimes plasma moves chemicals, such as adrenaline, from one part of the body to another. Adrenaline is a chemical that gives your heart and muscle cells extra strength and energy.

Red blood cells perform a very important job. They carry oxygen to your cells. Oxygen makes it possible for your cells to get energy from food. When red blood cells are carrying oxygen, they are bright red. After they have delivered the oxygen, they turn darker red in color.

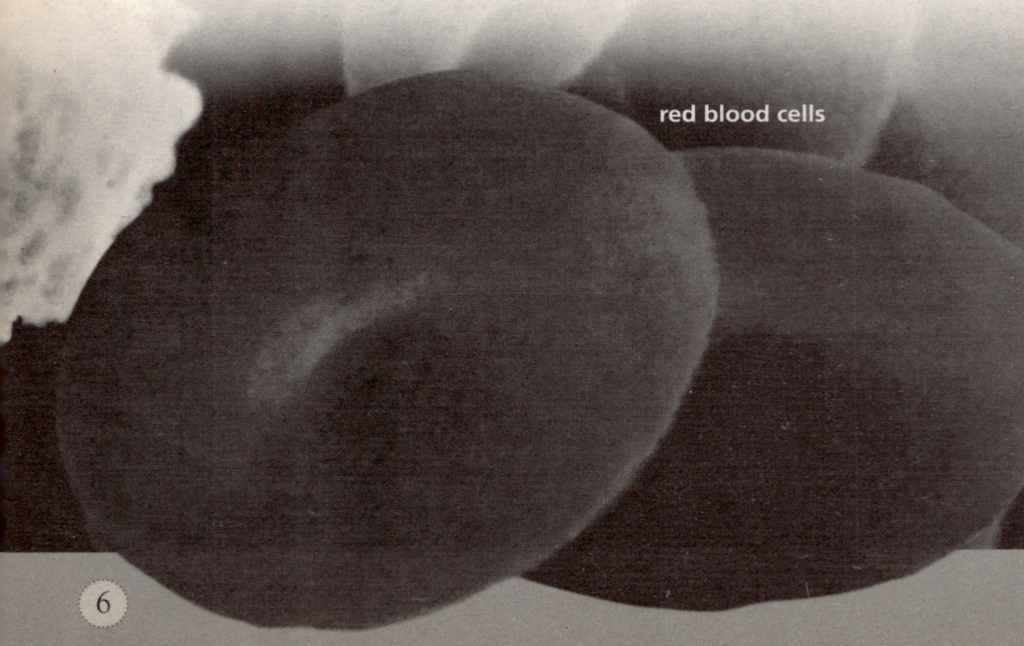

red blood cells

Parts for chewing and swallowing

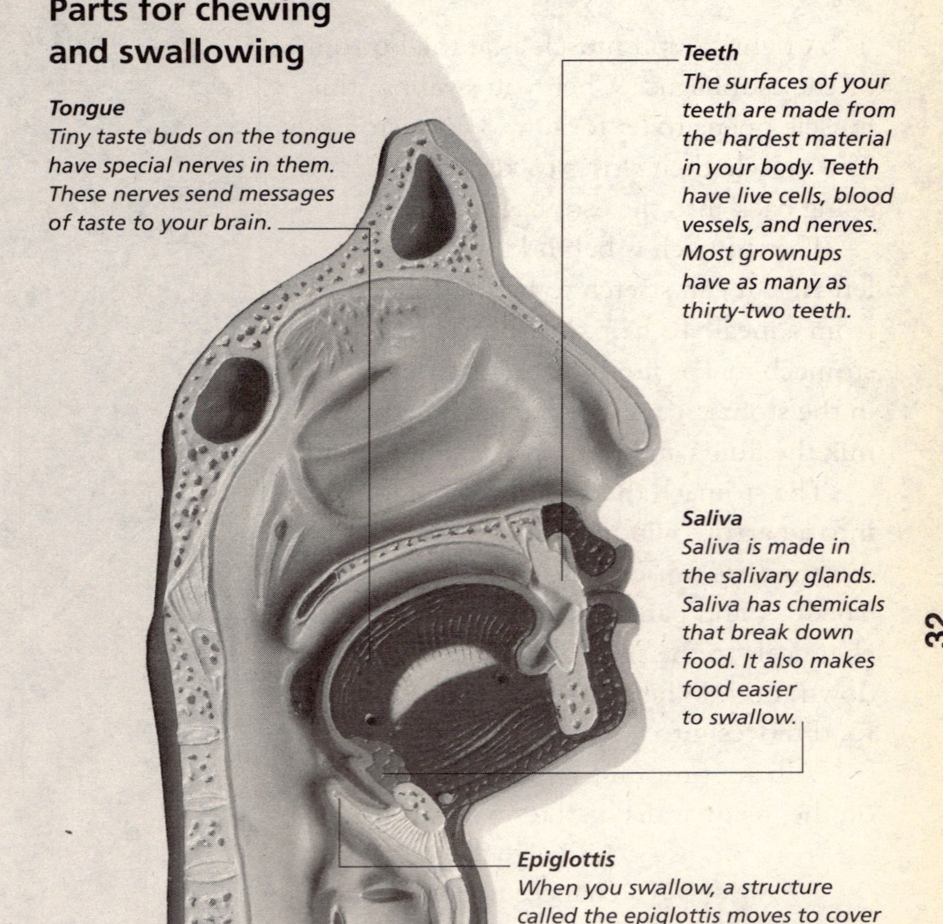

What is the digestive system?

When you eat, food passes through many organs in the digestive system. Each organ has certain parts to help it do its job.

Food must be changed before your cells can use it. Your body digests, or breaks down, food into very small pieces. The food can then enter the blood to get to the cells. There are several steps to digestion, so many organs need to work together.

Mouth and Esophagus

The first step of digestion is chewing. Chewing breaks the food into smaller pieces, making the digestive system's job easier. The tongue moves food around the mouth so that it can be chewed by the teeth.

Then it pushes the pieces of food to the back of the mouth, where they are swallowed.

The **esophagus** is a tube that moves food from the mouth to the stomach. Rings of muscle in the esophagus push food along.

As the food passes each ring of muscle, the muscles behind the food close up. It's a bit like the way toothpaste gets squeezed out of its tube. This pushing moves the food from the esophagus to the stomach in two to three seconds.

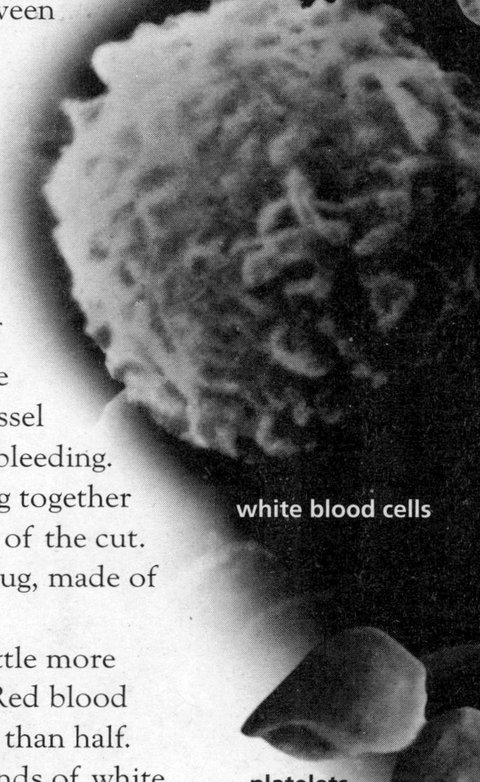

White blood cells protect your body against germs. One of the ways they do this is by wrapping around germs and breaking them down. Sometimes these cells work with other systems of the body to fight germs. Some white blood cells make chemicals that kill germs. Other white blood cells fight germs outside the blood vessels by squeezing between your body cells. The number of white blood cells in your body is always changing. To fight an infection, your body makes more white blood cells.

Platelets are pieces of cells that are found in the blood. When a blood vessel is cut, platelets stop the bleeding. They do this by bunching together and sticking to the edges of the cut. This forms a clot, or a plug, made of long, sticky threads.

Plasma makes up a little more than half of the blood. Red blood cells make up a little less than half. Platelets and different kinds of white blood cells make up a tiny fraction of the blood.

Arteries and Capillaries

Your circulatory system uses blood vessels to reach all the cells in your body. Did you know your body contains enough blood vessels to stretch around Earth more than twice? The three kinds of blood vessels in your body are arteries, capillaries, and veins.

Arteries carry blood from your heart to other parts of your body. This blood contains the oxygen needed by your body's cells. When your heart pumps blood into arteries, their thick, muscular walls stretch. Your arteries branch into narrower and narrower vessels.

Blood vessels of the heart

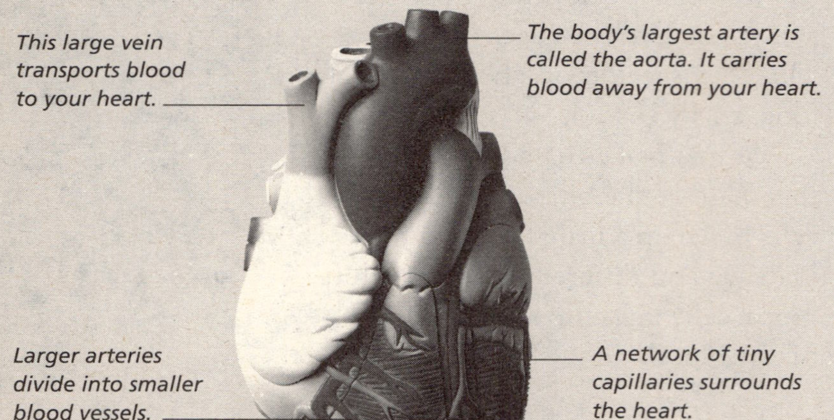

This large vein transports blood to your heart.

The body's largest artery is called the aorta. It carries blood away from your heart.

Larger arteries divide into smaller blood vessels.

A network of tiny capillaries surrounds the heart.

Your body has more parts than insect and worm bodies. Your respiratory and circulatory systems work together to get oxygen to your cells. The respiratory system moves the oxygen to the air sacs in your lungs. The circulatory system's blood picks up the oxygen there and moves it to all of your cells.

Gas exchange in an air sac

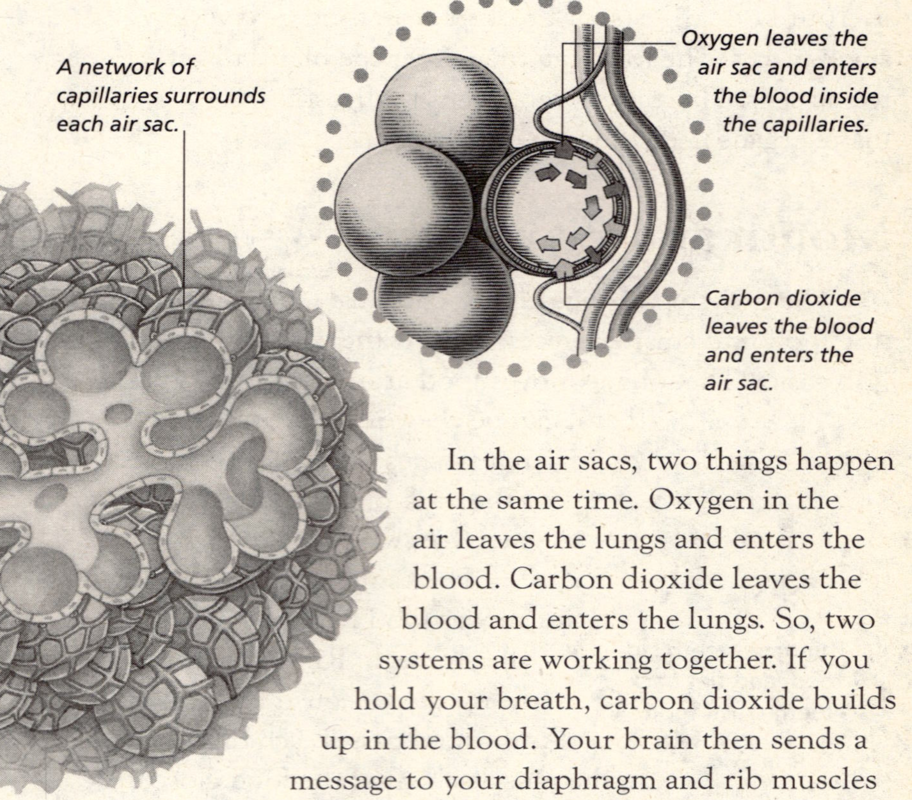

A network of capillaries surrounds each air sac.

Oxygen leaves the air sac and enters the blood inside the capillaries.

Carbon dioxide leaves the blood and enters the air sac.

In the air sacs, two things happen at the same time. Oxygen in the air leaves the lungs and enters the blood. Carbon dioxide leaves the blood and enters the lungs. So, two systems are working together. If you hold your breath, carbon dioxide builds up in the blood. Your brain then sends a message to your diaphragm and rib muscles telling them to breathe. When this happens, more than two systems are working together.

34

How do the respiratory and circulatory systems work together?

Almost all living things need oxygen so their cells can get energy. Many simple animals need only one system to do this job. Insects use a respiratory system to get oxygen from the air and move it around their bodies through tubes. Worms use a circulatory system that transports oxygen through their blood.

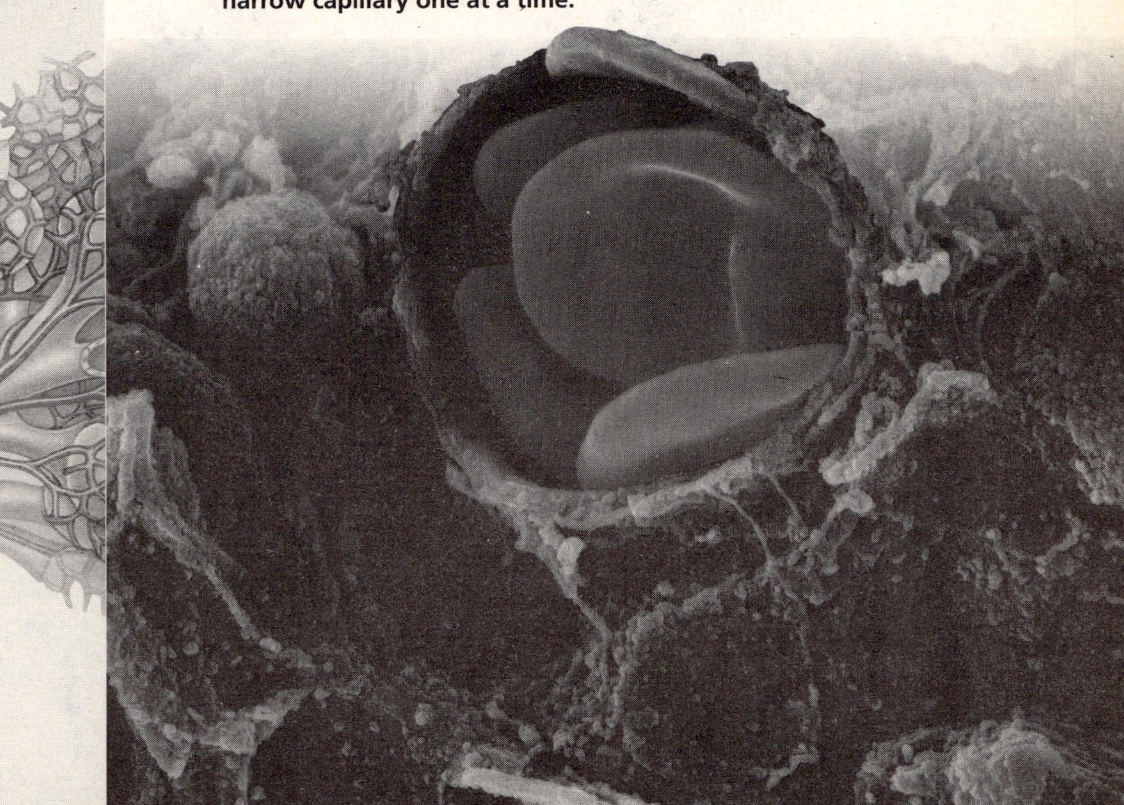

The smallest and narrowest type of blood vessel is called a **capillary.** Some capillaries are so narrow that red blood cells must move through them one by one.

The walls of capillaries are only one cell thick, so gases can pass right through them. The oxygen in your blood is able to reach your cells by passing through these thin walls. Carbon dioxide and other wastes move from your cells to your capillaries.

Bloods cells move through a narrow capillary one at a time.

Veins

Capillaries join together to form tiny **veins.** Then the tiny veins join together to become larger veins. Veins transport blood from cells back to the heart.

Veins have thicker walls than capillaries but thinner walls than arteries.

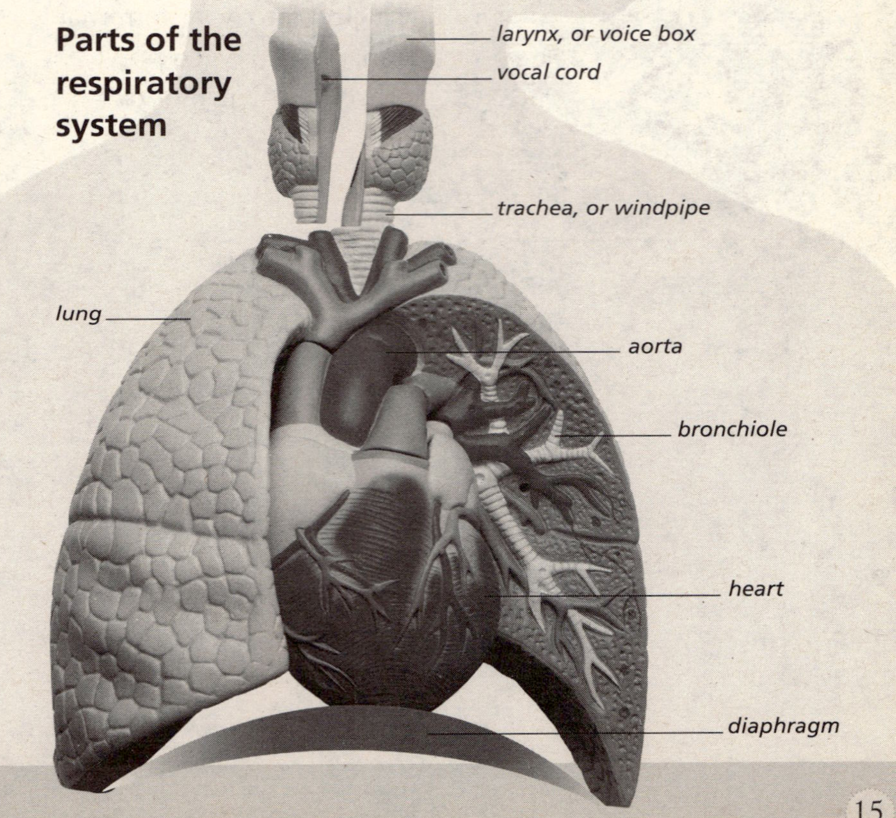

Veins have valves. **Valves** are flaps that act like doors that open in only one direction. This keeps blood flowing in only one direction. The valves open to let blood flow to the heart. Arteries and capillaries do not have valves. The pumping of the heart keeps blood moving in the right direction through the arteries and capillaries.

At the end of the bronchioles are bunches of **air sacs.** There, oxygen enters the blood and carbon dioxide leaves the blood. The walls of the air sacs are so thin that these gases can easily pass through them. The air sacs are also called alveoli.

The diaphragm is a dome-shaped muscle that makes up the bottom of the chest area. This muscle moves down and flattens out to draw air into the lungs.

Cilia are parts of cells that look like tiny hairs. They are found on the inside of the trachea and on many other parts of the respiratory system. Cilia move back and forth to push dirty mucus out of the lungs. The mucus then enters the throat, where it is swallowed.

Parts of the respiratory system

What is the respiratory system?

Parts of the Respiratory System

Your respiratory system works whenever you breathe, talk, smell, sing, or laugh. Its main job is to carry gases from the air to your blood. Many parts of the respiratory system are covered in mucus. **Mucus** is a thick, sticky fluid that traps dust and germs that may be in the air.

When air comes in through the nose or mouth, it enters the sinuses, which make the air warm and damp. The nose has hair and mucus to trap dust and germs.

Air goes from the sinuses to the back of the throat and into the larynx, or voice box. Two vocal cords stretch across the larynx. The sound of your voice is the sound of the vocal cords vibrating as you breathe.

The **trachea,** or windpipe, is a tube that moves air from the larynx to the lungs. The trachea branches into two tubes called bronchi, which go into the lungs. The bronchi branch into smaller and smaller tubes called **bronchioles.** The bronchioles can swell up because of a disease called asthma. Asthma keeps air from moving easily through the lungs, making breathing very difficult.

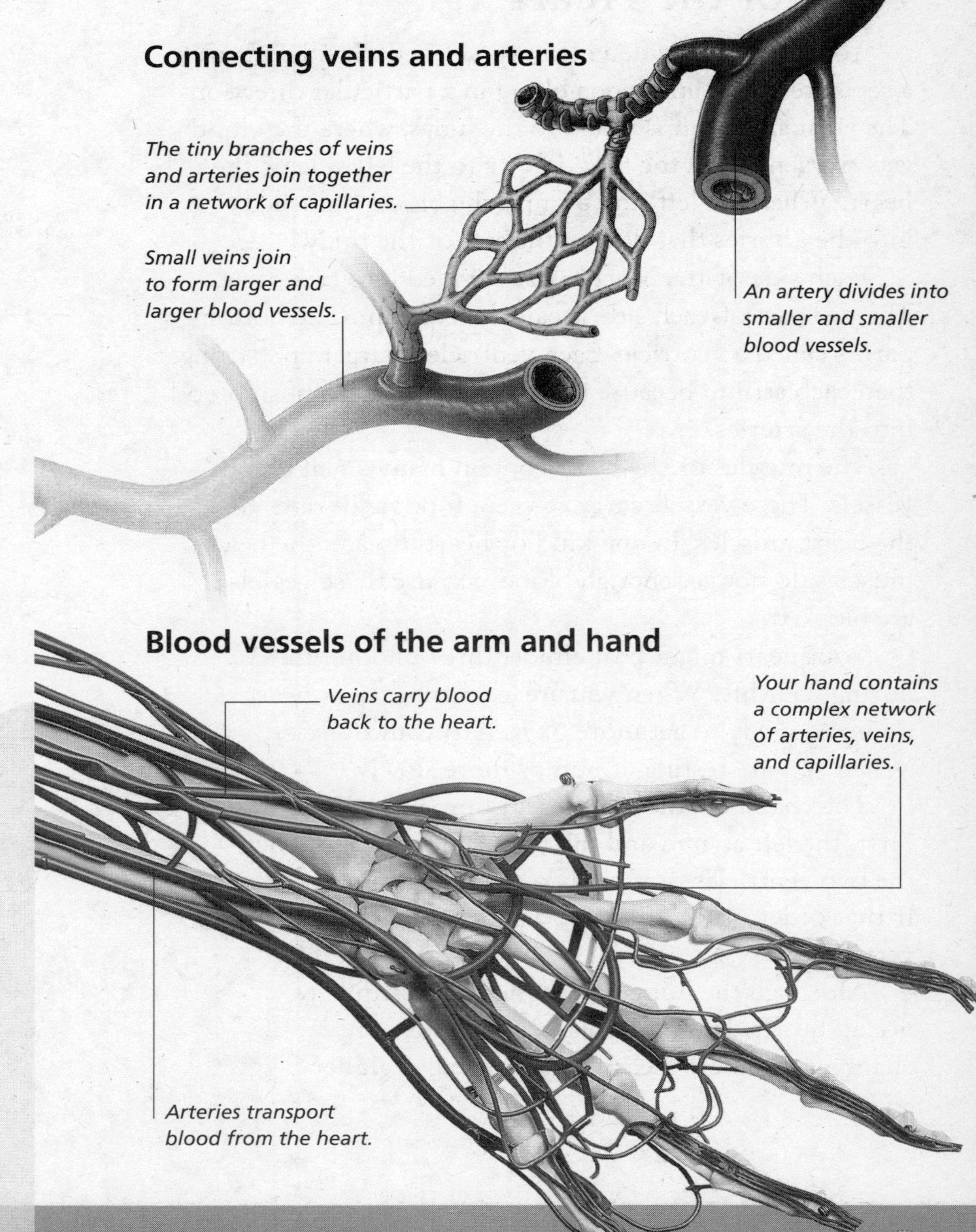

Parts of the Heart

Your heart is divided into two sides. Each side acts as a separate pump and sends blood in a particular direction. The right side pumps blood to the lungs, where the blood gets oxygen. Then the blood flows to the left side of the heart. When the left side pumps, the blood is pushed into the arteries that flow to the rest of the body.

Each side of the heart is also divided into two parts. The top part of each side is called an atrium. The bottom part is called a ventricle. Each ventricle is larger and stronger than each atrium because the ventricles need to push blood into the arteries.

The muscles of the heart contain many small blood vessels. These vessels carry oxygen, food, and water to the heart muscles. In one kind of heart disease, the heart muscles do not get enough blood because these vessels are blocked.

Your heart might beat almost three billion times during your life. When you are exercising, your heart pumps quickly to get more oxygen to your muscles. When you are resting, it pumps more slowly.

The chambers of your heart pump in a certain order. First, the left atrium and the right atrium pump. Then the two ventricles pump. Then the order is repeated. If that order is not followed, a person can become very sick.

Although the human heart has four chambers, not all hearts do. Amphibians' hearts have three chambers. Spiders' hearts have one big chamber.

Like your veins, your heart has valves that keep blood flowing one way. There are four one-way valves in your heart. The beating of your heart is the sound of the valves.

Circulation of blood inside the heart

38

Science

Science

Sunflowers
and the Story of Plants

by Pat Fridell

Genre	Comprehension Skill	Text Features	Science Content
Nonfiction	Cause and Effect	• Captions • Labels • Diagrams • Glossary	Plants

Scott Foresman Science 5.4

PEARSON

Scott Foresman

scottforesman.com

DK

ISBN 0-328-13926-2

90000

9 780328 139262

What did you learn?

Vocabulary

embryo
growth hormone
phloem
photosynthesis
pollen
pollination
spore
tropism
xylem

1. What are the three main parts of a seed? Tell what job each part does.

2. What process do plants use to make food? Name three things plants need for this process to happen.

3. How do stems and roots help a plant?

4. **Writing** in Science Human beings use plants for many things. Write to explain how plants are useful. Use the sunflower or another plant as an example to help explain your ideas. Include details from the book to support your answer.

5. **Cause and Effect** Tell what causes each of the three kinds of tropism: phototropism, gravitropism, and thigmotropism. Then tell what effect the tropism has on a plant's growth.

Picture Credits
Every effort has been made to secure permission and provide appropriate credit for photographic material.
The publisher deeply regrets any omission and pledges to correct errors called to its attention in subsequent editions.

Photo locators denoted as follows: Top (T), Center (C), Bottom (B), Left (L), Right (R), Background (Bkgd).

15 Eric Crichton/Corbis; 21 Kevin Schafer/Corbis.

Unless otherwise acknowledged, all photographs are the copyright © of Dorling Kindersley, a division of Pearson.

ISBN: 0-328-13926-2

Glossary

embryo	a new plant inside a seed
growth hormone	a kind of chemical that causes cells to grow
phloem	plant tissue made up of tubes that carry sugar away from the leaves
photosynthesis	the process in which plants use light, carbon dioxide, and water to make sugar and oxygen
pollen	a grainy yellow powder made in tissue at the top of a flower's stamen
pollination	the movement of pollen from the plant stamen to the pistil
spore	a single plant cell that can grow into a new plant
tropism	the way plants change growth direction in response to the environment
xylem	plant tissue made up of tubes that carry water and minerals from roots to leaves

Sunflowers
and the Story of Plants

by Pat Fridell

What comes to mind when you think about plants?
Beautiful flowers? A tree you like to climb? A salad, maybe?
If you take a closer look, you'll discover that plants are
complicated life forms. Like animals, plants have needs that
must be met if they are to survive. They need air, water,
sunlight, and minerals. They also need to reproduce to make
new plants.

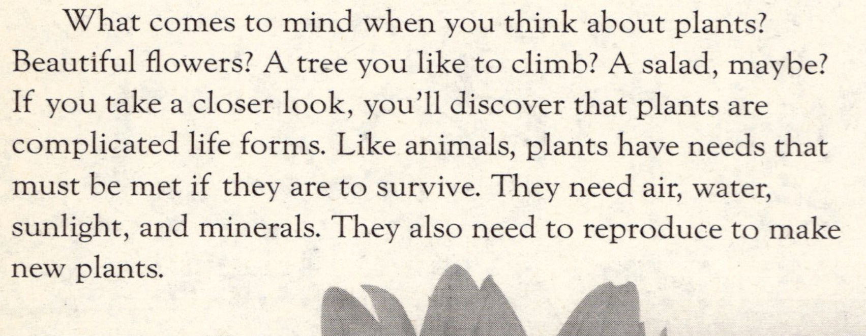

There are different kinds of asexual reproduction. Plants
such as strawberries reproduce by growing new plants on
long stems called runners. Others, such as the tiny duckweed
plant, reproduce by budding. Small buds from the plant
drop off and grow into new plants.

Plants are amazing life forms. You may just think of
them as pretty flowers, but there's really much more going
on. Plants can move to follow the Sun. They breathe and
make their own food. And they make food for us too. So
the next time you're in the garden or at the flower shop, take
a good look at all the plants. They're full of surprises!

Other Ways of Reproducing

Plants that do not make flowers, such as mosses and ferns, reproduce using **spores.** A spore is a single plant cell that can develop into a whole new plant.

Some plants don't have egg cells and sperm cells. They reproduce by asexual reproduction. These plants don't need two parents to make a new plant. Since there is only one parent in this type of reproduction, the new plants look exactly the same as the plant that produced them.

To meet these needs, plants have several systems at work inside of them. They have a system of tubes that move food and water from one part of the plant to another. They have a way of taking in air, getting the gases they need from it, and then getting rid of what they don't need. Sometimes plants can even move to get what they need!

Sunflowers are beautiful plants that use all of these systems to survive. By learning about the sunflower, we can learn about all plants.

Sunflowers, standing twelve to fifteen feet tall, are giants in the garden. Their name comes from the way the plant turns its flower face. The large flower follows the Sun as it moves across the sky from east to west. The sunflower's scientific name, *Helianthus*, comes from the Greek words *helios*, meaning "Sun," and *anthos*, meaning "flower."

Long ago, people discovered that plants, including wild sunflowers, are useful to humankind. About eight thousand years ago, Native Americans began gathering wild sunflowers for food and medicine. About three thousand to four thousand years ago, they began growing and improving sunflowers to make them even more useful.

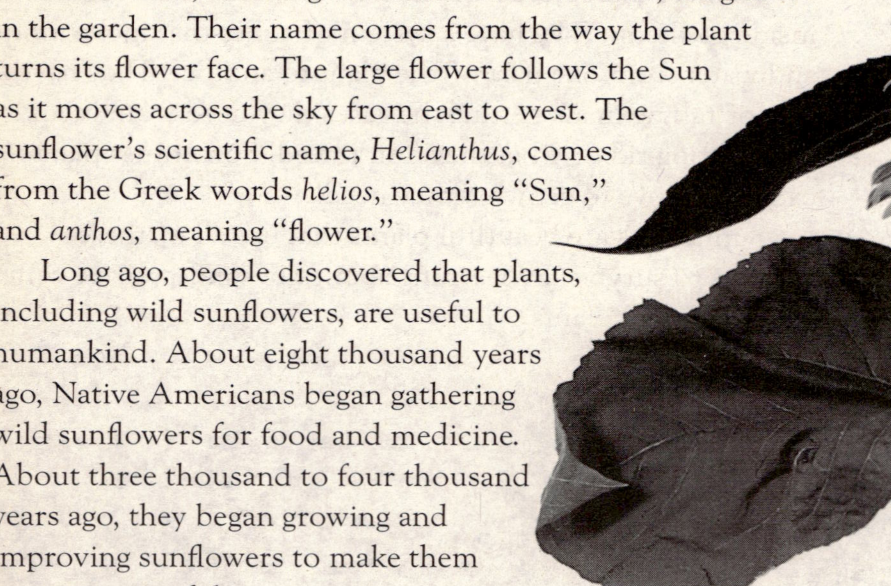

Sunflowers turn their faces toward the Sun.

Seeds Drop and Scatter

If left alone, developed seeds drop to the ground and begin to grow. Sometimes seeds are scattered, or moved away from the parent plants. Some seeds are scattered by the wind. Coconuts, which are very large seeds, float on the ocean to their new homes. Animals can also help to scatter seeds. Fruit surrounding some seeds helps attract animals, which eat the fruit and then scatter the seeds. Some seeds stick to the fur of passing animals and are carried away.

Coconuts are large seeds that are transported by the ocean.

Once pollination takes place, a tube grows from the pollen down to the egg cells in the bottom of the pistil. Special cells called sperm cells, which carry DNA, travel down the tube and join the egg cells. The egg cells also contain DNA. When the sperm and egg cells join, fertilization occurs and a seed develops. This is the beginning of a new plant.

Today in the United States, sunflowers are perhaps best known as a snack food. We munch and crunch raw, roasted, and salted sunflower seeds. Birds like these seeds too, and many people put them in their bird feeders. Sunflowers are also used to make vegetable oil. This oil is in many things we use, from salad dressing to paint.

Plants

Now let's take a closer look at all plants, and at the same time get to know the sunflower.

Seeds

Plant seeds have three main parts: the seed coat, the **embryo,** or baby plant, and stored food called endosperm. The seed coat covers the seed and protects the embryo and the stored food. Cotyledons store the food for the embryo to use when it is growing. Plants with one-part cotyledons, such as tulips, are called monocots. Plants with two-part cotyledons are called dicots. Sunflowers are dicots.

Some plants, such as certain maple trees, don't have both stamens and pistils. These plants' flowers are called imperfect flowers. Flowers that do have both a stamen and a pistil are called perfect flowers.

When pollen moves from the stamen to the pistil, the process is called **pollination.** Wind or water can move the pollen. Animals such as insects, bats, birds, and bees can move pollen too. For example, if a honeybee sees the bright yellow of a sunflower, it might land on the flower to collect pollen for itself. As the bee crawls across the florets, its body and legs become covered with pollen. The bee flies from one flower to another. Some of the pollen rubs off its body into the florets of other sunflowers.

A bee collects pollen from many different flowers.

Flowers and Reproduction

Let's take a look at flowers. Beautiful flowers can capture people's imagination. The artist Vincent van Gogh painted the large, bright yellow flowers of the sunflower. He liked their rich color.

The center of each sunflower head is actually made of hundreds of tiny flowers. A sunflower is called a composite flower because it is made up of these tiny flowers, or florets.

The flower is where sexual reproduction takes place. It is the flowers that have the job of reproduction and the job of passing on DNA to the next generation. It takes a male part and a female part to reproduce. The stamen is the male part of a flower. This is where the powder called **pollen** is located. The pistil is the female part of the flower.

A seed that is planted starts growing when the soil temperature is right. For example, a sunflower seed needs a soil temperature of at least 46° Fahrenheit. Seeds also need the right amount of wetness in the soil to start growing. When conditions are right, a tiny stem grows up into the air. Tiny roots grow down into the soil. But a seed can only wait so long for the conditions to be right.

While it waits, the seed uses the food stored in its cotyledon. If the conditions are not right for the seed to start growing before this food runs out, the seed will die.

Leaves, Roots, and Stems

Above ground, the first leaves open out from the new stem. Plants make their own food, and they use leaves to do it. Leaves are made up of layers of different tissues.

Let's take a closer look at leaves. The outside layer of a leaf is the epidermis. Just as your skin protects you, the epidermis on a leaf protects the plant.

phototropism. You may have seen a houseplant turn itself toward a bright window as it tries to get more of the light it needs to grow.

Plants change direction in other ways too. For example, roots grow down and stems grow up. This is called gravitropism. The growth is either downward toward the pull of gravity or upward away from it.

You can see another kind of tropism when you see a vine climbing a pole or fence. This tropism is called thigmotropism. The plant senses when it touches an object and wraps around it.

Plants Move

Tropism is what happens when the environment causes plants to change the direction in which they are growing. Sunflowers turn their flower heads to face the Sun. As the Sun moves across the sky, the flower heads turn to follow it. Whenever plant growth is affected by light, it is called

On the underside of a leaf are tiny openings that let air in and out. Inside a leaf is spongy tissue. Air, which plants need for photosynthesis, passes through this tissue.

Look at the tubes made of cells in the diagram. They carry food and water to all the parts of a plant. In this way they are a bit like our blood vessels.

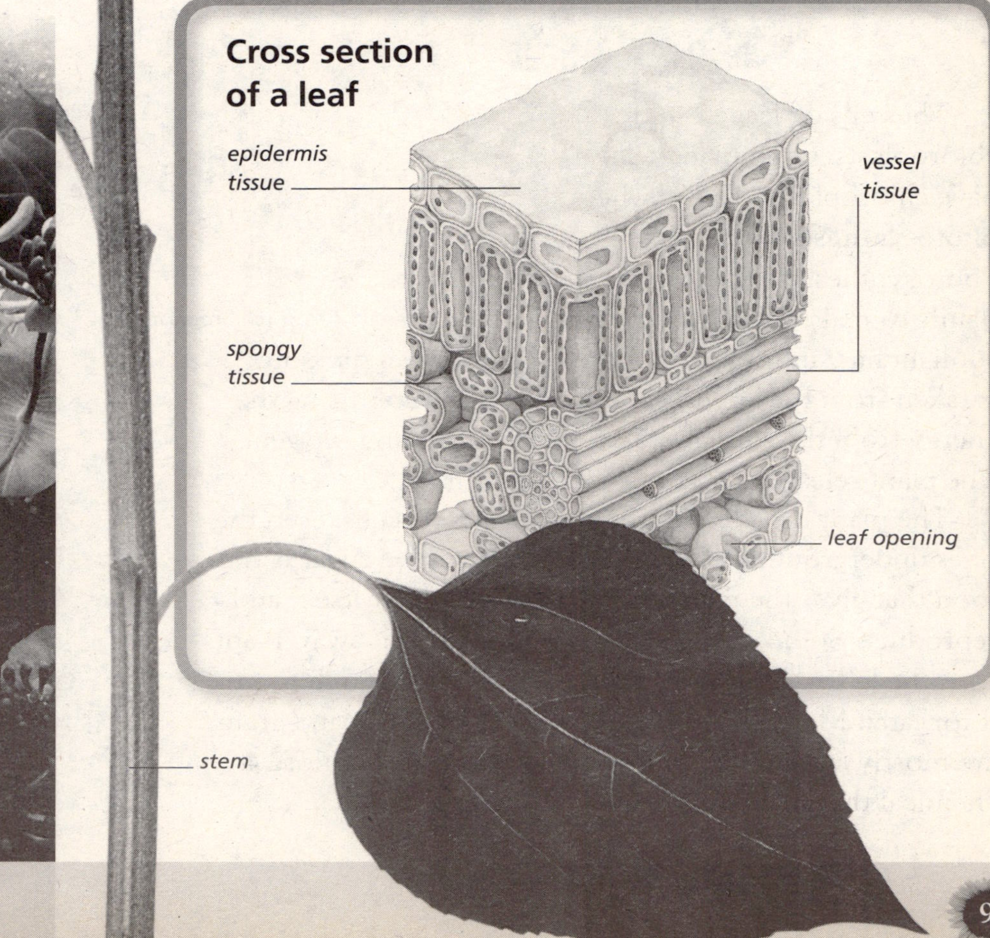

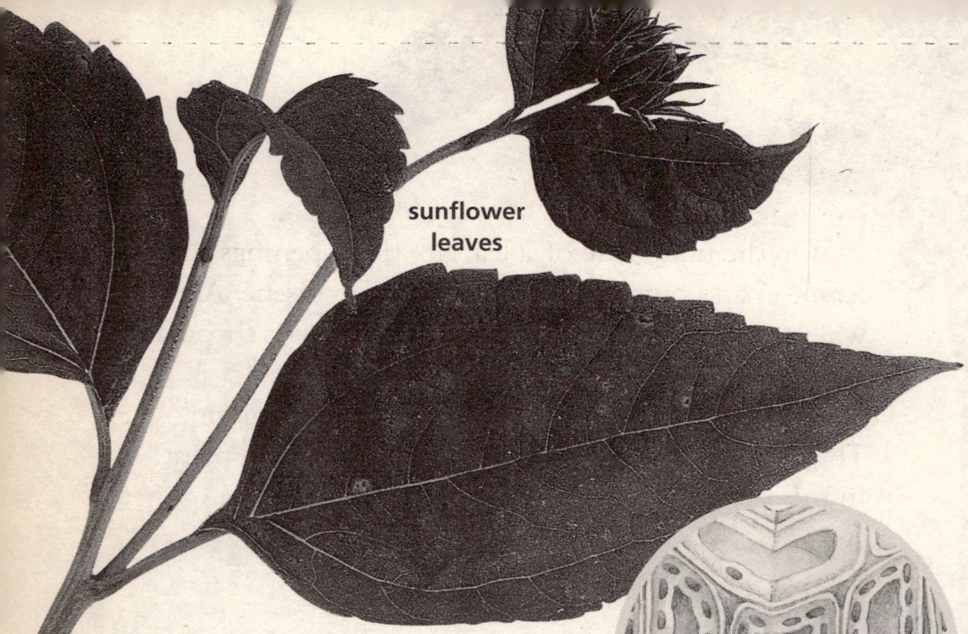
sunflower leaves

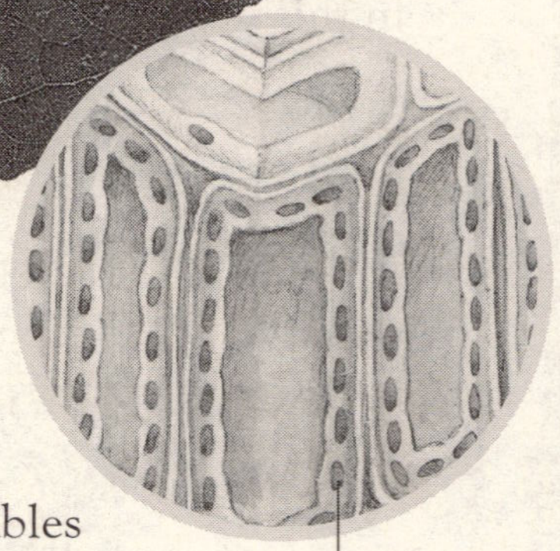
chloroplasts

The cells of leaves hold chloroplasts. Only plant cells have chloroplasts. This is where **photosynthesis** takes place. Photosynthesis is the process that enables plants to make their own food. The leaves use sunlight, air, and water to make sugar. Carbon dioxide is taken from the air. It is combined with water using the energy from the sunlight. This makes sugar and oxygen. The plant releases the oxygen into the air.

The plant then moves the sugar to all its cells, even the ones underground that can't get sunlight. The sugar is the food that gives the plant energy to grow, repair itself, and reproduce. Some of the sugar is not used right away. Plants turn the leftover sugar into a chemical called starch to save it for later. Many of our foods, such as potatoes and grain, are mostly starch. Plants also turn sugar into cellulose, a chemical that makes up plants' strong cell walls.

this same size, shape, and color. Seeds from the Russian giant sunflower will grow to look like their parents. They will be ten to twelve feet tall with a large, single yellow flower.

Growth hormones also affect plant growth. A **growth hormone** is a chemical made by the plant. It causes more cells to grow, and it makes plant cells grow larger.

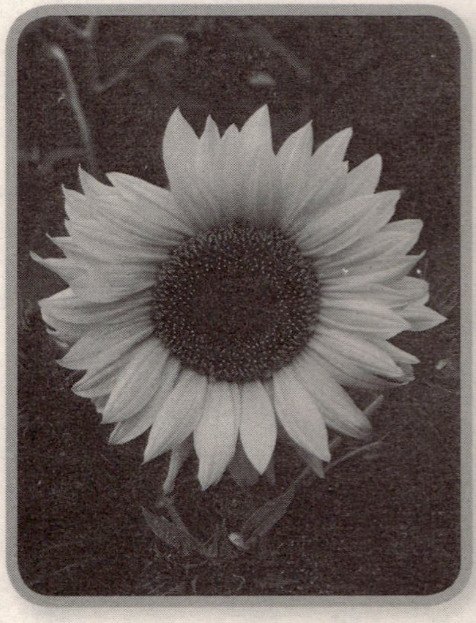
sunspot

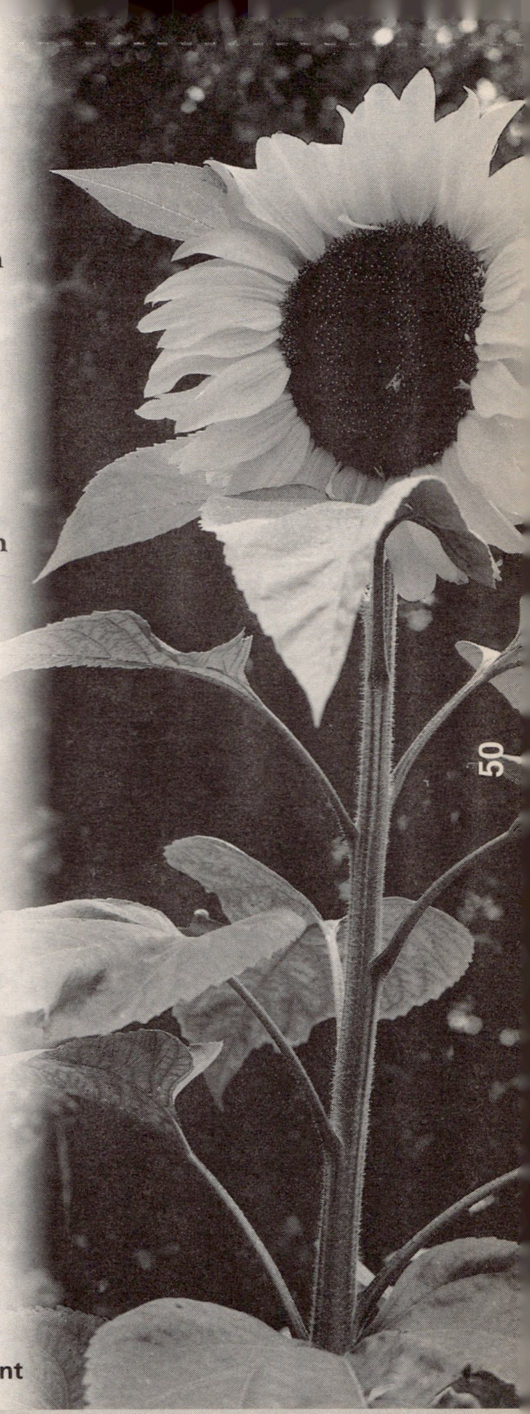
Russian giant

Plants Grow

Sunflowers can grow as high as fifteen feet. This is about as tall as a one-story house. It takes only about four months for a sunflower to become an adult plant. That means it goes from a seed to a flowering plant producing seeds in a single summer.

A plant's DNA helps control how it grows. DNA is in each cell of the plant. It carries the instructions that tell how fast or slow, tall or short a plant will grow. DNA also controls the shape of a plant. DNA from two parent plants is passed on to the next generation. New plants look and grow like the parent plants. The type of sunflower called sunspot is two feet tall. It has wide, golden yellow flowers with brown centers. Seeds from sunspot plants will grow into new plants

autumn beauty

teddy bear

beet

Roots

Now let's look at roots. One job of roots is to hold a plant in the ground as it grows. Another job is to take in the water and minerals that a plant needs to stay alive and keep growing. Not all plants have the same type of roots. Many trees and flowers, including sunflowers, have a fibrous root system. This means many roots grow out in all directions. Another type of root system is a taproot. A taproot is a big, thick root that grows straight down. It's what you eat when you chew a carrot, a beet, a turnip, or a radish! Roots grow longer because of special cells near their ends. These cells divide rapidly to push the root farther into the ground.

taproot

Stems

The stem is part of a plant's food and water transportation system. Food and water for the plant travel through tubes that act like our own blood vessels. These tubes are in the leaves, the stems, and the roots. They are tissues called **xylem** and **phloem.** Xylem carries water and minerals up from the roots, through the stem, and to the leaves. Phloem works the other way. It carries the sugar made in photosynthesis away from the leaves to the rest of the plant. Plants that have xylem and phloem, such as sunflowers and all other flowering plants, are called vascular plants.

You can easily see xylem and phloem in many plants when you look at the pattern of veins in a leaf. You are looking at phloem when you look at the bark of a tree. Tree bark is dead phloem that protects live phloem behind it.

INSIDE ECOSYSTEMS

by Mary Jefferson

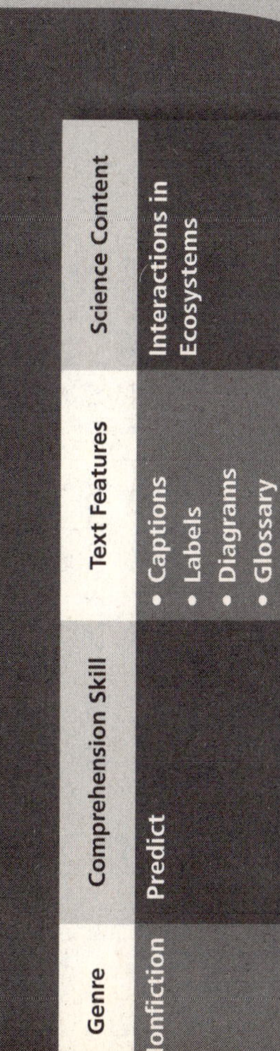

Genre	Comprehension Skill	Text Features	Science Content
Nonfiction	Predict	• Captions • Labels • Diagrams • Glossary	Interactions in Ecosystems

Scott Foresman Science 5.5

PEARSON

Scott Foresman

scottforesman.com

What did you learn?

Vocabulary

community
cycle
ecosystem
energy pyramid
habitat
niche
population

1. Arrange the following elements in order, from the smallest to the largest: ecosystem, organism, community, population, biome.

2. You have learned that more plant and animal species are found in rain forest biomes than in all other biomes. What factors of an ecosystem make it well suited for organisms to live and thrive?

3. Where is more energy found in a food web: at the level of carnivores, or at the level of decomposers?

4. **Writing** in Science You read about animals and plants that often live together in close relationships. Some of these relationships are helpful to the organisms and some are harmful. Write to explain one helpful relationship between two species and one harmful relationship between two species. Include details from the book to support your answer.

5. **Predict** Predict what would happen to a coastline that is protected by a coral reef if that reef were destroyed by a storm.

Picture Credits
Every effort has been made to secure permission and provide appropriate credit for photographic material.
The publisher deeply regrets any omission and pledges to correct errors called to its attention in subsequent editions.

Photo locators denoted as follows: Top (T), Center (C), Bottom (B), Left (L), Right (R), Background (Bkgd).

Opener: Peter Herring/©Image Quest Marine; 1 Getty Images; 4 Digital Vision; 5 IMAGINA/Atsushi Tsunoda/Alamy Images; 7 Getty Images; 8 Francois Gohier/Ardea; 9 (R) Getty Images; 10 (BC) Digital Vision, (BL) ©Jerry Young/DK Images; 11 (B) Francois Gohier/Ardea.com; 12 (BL) Getty Images; 13 Jim Zipp/Photo Researchers, Inc.; 14 Getty Images; 15 Peter Herring/©Image Quest Marine; 17 Steve Bloom/Alamy Images; 19 (C, CR) ©Jerry Young/DK Images; 20 (CB, CBL) ©Jerry Young/DK Images.

Scott Foresman/Dorling Kindersley would also like to thank: 19 (CL) Jerry Young/DK Images; 20 (C) Philip Dowell/DK Images; 22 (BR) Natural History Museum, London/DK Images.

Unless otherwise acknowledged, all photographs are the copyright © of Dorling Kindersley, a division of Pearson.

ISBN: 0-328-13929-7

Copyright © Pearson Education, Inc.

Glossary

community	all the populations in one area
cycle	a repeating process or flow of material through a system
ecosystem	all the living and nonliving things in an area
energy pyramid	a diagram that shows the amounts of energy at each level of a food chain
habitat	the place where an organism lives
niche	the role an organism has in an ecosystem
population	all members of one species in one area at one time

INSIDE ECOSYSTEMS

by Mary Jefferson

What is an ecosystem?

An **ecosystem** is all the living and nonliving things
in an area. The park on your way to school is an ecosystem,
and so is your home. The desert is also an ecosystem.

An ecosystem is filled with different populations.
A **population** is a group of organisms of one species
that live in an area at the same time. A population could
be all the lizards or all the cactuses in an area.

What are some nonliving parts
of this desert ecosystem?

Oxygen and Carbon Dioxide

Oxygen is the second most common gas in the
atmosphere, after nitrogen. There is much less carbon
dioxide in the air. Both oxygen and carbon dioxide
constantly move through ecosystems, and both are
necessary for life.

Plants need carbon dioxide. They take it in and give
off oxygen in a process called photosynthesis. Some
microorganisms also release oxygen in this way.

Animals need oxygen to live. They take it in and give
off carbon dioxide during the process of respiration, or
breathing. Respiration combines oxygen with food to
produce carbon dioxide and water. Carbon dioxide is
also released by combustion, or burning.

oxygen–carbon dioxide cycle

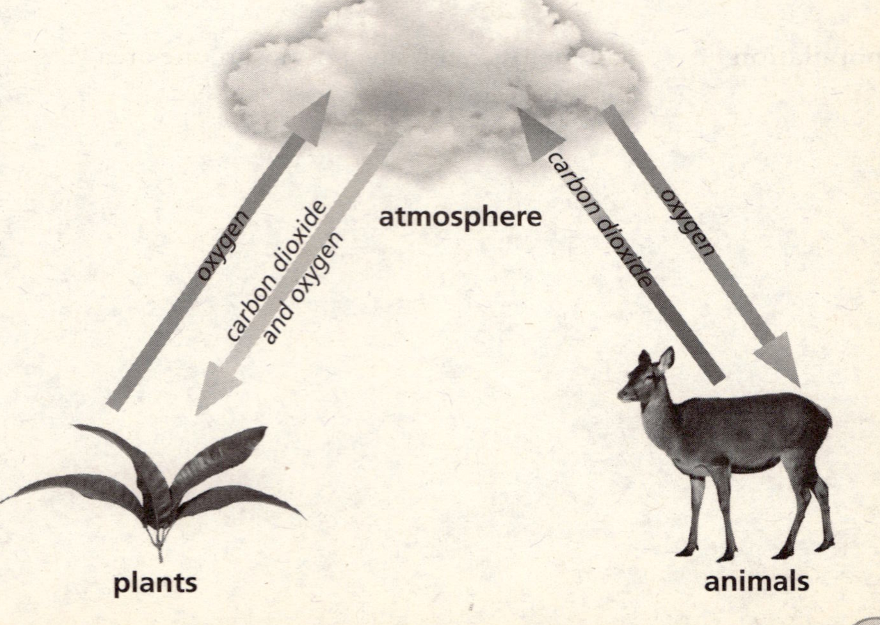

Nitrogen

An important cycle in nature is the nitrogen cycle.
All cells in plants and animals need nitrogen. Almost
$\frac{8}{10}$ of Earth's atmosphere is made up of nitrogen gas.

The nitrogen cycle starts with nitrogen gas in the air.
Bacteria in the soil turn the gas into a form that plants can
use. Then plants absorb it through their roots. Herbivores
get their nitrogen by eating these plants, and carnivores get it
by eating the herbivores. When an animal or plant dies,
or when an animal produces waste, the nitrogen returns to
the soil to start the cycle again. Nitrogen can also be made
into a usable form by lightning and brought to the ground
by rain. Some special plants can also take it directly from
the air. Humans contribute to the nitrogen cycle too,
by putting nitrogen-rich fertilizers in the soil.

nitrogen cycle

All the populations of an area make up a **community.**
Members of a community depend on each other. In a desert,
the kangaroo rat depends on the seeds of plants for food.
The rattlesnake feeds on the kangaroo rat, and the hawk
makes a meal of the rattlesnake.

Air, water, soil, temperature, and sunlight are the
nonliving parts of an ecosystem. They help the organisms
in an ecosystem survive. If a population gets too large,
some members may not find enough to eat. The population
may die out or move to another area.

desert tortoise

What are biomes?

A biome is a large ecosystem with basically the same climate and species all through it. A single biome may cover many countries. A desert biome covers many African and Asian countries. Several South American countries are in a tropical rain forest biome.

There are two kinds of rain forests—tropical and temperate. Tropical rain forests are found near the equator. They are always hot and very wet. Temperate rain forests are also wet, but much cooler. There is a temperate rain forest in Washington State and one in western Canada.

Earth's biomes

- polar
- tundra
- taiga
- tropical rain forest
- deciduous forest
- grassland
- desert
- mountain

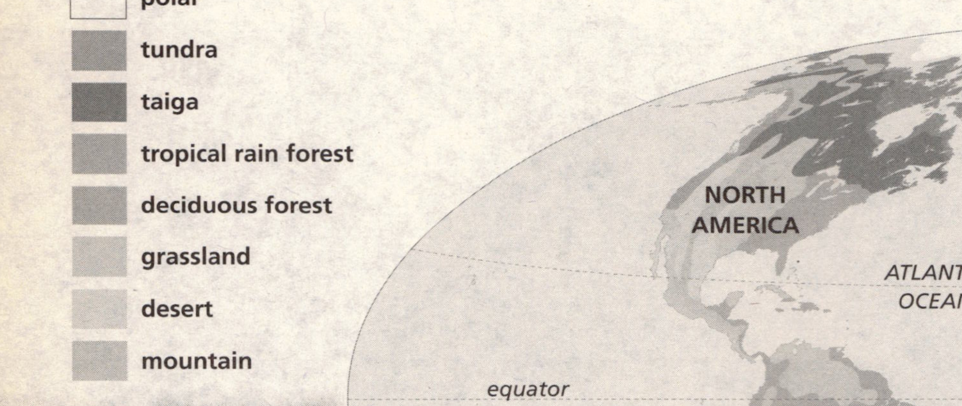

Cycles in Ecosystems

Nature Recycles

All organisms create waste. All organisms eventually die. Imagine what Earth would be like if waste and dead matter were never removed.

Certain organisms serve as garbage collectors. They are called decomposers. Their niche, or job, is to clean up an ecosystem by eating waste material and dead matter. They break matter down and return it to the soil in the form of minerals and nutrients. There it can be reused by growing plants. In this way decomposers are an important part of the life cycle. A **cycle** is a repeating process or flow of material through a system. In an ecosystem, there is a constant cycle of minerals and nutrients from living things to the soil and back again.

Dead matter is also broken down by something that's not an organism: fire. When trees and plants burn, the ashes fertilize the soil.

Fungi and bacteria decompose a tree trunk, returning its nutrients to the soil.

The Energy Pyramid

Energy in an ecosystem starts with sunlight. It passes to producers, herbivores, carnivores, omnivores, and finally to decomposers. But not all the energy at each stage of the food chain makes it to the next step.

An **energy pyramid** is a diagram that shows how energy moves through the levels of a food chain. It shows how the amount of energy decreases as matter moves higher and higher in the chain. When the energy decreases, it does not disappear. It is used up in the everyday activities of the organisms.

For example, an insect might eat a plant, and then fly for a while before being eaten by a bird. By the time the bird eats the insect, the insect has used energy for flying, breathing, and other activities. Only part of the insect's energy from the plant is left to pass to the bird and up the food chain.

Each organism in an ecosystem has a niche and a habitat. A **niche** is the role an organism has in a habitat. A **habitat** is the home of a group of plants and animals in the natural world. A hawk in a temperate forest habitat has the niche of a hunter. It eats small mammals and snakes. Its droppings fertilize the soil. Its nest has eggs that snakes and squirrels use as food.

The relationships in an ecosystem help keep it balanced. If one or more species increases its numbers, the balance is affected. If there are too many hawks and not enough mice, the hawks will die out or move to another habitat. Humans also affect the balance of an ecosystem. For example, too much logging destroys habitats for many plants and animals.

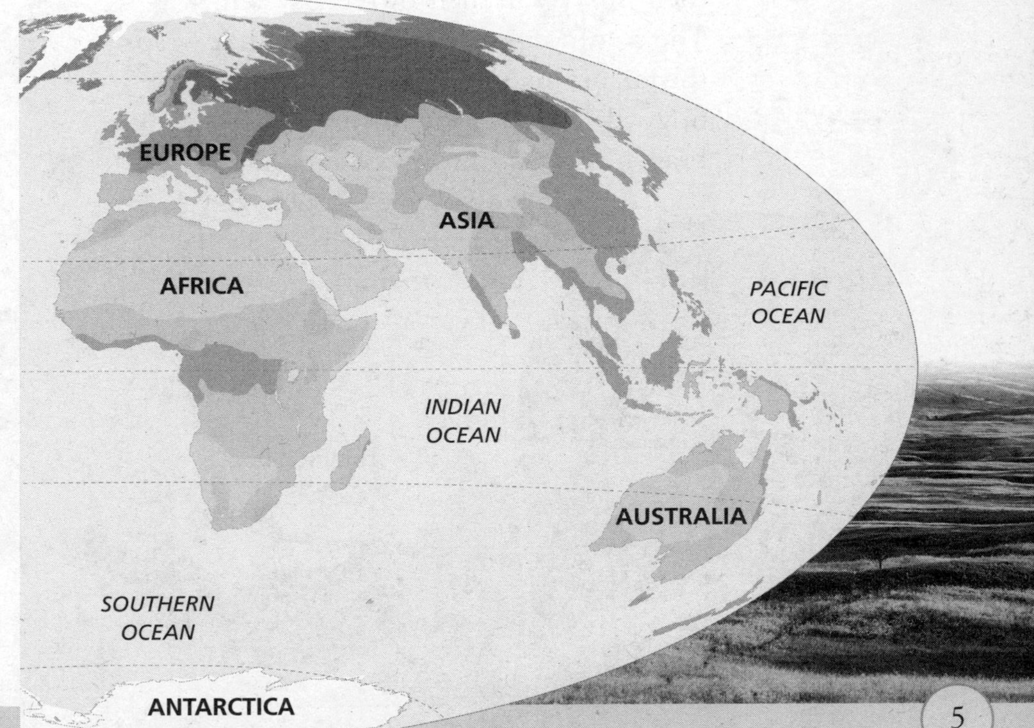

Land Biomes
Tropical Rain Forest

Ecosystems that lie near the equator are always warm and wet. The constant sunlight and rain help many plants and trees grow. The result is a tropical rain forest. Tropical rain forest biomes cover less than $\frac{1}{10}$ of Earth's surface. Yet they contain up to $\frac{7}{10}$ of Earth's plants and animals. A single tree often provides a habitat for dozens of flowers, mammals, birds, and insects.

Animals have structures that help them survive in their own ecosystem. The common boa has a strong tail. It wraps the tail around a branch and lifts its body upward. Then it wraps around another branch and lifts the rest of its body up behind it. Some types of boas have small pits on their heads that allow them to sense the heat of their prey.

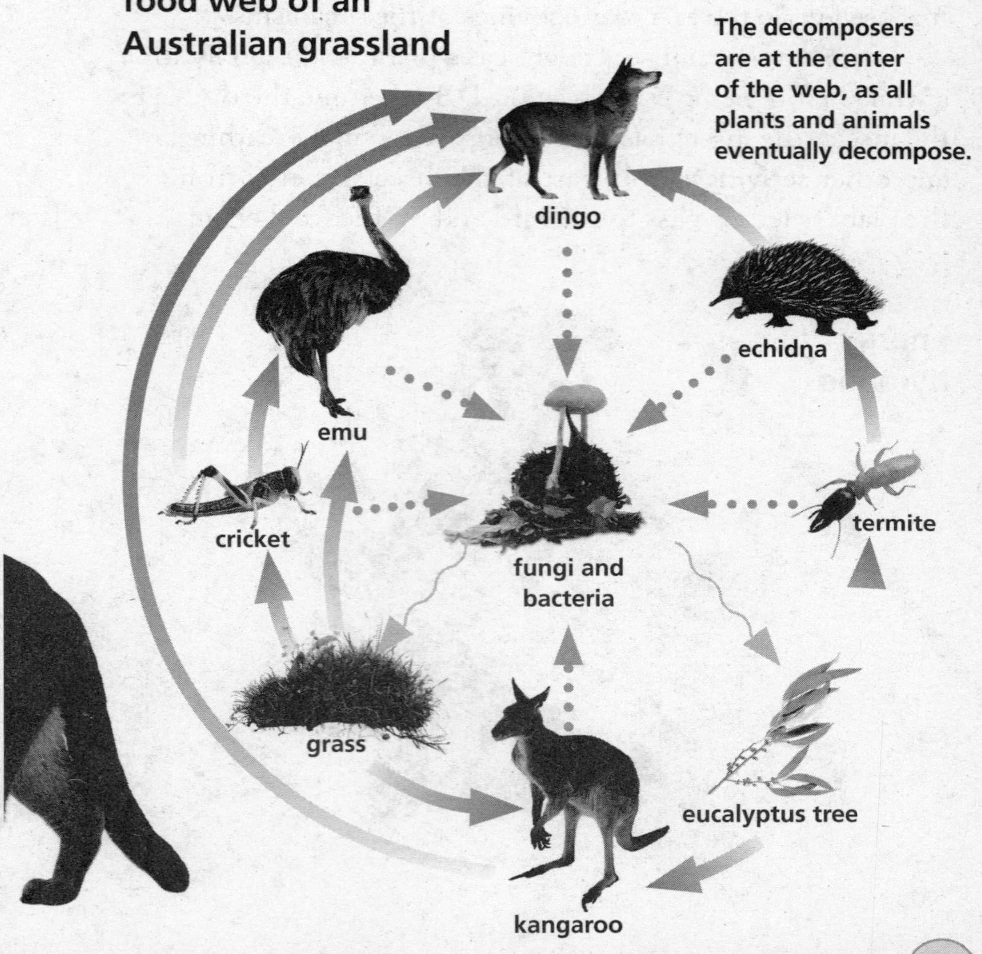

common boa

Some food chains are very short. They involve only a plant and a decomposer. Others are very long and may involve more than one carnivore or omnivore. A food chain is only one simple energy process. A food web is more complex. It contains all the food chains within one ecosystem.

Examine the simplified food web below. Identify the producers and the consumers. Then identify the herbivores, carnivores, and the one omnivore. Which organisms are decomposers?

food web of an Australian grassland

The decomposers are at the center of the web, as all plants and animals eventually decompose.

Moving Energy

Food Chains and Food Webs

All living organisms need energy. Energy moves between organisms in food chains or food webs.

Producers are organisms that make their own food. Plants and some microorganisms make food through photosynthesis. Consumers cannot make their own food. They must eat other organisms to get energy. All animals are consumers. Herbivores eat only plants. Carnivores eat only other animals. Omnivores eat plants and animals. Decomposers, such as fungi and bacteria, eat waste or dead organisms.

When food is eaten, both matter and energy move from one organism to another. When this process involves several organisms, it forms a food chain.

Almost all food chains on land start with plants. Ocean food chains usually start with plankton, which are microorganisms much like plants. Bacteria are the basis of deep-sea food chains.

Deciduous Forest

Deciduous forest biomes are common in the northern United States, northeastern Asia, and across Europe. Oaks, maples, and elms need much less rain than rain forest trees. Deciduous trees lose their leaves in the fall to save food and water during the winter.

Some mammals in these forests also save energy during the winter. Snakes, frogs, and salamanders hibernate underground. This means they fall into a deep sleep during which they do not need to eat.

If too many of one species are found in an ecosystem, the balance between hunter and hunted breaks down. For example, if too many predators are competing for a small number of prey animals, some of the hunters may starve.

The brown bear is one of the largest predators in a deciduous forest.

Grassland

Tall grasses once covered large areas of the middle part of the United States. Some grasses grew to be two meters tall. These biomes are called grasslands. Today, much of this land has been plowed under for farms.

Grassland biomes have few trees. Trees need a lot of water, and grasslands do not get much rain. Also, the thick root systems of the grasses that live there prevent trees from growing. Grassland soil is extremely fertile, which is why it is good for farming.

Grassland animals include buffalo, antelope, and prairie dogs. They all eat the grass and in turn are hunted by wolves and coyotes. Wolves were nearly wiped out by humans in the United States during the twentieth century. Now they are making a comeback in Yellowstone National Park and in Idaho. They feed on elk, which are also grassland animals. Wolves prevent elk herds from growing too fast.

The giant anteater lives in the grasslands of South America.

A Close Relationship

Organisms do not always compete. Two species can live in symbiosis, or a long-term relationship. In symbiosis, one species always gains something. The other species may gain something, or it may lose something. Or, it may not be affected by the relationship.

In Africa, zebras have a helpful symbiosis with a type of bird. The birds ride around on the zebra's back, eating insects that live in the zebra's fur. When predators are near, the bird makes noise, alerting the zebra. Both animals gain something.

Parasites are plants or animals that live on other organisms. They get food, but they give nothing in return. The fleas on your pets are parasites.

Sometimes symbiosis is necessary for both species to survive. Many flowering plants need insects to spread their pollen to make new plants. The insects get food from the nectar that plants make.

These birds warn the zebra of danger.

Organism Interactions

Competing Organisms

Plants and animals in an ecosystem compete for water, light, food, mates, and space. Those that win survive and reproduce. Those that lose die or move to a new ecosystem.

Competition takes place between organisms of the same species. It also takes place between different species. For example, two herons may continually compete for the same fish while wading in a river. If one heron always manages to catch the fish first, then the other heron will need to find another fishing spot. In a forest, hawks, wolves, and snakes may all hunt the same kinds of mice. If there are not enough mice, only the best hunters will have enough to eat.

Plants compete for water and sunlight. If a plant with a large root system grows in an ecosystem with a plant with a small root system, which species do you think will grow better? Why?

The bilby is a mammal native to Australia. When rabbits were introduced to Australia, they competed with the bilbies for food and habitat. The bilby is now an endangered species.

Taiga

A taiga is a forest biome that is found in very cool areas. Taigas lie across northern Canada and Russia. They are much drier than deciduous forests. Most trees in taiga ecosystems are species with needles, such as pine and fir. Needles are long, thin leaves that make food for the tree in the same way that other leaves do. They have much less surface area than most leaves, so they don't lose as much water. The needles also have a waxy coating, which helps them hold in water during dry periods.

Communities of bear, elk, moose, and wolves live in taiga ecosystems. Their fur and their large size help these animals keep warm during the cold winters.

The dark green color of needles helps absorb the heat of the Sun.

Desert

A desert is an area that receives less than twenty-five centimeters of rain or snow each year. But a desert does not need to be hot, sandy, or lifeless. It can be cold or rocky, and have a large variety of living creatures.

All desert species have to find ways to get what little water is available. The root systems of desert plants are often close to the surface. This helps them soak up the rain quickly before it evaporates. Cactuses have leaves like waxy needles. Animals in hot deserts don't move much during the hottest part of the day. Some snakes, beetles, and small mammals dig into the cool sand or earth. Others rest quietly under rocks or vegetation. Most wait until dark to hunt.

Large ears help the African fennec fox to lose heat in its hot desert home.

Deep-Sea Ecosystem

The deep-sea ecosystem is cold, dark, and under great pressure from all the ocean water above it. Animals that live in deep-sea biomes do not eat living plants. Why? No sunlight reaches that deep, so plants cannot grow. Some organisms at this depth eat dead plants and animals that sink down from above. Near hot vents on the ocean floor, bacteria make their food from chemicals in the water coming out of the vents. Then the bacteria become food for larger animals.

It is hard for organisms to see in such a dark environment. Some deep-sea animals have well-developed eyes to help them see in the dark. Some of these animals create their own light with special organs. This light helps attract mates and prey.

Pressure increases as the water depth increases. Deep-sea organisms are adapted to this pressure. In fact, they are so well suited to high pressure that they can't survive the lower pressures at the ocean's surface.

The deep-sea anglerfish has a rod that dangles in front of its mouth. The end of the rod glows in the dark to attract prey.

Coral Reef Ecosystem

A coral reef ecosystem is like a small city. Its residents include clams, crabs, eels, fish, octopuses, and sharks.

Corals are tiny animals that get food from algae that live inside them. The algae make food from sunlight. In turn, the algae eat the waste products from the coral. As corals die, their hard outside coverings build up to make a reef.

Coral reefs grow in shallow water with lots of sunlight. Large coral reefs are found near Florida and in Australia.

Like salt marshes, coral reef ecosystems protect the land from storm waves. The study of some organisms that grow in reefs has led to new medicines. In addition, many fish that we catch for food live in and around coral reefs.

Coral reefs are home to many types of animals.

Tundra

Tundra biomes are found in northern areas of the world. They are cold and get little rain. There are few trees, and the grasses do not grow very high.

In a tundra—as in any ecosystem—a population of organisms can grow to only a certain size. Limited supplies of food, water, space, and shelter control how big a population gets. If a population becomes too large, there will not be enough resources for all its members. The ecosystem will become overcrowded, and organisms may die or move away. The number of organisms that can be supported by the resources in an ecosystem is called the carrying capacity.

Carrying capacity in the tundra is limited by the cold weather. The soil is frozen most of the time. Only the top layer thaws enough for plants to grow. But they can't grow very tall, and trees can hardly grow at all. This limits food and shelter for many populations of animals.

A thick coat keeps the musk ox warm.

Water Biomes

River Ecosystem

A river ecosystem contains a variety of animals. These include fish, crayfish, otters, ducks, turtles, and insects. Not all animals can live in fast-flowing rivers. Some must live where the water flows more slowly. All organisms have trouble living in polluted waters.

The kinds of plants and animals that live in rivers are different from those that live in oceans. This is because some species need fresh water, while others need salt water.

Fish live entirely in the water. Species such as the river otter live both in and out of the water. The otter is an animal that can hunt on land. But its long, sleek body also makes it a fast swimmer. It can close its nose and ears while it swims after fish.

river otter

Wetlands are home to many reptiles, including alligators and crocodiles.

Wetland Ecosystem

A wetland may be part land and part water. Or it may be covered with water only at certain times of the year. The Florida Everglades is a huge wetland. It holds vast swamps as well as large areas of tall grass. Everglade animals include alligators, fish, deer, snakes, frogs, and wading birds such as herons and egrets. Wetlands act as water purifiers. They are full of plants and tiny organisms that filter the water. This keeps the water clean for all the organisms that live there.

An estuary is a meeting place between a river and an ocean. Many wetlands are estuaries, and the ocean's tides flow in and out of them every day. These wetlands are called salt marshes, even though their water is not as salty as ocean water. Salt marshes act as a buffer between the land and violent ocean storms.

How Ecosystems Change

by Ellen Chapman

Genre	Comprehension Skill	Text Features	Science Content
Nonfiction	Cause and Effect	• Captions • Labels • Maps • Glossary	Changing Ecosystems

Scott Foresman Science 5.6

PEARSON

Scott Foresman

ISBN 0-328-13932-7

9 780328 139323

90000

scottforesman.com

What did you learn?

1. What fish was introduced to Maryland's ponds in 2002? What happened?

2. Why is each offspring different from others that have the same parents?

3. What is an example of a behavioral adaptation?

4. **Writing** in Science Most bacterial diseases can be treated by antibiotics. But some bacteria have adapted and changed, and have proven resistant to treatments. Write to explain what kind of adaptation this is, and what effect it might have on how diseases are treated. Use details from the book to support your answer.

5. **Cause and Effect** The giraffe's body has changed over many years. What was the cause of this change?

Picture Credits
Every effort has been made to secure permission and provide appropriate credit for photographic material.
The publisher deeply regrets any omission and pledges to correct errors called to its attention in subsequent editions.

Photo locators denoted as follows: Top (T), Center (C), Bottom (B), Left (L), Right (R), Background (Bkgd).

Opener: Vince Streano/Corbis; 1 Getty Images; 2 (CB) Robert Noonan/Photo Researchers, Inc., (BC) Maurizio Lanini/Corbis; 3 Vince Streano/Corbis; 11 (TL) Paul A. Souders/Corbis, (C) Lee Snider/Photo Images/Corbis; 12 Custom Medical Stock Photo; 14 U.S. Fish & Wildlife Service.

Unless otherwise acknowledged, all photographs are the copyright © of Dorling Kindersley, a division of Pearson.

ISBN: 0-328-13932-7

Copyright © Pearson Education, Inc.

All Rights Reserved. Printed in the United States of America. The blackline masters in this publication are designed for use with appropriate equipment to reproduce copies for classroom use only. Scott Foresman grants permission to classroom teachers to reproduce from these masters.

2 3 4 5 6 7 8 9 10 V004 13 12 11 10 09 08 07 06 05

Glossary

behavioral adaptation   a change in the way members of a species act that helps them to survive

extinct   when every member of a species has died and there are no members of that species left alive anywhere on Earth

inherit   to receive genes from one's parents

mutation   a random change in an organisms genes

pesticide   a poison that kills insects

structural adaptation   a change in a body part of an organism that helps it to survive

How Ecosystems Change

by Ellen Chapman

Ecosystems Change
Animals Change Ecosystems

In the 1860s, an amateur scientist near Boston accidentally introduced the gypsy moth caterpillar, an insect native to Europe, into the ecosystem. More than one hundred years later, this forest pest has spread throughout much of the eastern United States. It feeds on forest foliage, especially oak and aspen trees. In some areas, and in years when the caterpillars are most active, up to $\frac{1}{5}$ percent of trees in a particular forest may die.

The gypsy moth caterpillar can harm the environment. However, some animals change ecosystems in a helpful way. When animals such as earthworms burrow through the ground, they make holes that let more moisture into the soil. This helps plant roots to grow.

Gypsy moth caterpillar activity causes damage to trees.

Other organisms that are close to being extinct are called endangered species. Organisms that are in less danger are called threatened species. The blue whale, the largest mammal that has ever lived, is an endangered species. For years it seemed as if this giant would become extinct. Beginning in the late 1800s, it was hunted for the oil its body contained. There may have been up to 350,000 blue whales in the world's oceans at that time. By 1931, they were highly endangered. Almost all of them had been killed. In 1966, the International Whaling Commission banned the hunting of blue whales. Today it is estimated that there are about ten thousand blue whales.

Ecosystems are always changing. Sometimes the change is natural. But often the change is caused by humans. These changes can be dangerous, causing whole species to disappear from the Earth forever. People must be careful in the way they treat the world and remember that it is shared with many other living things.

The blue whale is an endangered species.

One recent example of extinction in the United States
is the dusky seaside sparrow, which became extinct in 1987.
It had lived on the east coast of Florida, but its habitat
was reduced as highways and building development spread
to more areas. From now on, scientists will only know
about the dusky seaside sparrow from reading records
kept about it.

Animals that became extinct a very long
time ago can be studied by their
fossils. Fossils are remains of plants
and animals that are no longer living.
There are many different reasons why
species become extinct. Fossils give
scientists information about what past
ecosystems and species were like and
what caused their extinction.

Fossils have also shown
scientists that many species have
become extinct in the past. In any
ecosystem, some organisms will
survive, and some will not.

**The dusky seaside sparrow
became extinct in 1987.**

People Change Ecosystems

Your backyard is an ecosystem. Think of how many
ways it changes. Sometimes it is noticeable, and sometimes
it is not. If you plant a vegetable garden, you are changing
the ecosystem. You are providing food for yourself, but also
taking away open space and nutrients from other animals.

When you cut down a tree, organisms that relied on
it for everything from food to shade must turn elsewhere.
They will have to adapt to the changed ecosystem. Their new
ways of living will change how other organisms live in the
ecosystem as well.

Ecosystems can be changed by people on a much larger
scale as well. What if a forest fire wiped out a forest? What
happens when **pesticides** kill all the insects in an ecosystem?
In Maryland in 2002, it was discovered that the snakehead
fish, a meat-eater native to Asia, had been introduced to a
local pond. This new fish, nicknamed the "walking fish"
because it has the ability to survive out of water and
walk from pond to pond, has completely changed the
pond's ecosystem.

Species Change

All organisms pass on traits to their young. These traits may change over time to help a species survive.

Inheriting DNA

Heredity is the process by which plants and animals **inherit** half of their genes from each parent. The genes control the way the organisms grow. But each offspring of the same parents is different because each one receives a unique mix of genes. This is one way offspring can change from generation to generation.

Children usually look a bit like each of their parents. But sometimes offspring show traits that neither of their parents have.

A child might be born with red hair, when both parents have brown hair. Nevertheless, this is still an inherited trait, because children get all of their genes from their parents.

DNA has the structure of a double helix.

What is extinction?

If a plant or animal is not adapted to changes in its ecosystem, it will try to move, or migrate, to another place. But if the organism cannot move, or there is nowhere left to go, the size of its population will shrink, and the species may become **extinct.** That means that there are no members of its kind alive. Many species are becoming extinct as people move into other organisms' habitats, taking away their homes and food supplies.

Dinosaurs are probably the best-known extinct animals.

You may have heard of "strep throat" and may have even had it. The illness is caused by the streptococcus bacteria. The bacteria produce toxins, which can harm the body. In most cases, medicines called antibiotics can kill streptococcus. But one type of the bacteria has adapted and now survives some antibiotics. This makes it very hard to cure, and dangerous to people.

Today many bacteria are adapting to survive antibiotics. Scientists are always looking for new medicines to use when bacteria adapt to the old ones.

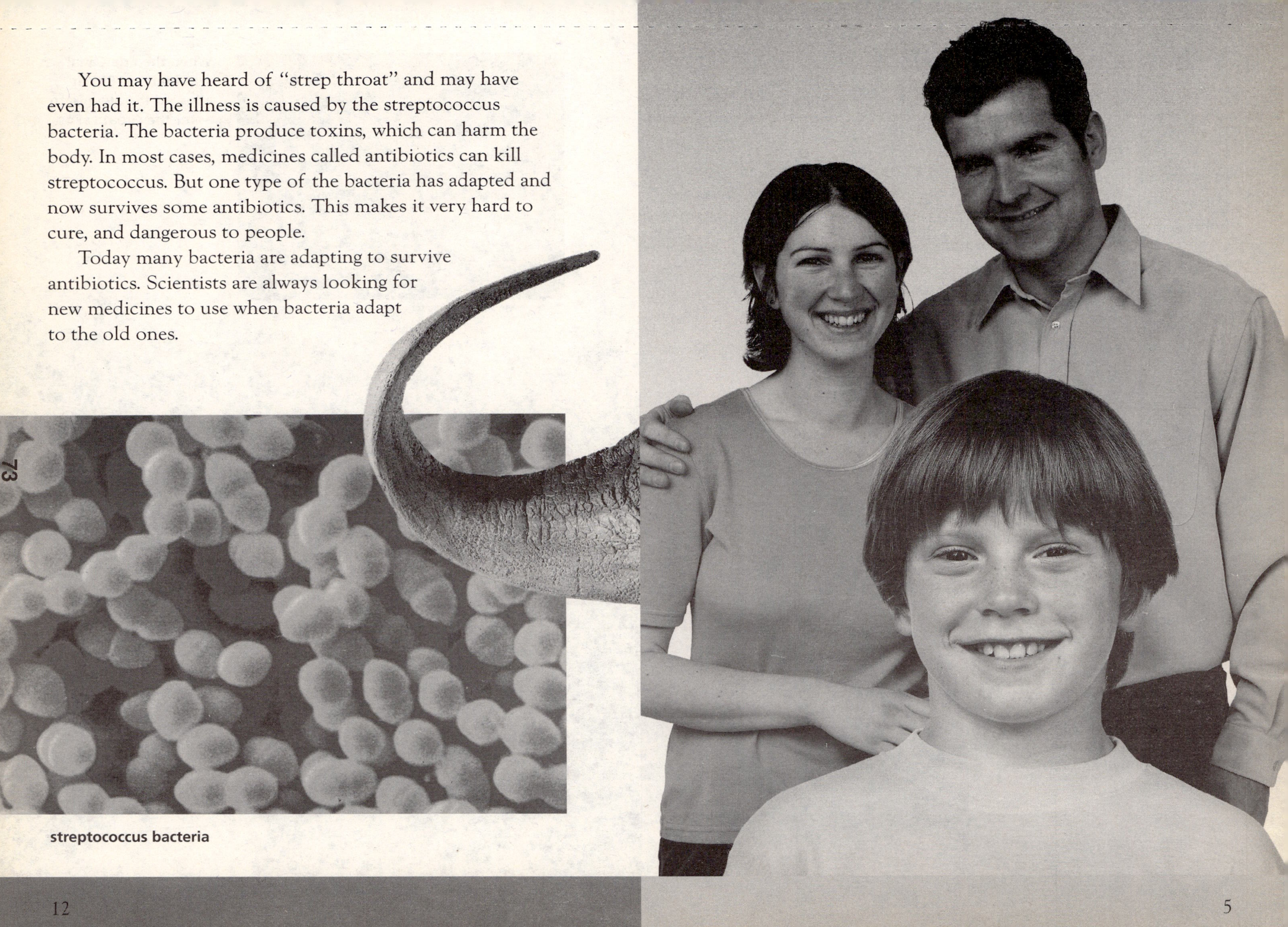

streptococcus bacteria

73

What is not inherited?

Genes can determine much of what an organism is like. But the ecosystem also plays a role in how the organism grows. The color of organisms can be affected by their ecosystems. For example, plants need light to develop chlorophyll, which makes leaves green. Without enough light, some leaves can be a lighter shade of green.

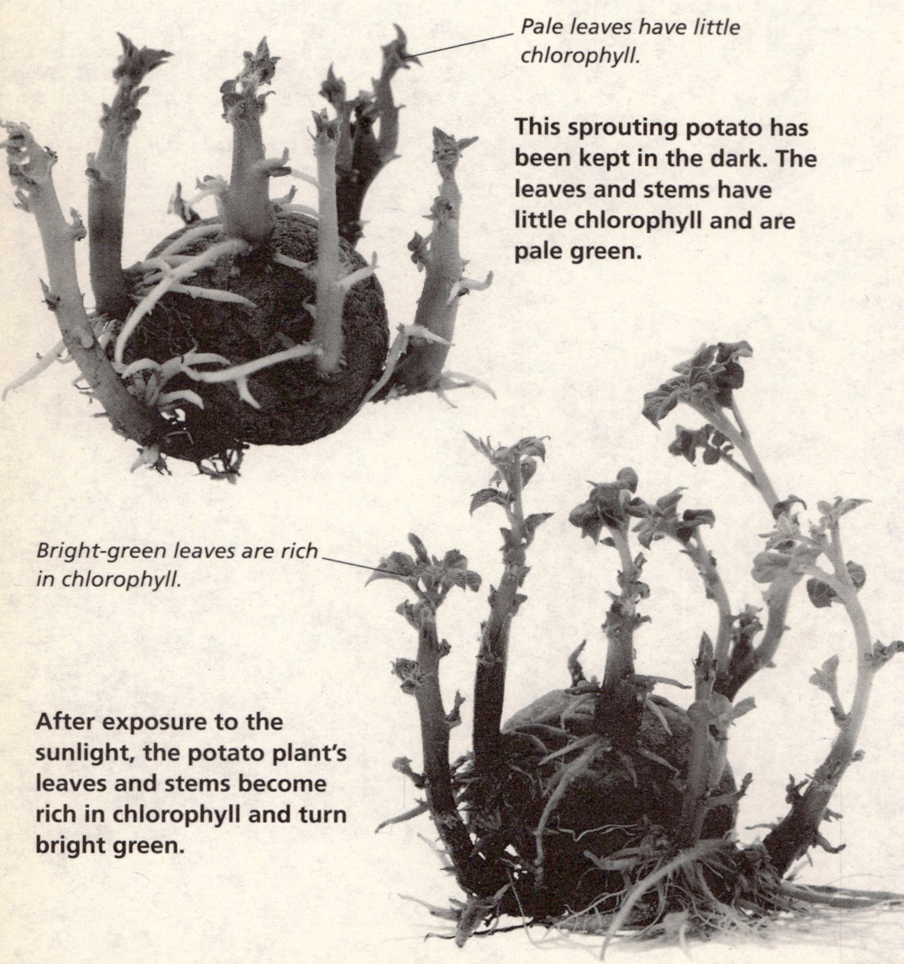

Pale leaves have little chlorophyll.

This sprouting potato has been kept in the dark. The leaves and stems have little chlorophyll and are pale green.

Bright-green leaves are rich in chlorophyll.

After exposure to the sunlight, the potato plant's leaves and stems become rich in chlorophyll and turn bright green.

When the Erie Canal was built in 1825, it allowed the alewife to enter the Great Lakes.

Changes Causing More Changes

When an organism changes, it can affect other organisms. This can cause the other organisms to change as well.

Behavior Changes

The way animals act can change for many reasons. Their actions might change if there has been a change in the number or types of animals in their ecosystem. For example, if one animal that is prey for a predator moves out of an ecosystem, the predator must find a new source of food. It may begin hunting a different animal. This new behavior might change the ecosystem a lot.

Population Changes

Organisms that are introduced into an ecosystem bring many changes. The alewife is a fish that originally bred in rivers, but made its home in the Atlantic Ocean. It is believed that in the 1800s, the alewife followed the Erie Canal when it left the ocean for a short time to breed. It eventually made its way to the Great Lakes. The fish never returned to salt water and became a major species of lake fish in its new home. In fact, the ecosystem of some of the Great Lakes is now very dependent on the alewife because it eats zooplankton, keeping the lakes clean. It also serves as food for larger organisms, such as salmon. Scientists know that removing the alewife from its adopted ecosystem would cause lots of problems. Instead, they are focusing on keeping the alewife population stable.

Adaptations

When ecosystems change, organisms that are best adapted to the change will fit into the ecosystem the best. One way that this can happen is for a **mutation,** or random change, to take place in an organism's genes. Often the mutation is harmful to the organism or has no effect. But sometimes the change helps the organism survive, so the change can be passed on to its offspring. The organisms that are best adapted to compete for food and shelter in a changed ecosystem survive very well. For example, if an ecosystem suddenly becomes colder, members of a species that are best adapted to the new temperature will survive.

The penguin is a bird that does not fly. Its wings have become flippers, and its feet are webbed. Both of these adaptations have enabled it to be at home in the sea.

Structural Adaptations

Some of these adaptations are called **structural adaptations.** This means a change in a body part of an organism that helps it survive in its ecosystem. For example, it is thought that giraffes with long necks were better at getting food from the tops of trees in the African savannah. The giraffe's ancestors had shorter necks. Then one was born with a slightly longer neck, allowing it to reach food that the other animals could not. This advantage was passed on through genes to new generations of giraffes. Over many years, many slight changes like this gave the giraffe the very long neck it has today. This process is called natural selection. Helpful adaptations are passed on, or selected, by nature.

Behavioral Adaptations

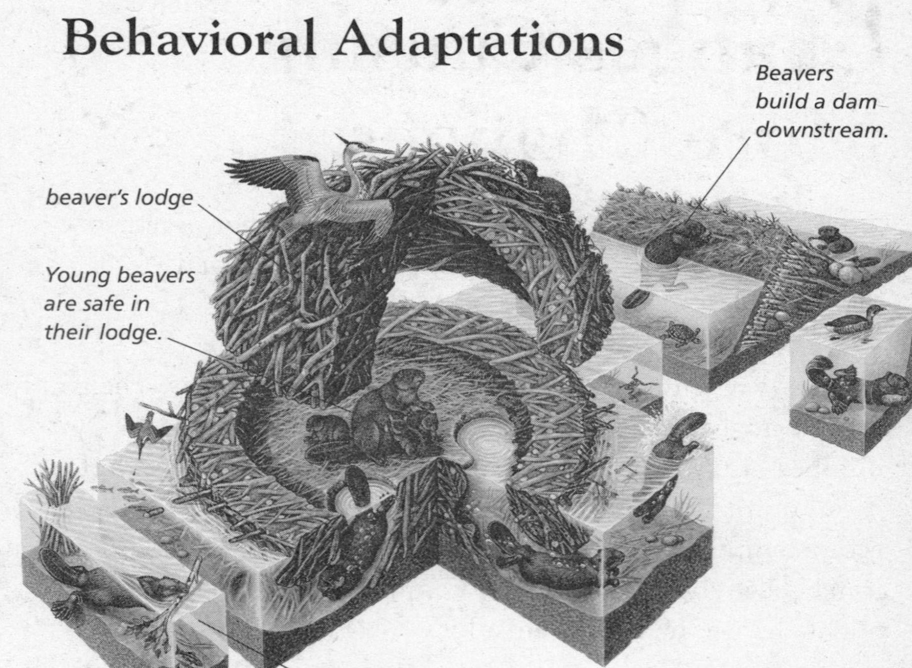

Beavers change the environment by damming streams.

Another way organisms are adapted to changed ecosystems is by **behavioral adaptations.** These are changes in the way an organism acts that help it to survive. They are sometimes called instincts. For example, beavers are born knowing how to build dams. They inherit this instinct from their parents. The instinct to build a dam is a helpful adaptation that was caused by natural selection. Some behaviors are learned, not inherited. For example, chimpanzees sometimes use leaves to get water out of hollow trees. They crumple the leaves up and use them like sponges. This behavior is learned, and parents teach it to their offspring.

Earth's Water

by Jocelyn Vial

Genre	Comprehension Skill	Text Features	Science Content
Nonfiction	Sequence	• Captions • Diagrams • Maps • Glossary	Water on Earth

Scott Foresman Science 5.7

What did you learn?

1. What causes ocean water to vary in temperature from place to place?

2. Compare precipitation and evaporation.

3. What role do temperature and pressure play in forming clouds?

4. **Writing** in Science Ocean water has higher salinity than swimming pool water. Write to explain why some water has higher salinity than other water. Include details from the book to support your answer.

5. **Sequence** What are the four steps in treating water for human use? Write them in order.

Vocabulary

aquifers
condensation
evaporation
precipitation
reservoir
salinity
sleet
sublimation
water table

Picture Credits
Every effort has been made to secure permission and provide appropriate credit for photographic material. The publisher deeply regrets any omission and pledges to correct errors called to its attention in subsequent editions.

Photo locators denoted as follows: Top (T), Center (C), Bottom (B), Left (L), Right (R), Background (Bkgd).

Opener: Getty Images; 1 Digital Vision; 2 (B) Getty Images; 4 (B) Getty Images, (T) Jack Sullivan/Alamy Images; 6 (B) Getty Images; 7 (T) K.M. Westermann/Corbis; 8 (B) Getty Images, (CR) Digital Vision; 9 Getty Images; 10 (B) Getty Images; 12 (B) Getty Images; 14 (B) Getty Images; 15 (T) Digital Vision, (CL) Digital Stock; 16 (B) Getty Images; 18 (B) Getty Images; 20 (B) Getty Images, (T) Digital Vision; 22 (B, TL) Getty Images, (TR) Paul Katz/Index Stock Imagery; 23 (TR) Jim Reed/Photo Researchers, Inc., (B) Rex Features, Limited; 24 (B) Getty Images.

Unless otherwise acknowledged, all photographs are the copyright © of Dorling Kindersley, a division of Pearson.

ISBN: 0-328-13935-1

Glossary

aquifers	underground layers of sand, gravel, and rock that contain water.
condensation	process of water vapor changing from a gas to a liquid.
evaporation	changing of liquid water to water vapor.
hydrosphere	all the waters of Earth.
precipitation	process of water vapor in clouds returning to Earth as rain, snow, sleet, or hail.
reservoir	lake that stores water for people to use.
salinity	the amount of salt in water.
sleet	pellets of ice that form when rain freezes as it falls.
sublimation	process of ice changing directly into water vapor without first becoming a liquid.
water table	top level of groundwater in an aquifer.

Earth's Water

by Jocelyn Vial

The Oceans

The Hydrosphere

Most of Earth's surface is covered by water. No other planet in our solar system has this feature. All the waters on Earth form the hydrosphere. Almost all of the hydrosphere is ocean water. Fresh water makes up only about $\frac{3}{100}$ of the hydrosphere.

oceans of the world

Hail forms when raindrops are blown back up into the freezing air at the top of a cloud. If this continues to happen, the raindrops can form balls of ice called hail. Hailstones sometimes grow as large as baseballs.

Earth's hydrosphere is a very busy place. We're lucky that it is, because if it weren't, humans couldn't survive. You may have heard people say, "Well, we needed the rain," after a storm. Now you know how right they are!

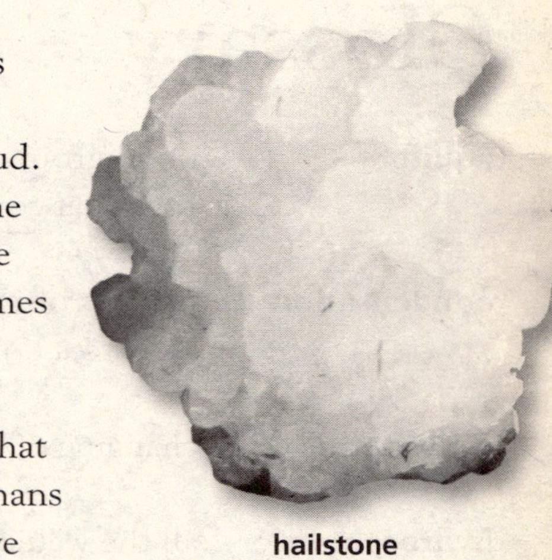

hailstone

These cars were damaged by a fierce hailstorm.

The oceans and seas cover more than three-fourths of Earth. The Pacific Ocean is the largest. Next in size are the Atlantic, Indian, Southern, and Arctic oceans. The Arctic is the smallest major ocean, but there are many smaller seas. As you can tell from the map, all Earth's oceans are connected.

Each ocean is a little bit different from the others. For example, in the western hemisphere, mountain ranges are near the Pacific, so few rivers flow into this ocean. Many large rivers flow into the Atlantic, however. Some oceans have more storms than others. Fierce tropical storms, called cyclones, break out several times a year in the Indian Ocean.

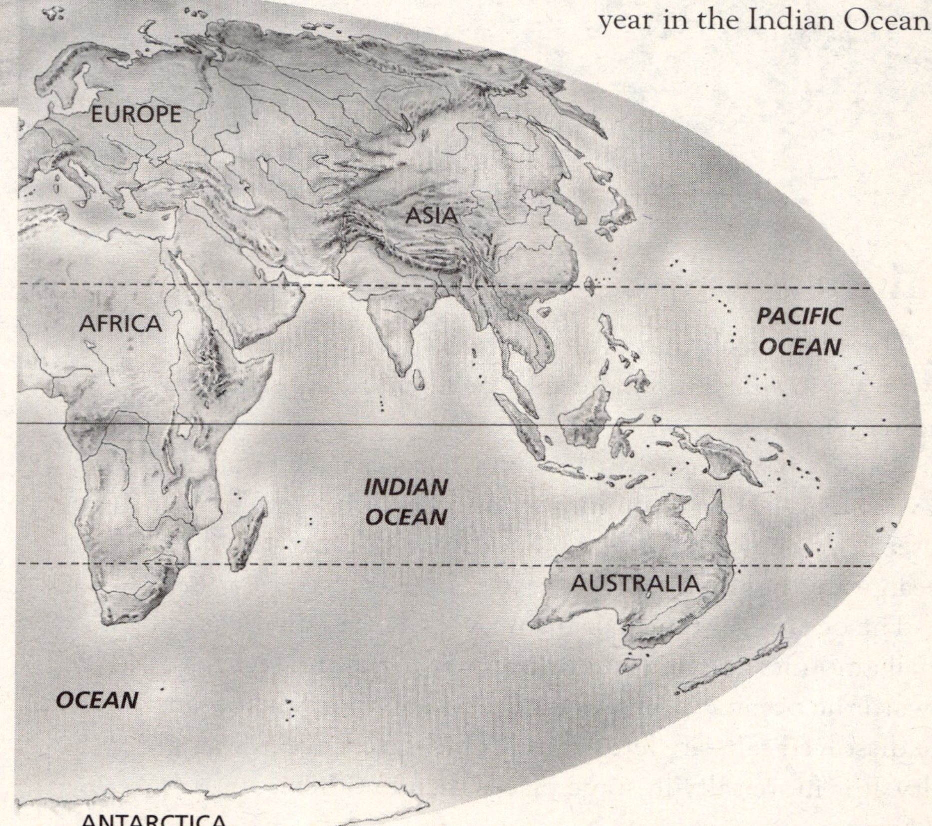

snow

sleet

Precipitation

The form of precipitation that falls depends on the temperature. For example, both sleet and hail are made of ice pellets. **Sleet** forms when rain freezes as it falls. Sleet falls in cold weather. Hail is also frozen, but it falls during thunderstorms, when the weather is warm.

Most rain starts as snow. That's because most clouds form high above the ground, where cold air causes ice crystals to grow. When the crystals get too large, they fall from the cloud. The ice crystals will fall to the ground as snowflakes if all the air between the cloud and the ground is cold. But if the air gets warmer near the ground, the ice turns to rain. If the air becomes cold again very close to the ground, the rain may freeze into sleet.

The Dead Sea has very high salinity. This makes the water very dense, which means that people float easily in it.

Salinity

The water itself may also vary from ocean to ocean. Two ways in which the water may be different are salinity and temperature.

Salinity is a measure of how much salt is in the water. Have you ever been swimming in the ocean and gotten water in your mouth? If you have, then you know that ocean water has high salinity.

The oceans get their salt from rivers. Rivers dissolve small amounts of salt as they flow over rocks and soil toward the oceans. When water evaporates from the ocean, the dissolved salts are left behind. This makes ocean water salty. It is more salty in some places than in others.

The pictures on this page show some types of clouds. Some names are related to their distance from the ground. High-level clouds, such as cirrus clouds, form from five thousand to nearly fourteen thousand meters. They are made mainly of ice crystals because the air temperature is so cold at those heights.

The bases of mid-level clouds are between two and seven thousand meters above ground. Mid-level clouds, such as altocumulus clouds, are made mainly of water droplets. However, they can contain ice crystals if the air temperature is very low.

The bases of low-level clouds are usually below two thousand meters. Low-level clouds, such as stratus clouds, are made mostly of water droplets.

Clouds that grow vertically to very great heights are sometimes called thunderheads. Huge amounts of energy are released as water vapor condenses in these clouds. They can produce powerful thunderstorms.

The lowest type of cloud is fog. It forms at ground level. It is caused when cool air near the ground makes water vapor condense.

cirrus clouds

altocumulus clouds

stratus clouds

Clouds

Clouds are an important part of the water cycle. They release all forms of precipitation. Oceans, rivers, and lakes would be dry without clouds.

How Clouds Form

Clouds form when water vapor changes into tiny water droplets or crystals of ice. As you probably know, clouds come in many shapes and sizes.

Air pressure helps determine when clouds form. Air flows from areas of higher pressure to areas of lower pressure. When air moves upward into an area of lower pressure, the air cools. If it cools enough, water vapor will form water droplets or ice crystals.

Air temperature helps determine what makes up the clouds. If the air temperature is cooler, the cloud will more likely be made of ice crystals. Air temperature drops as height above ground increases. Even on hot summer days, many clouds are made of ice crystals. That's because air temperature high in the clouds can be much lower than air temperature near the ground.

Even though rivers deposit salt in the oceans, areas where they flow into the oceans are the least salty. Oceans are more salty where the water evaporates. The Sun can't evaporate the water fast enough to raise the salinity at most places where the rivers meet the oceans. Warm areas with few rivers have the saltiest water. There the Sun evaporates the water quickly, leaving a lot of salt behind.

transportation of salt

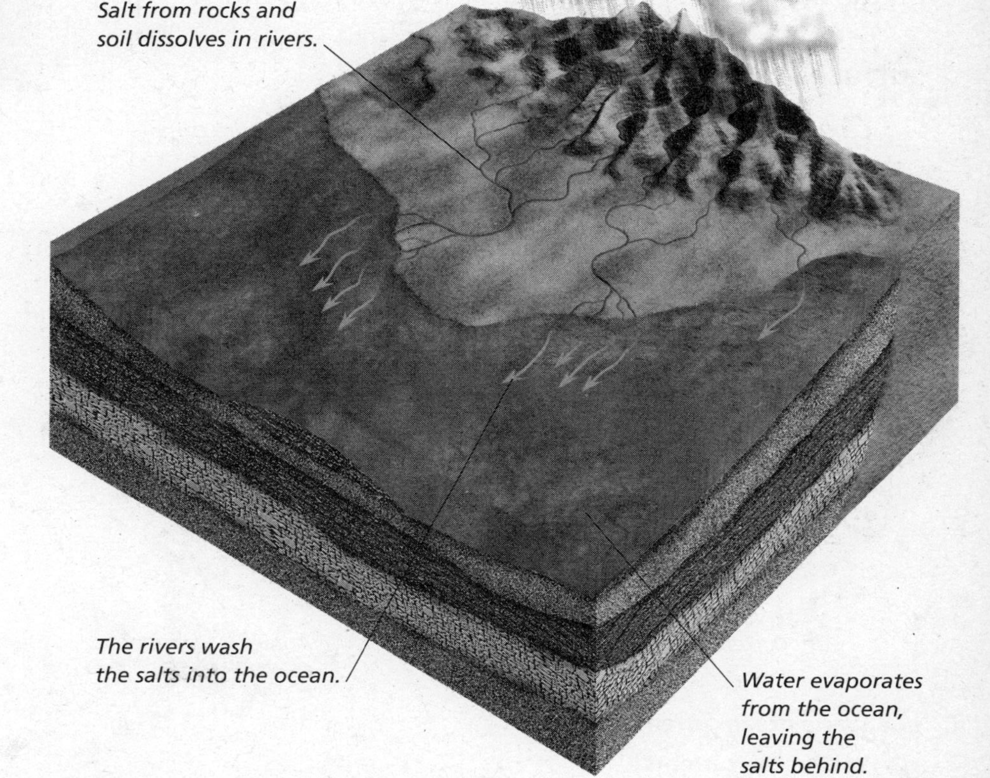

Temperature

Temperature also varies in ocean waters. The temperature of a place is affected by its distance from the equator. Near the equator, ocean temperatures are about 30° Celsius. Near the poles, they can be as cold as −2° Celsius.

Currents also play a role in water temperature. Some currents, such as the Gulf Stream, carry warm water toward the poles. The result is warmer water in a place where the air is very cold. Other currents, such as the California Current, carry cold water toward the equator, where the weather is very warm. Find the Gulf Stream and California Current on the map below. Use your finger to trace their flows.

surface currents

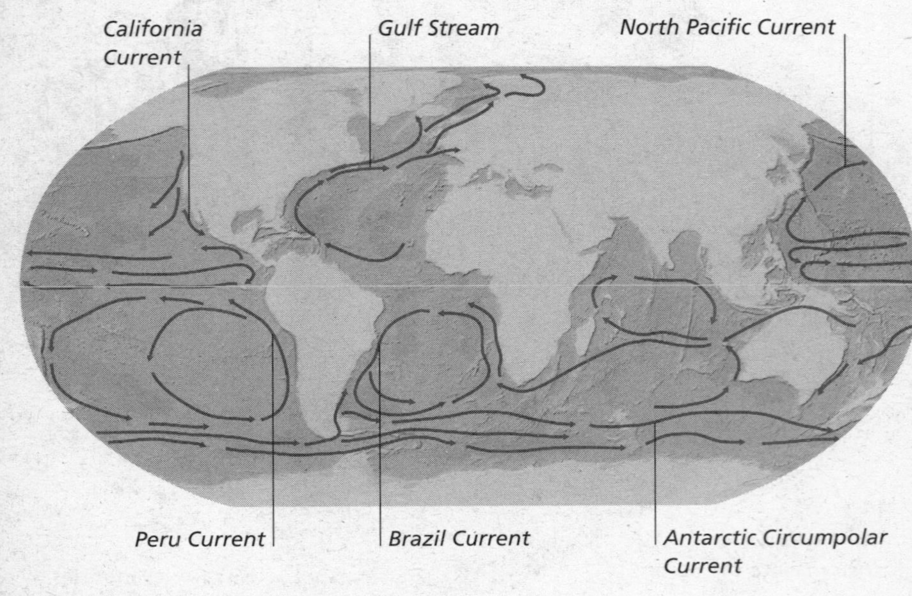

Some water disappears from the water cycle altogether. It is broken down by plants as they make their food. Other water is produced by organisms during respiration.

The Sun's energy powers every stage of the water cycle. Heat and light energy from the Sun cause water in oceans, rivers, and lakes to evaporate. The Sun's energy also causes ice and snow to melt.

paths of the water cycle

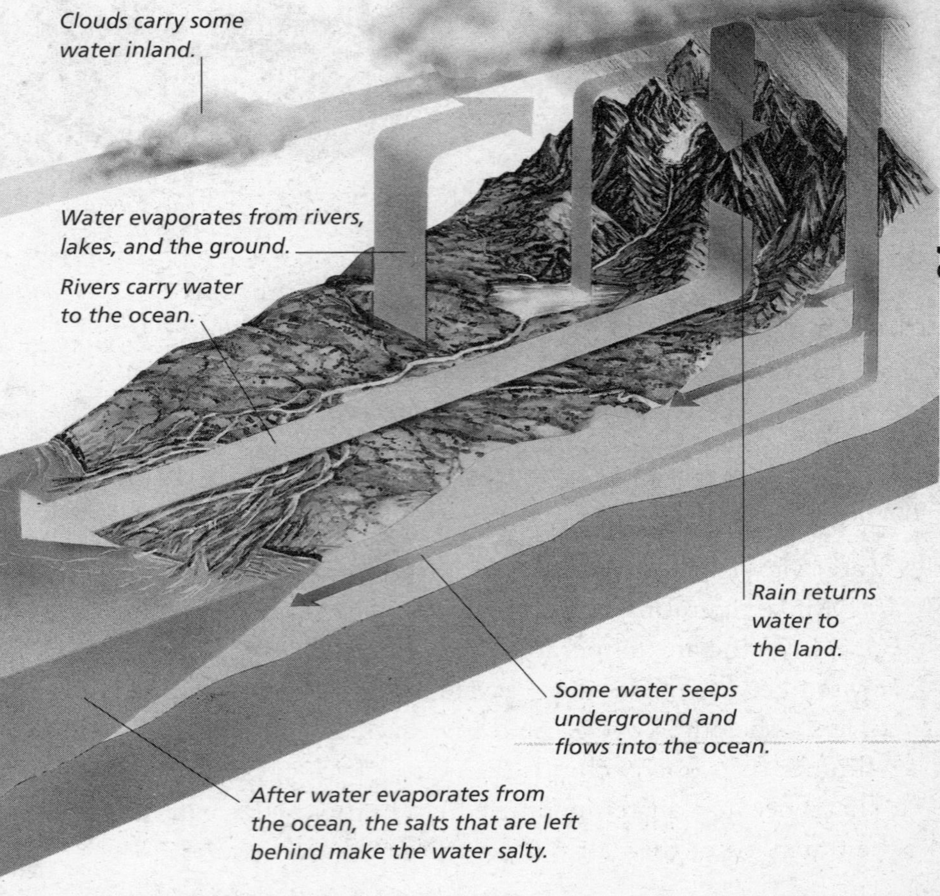

The Water Cycle

Earth's water does not sit still. It moves from the ground to the sky and back to the ground in a process called the water cycle.

Even though you cannot see it, you are surrounded by water all the time. This water is in the form of a gas called water vapor. Water vapor is in the air that surrounds you. As it moves through the water cycle, it changes form to become either solid, liquid, or gas.

There are several steps in the water cycle. During **evaporation,** liquid water from the oceans and rivers changes into water vapor and rises into the atmosphere. In **condensation,** water vapor changes back into liquid water to form clouds. This water may be dew on a leaf, or it may be water droplets in a cloud. During **precipitation,** water falls from clouds as rain, snow, sleet, or hail.

Sublimation is when ice changes directly from a solid into water vapor. It doesn't melt first and become water. You can observe sublimation in your freezer. Sublimation takes place when ice cubes shrink after being left in the freezer for a long time.

The ocean is the largest source of water that evaporates into Earth's atmosphere.

desalinization plant

Ocean Resources

Do you enjoy eating fish? What about shrimp or lobster? Americans eat quite a lot of seafood—a yearly average of fifteen pounds per person!

The oceans provide humans with many resources besides fish. One example is table salt. In some places, people get salt by channeling ocean water into shallow ponds. Over time, the water evaporates and salt remains. The mineral magnesium, which our bodies need to stay healthy, is also found in ocean water.

People can get safe drinking water through desalinization. Desalinization is the process of removing salt from ocean water. This process is costly, however. It is not usually done in places where people have other sources of drinking water.

salt

Fresh Water

Only a very small portion of Earth's water—less than 1 percent—is available for growing crops, drinking, and washing. Almost all usable fresh water starts as rain or snow. Some of this fresh water sinks into the ground. Some collects in rivers and lakes. Most fresh water is frozen in glaciers and polar ice caps, so it is very difficult for people to use.

The Water We Use

Drinking water needs to be fresh, or free of salt, to be safe. Some parts of the world have enough fresh water to meet people's needs. Other places have fresh water shortages. There is a limited supply of fresh water on Earth. You can help make the supply last longer by using water wisely.

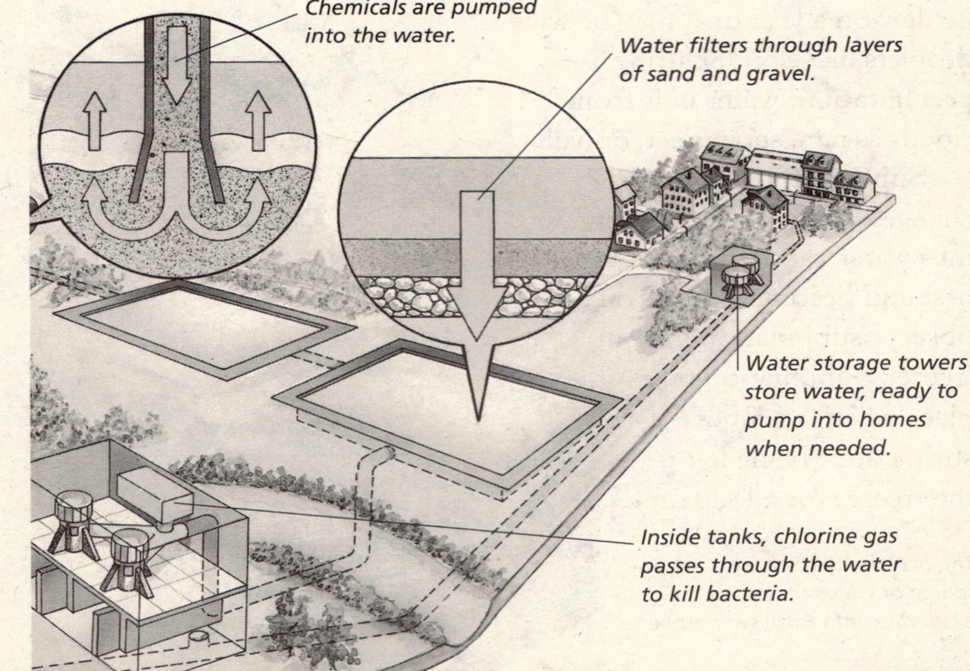

Next, dirt and other particles floating in the water need to be removed. To do this, chemicals are added to the water. The chemicals form tiny, sticky particles. These sticky particles work like magnets. They attract the dirt particles. The new particles of dirt and chemicals get heavier and sink to the bottom of the tank.

Then the water flows through filters. Some filters are made of layers of sand, gravel, and charcoal. As water passes through the filters, smaller particles that contain pollutants are removed.

Finally, another chemical is added to the water to kill germs. Many treatment plants use a chemical called chlorine. Chlorine is also used in swimming pools. Now the water is safe for people to use.

How We Get Our Water

Where does your drinking water come from? Many towns in the United States get their water from groundwater. Others use surface water.

Many materials dissolve easily in water. This makes water easy to pollute. As water flows over the land, it can dissolve and carry away all kinds of harmful chemicals. Because water can be so easily polluted, it must be treated before people can use it. People need a clean water supply to stay healthy.

The drawing on these two pages shows the steps in water treatment. First, water is pumped through pipes from the source, often a reservoir, into a treatment plant. There the water flows into a tank.

water treatment plant

Water is pumped out of the reservoir into the treatment plant.

Rainwater collects in a reservoir.

Clean water is pumped into homes and factories.

We can reduce the amount of water that we use by repairing leaky faucets and taking shorter showers. Can you think of other ways to conserve water?

We can also reuse water for many things. For example, gardeners can water plants with water that has already been used for showering or washing dishes. Unfortunately, this reused water is not safe to drink.

Groundwater

Rain or melted snow that soaks into the ground is called groundwater. Groundwater sinks deeper and deeper through soil and soft rock, until it hits layers of hard rock or clay. Groundwater cannot pass through these layers. They stop it like a dam. But groundwater can flow sideways, through layers of soft rock and soil, and over the hard rock or clay. Underground layers of rock and soil containing groundwater are called **aquifers.** Fresh water can be pumped out of aquifers through wells. Many people get their drinking water from aquifers.

water table

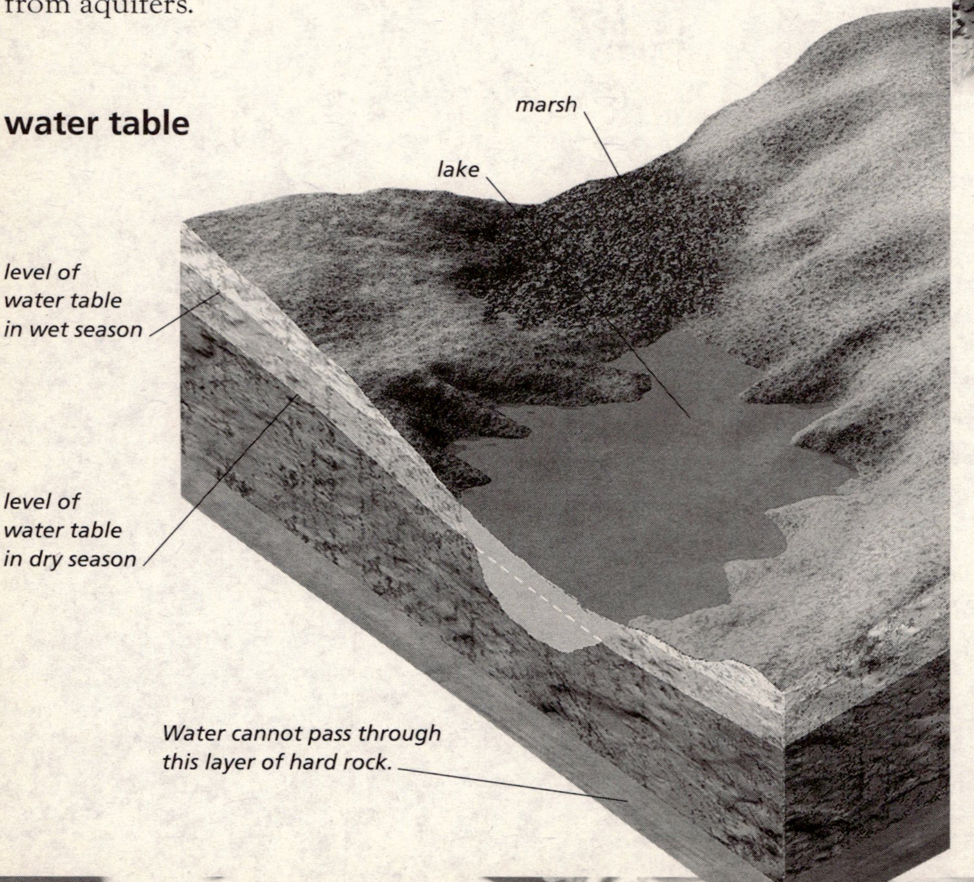

Glaciers and ice sheets form when snow doesn't melt in the summer for many years in a row. New snow just keeps piling up on top of the old snow. When enough snow builds up, its weight compresses, or squeezes, the bottom layers of snow into ice.

When glaciers and ice sheets reach the ocean, large pieces of ice can break off. These large, floating chunks are called icebergs. In 1955, an iceberg larger than the state of Maryland was discovered near Antarctica. It was more than three hundred kilometers long!

Glaciers look like rivers of ice.

iceberg

Ice

About seven-tenths of Earth's fresh water is frozen as ice. Most of this ice is in places such as Antarctica and Greenland, far from where most people live. So it is hard for people to use this ice as a source of drinking water.

Huge ice sheets, up to several kilometers thick, cover areas near the polar caps. The North Pole is covered by an ice cap that floats on the Arctic Ocean, with no land beneath it.

Glaciers are smaller areas of ice. Many glaciers are located in areas with high mountains. Glaciers are frozen rivers of ice that flow slowly downhill. Glaciers are huge and heavy. They change the landscape as they move. Over time, they carve out lakes and valleys.

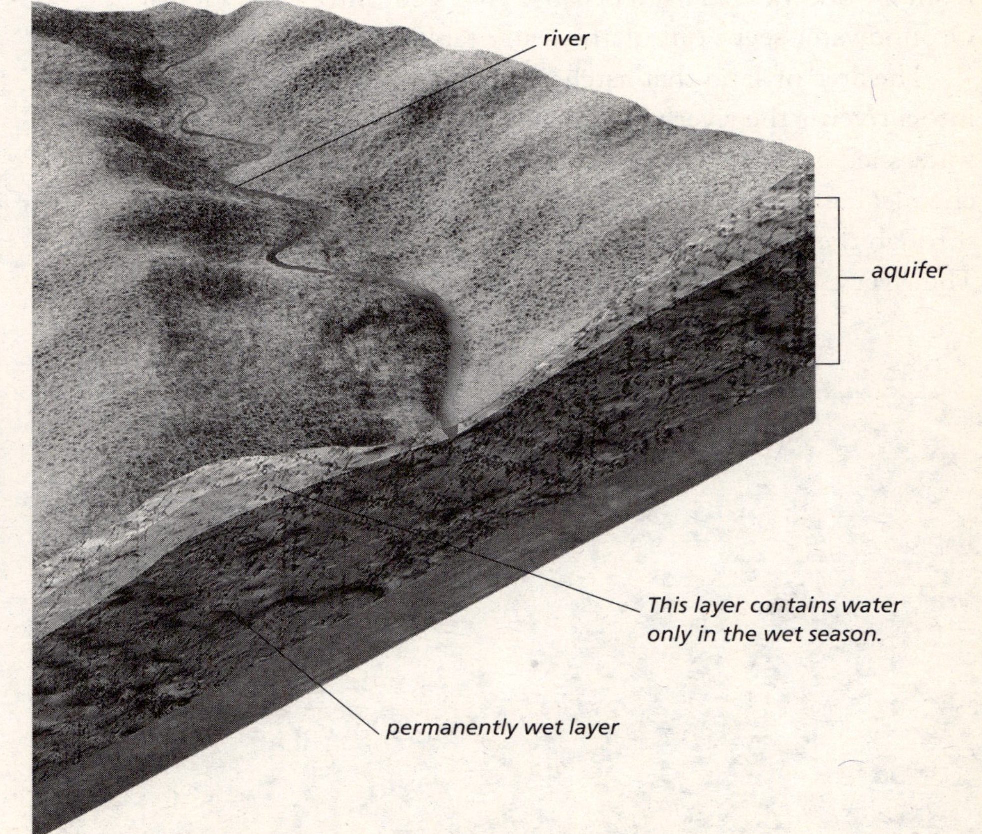

The top level of groundwater in an aquifer is called the **water table.** The level of a water table changes depending on the weather. The water table rises when rain or melting snow filters into it. The water table falls when there is a drought, or a long period without rain.

People sometimes lower the water table when they pump water out of an aquifer faster than snow or rain can replace it. This can cause aquifers to become dry, leading to water shortages. This is another reason why it is a good idea to use groundwater wisely and conserve it.

Rivers

Earth's surface water flows downhill in rivers and streams, from higher to lower areas. It is pulled downward by the same force that holds you on Earth—gravity.

When rain or melting snow soaks into the ground, it becomes groundwater. When it flows over the land, it is called runoff. Small brooks join to form larger streams as water flows downhill. Larger streams join to form rivers. Rivers eventually flow into the ocean.

Most river water comes from runoff, but some comes from groundwater. That's because rivers cut into water tables. Groundwater seeps out of the water table into the river.

The area of land that catches rain and snow and drains into a river is the river's watershed. What happens in a watershed can affect places far away. For example, suppose chemical fertilizers are used on a farm. Runoff flowing through the farm can carry the chemicals into a river. The river can carry the chemicals into other watersheds.

The Niagara River forms part of the border between the United States and Canada.

Water collected in a low spot in the mountains to form this lake.

Lakes

Suppose water flows into a place that is surrounded by higher land. The water will collect in the low spot, and a lake will form.

People can also make lakes. They can build dams, which are walls or other barriers that stop a river's flow. This is one way to get drinking water. A lake will form behind the dam. This kind of lake is called a **reservoir.**

Water leaves lakes as well. It can do this in three ways: by flowing into a river, by seeping into the ground, or by evaporating into the air.

Science

Changing Weather

by Jennifer Coates-Conroy

Genre	Comprehension Skill	Text Features	Science Content
Nonfiction	Draw Conclusions	• Captions • Maps • Diagrams • Glossary	Weather Patterns

Scott Foresman Science 5.8

PEARSON

Scott Foresman

scottforesman.com

ISBN 0-328-13938-6

90000

9 780328 139385

What did you learn?

1. How do temperatures change as you go up through the layers of the atmosphere?

2. Where do jet streams form?

3. What is the difference between a warm front and a cold front?

4. **Writing** in Science Scientists can use fossils to learn about past climates. Write to explain how this works. Include details from the book to support your answer.

5. **Draw Conclusions** Cool currents give the Hawaiian Islands a mild climate, even though the islands are located in the tropics. What affect do you think a current flowing north from the tropics might have?

Picture Credits
Every effort has been made to secure permission and provide appropriate credit for photographic material.
The publisher deeply regrets any omission and pledges to correct errors called to its attention in subsequent editions.

Photo locators denoted as follows: Top (T), Center (C), Bottom (B), Left (L), Right (R), Background (Bkgd).

1 Digital Vision; 2 Getty Images; 10 Digital Vision; 12 Digital Vision; 13 Corbis; 14 Getty Images;
15 (C) ©Bob Daemmrich/The Image Works, Inc.; 17 ©Jim Reed/Corbis; 23 Getty Images.

Unless otherwise acknowledged, all photographs are the copyright © of Dorling Kindersley, a division of Pearson.

ISBN: 0-328-13938-6

Copyright © Pearson Education, Inc.

All Rights Reserved. Printed in the United States of America. The blackline masters in this publication are designed for use with appropriate equipment to reproduce copies for classroom use only. Scott Foresman grants permission to classroom teachers to reproduce from these masters.

2 3 4 5 6 7 8 9 10 V004 13 12 11 10 09 08 07 06 05

Glossary

air mass	a large body of air with similar properties all through it
anemometer	an instrument that measures wind speed
barometer	an instrument that measures air pressure
climate	the average weather conditions in one place over a long time
convection current	when gases or liquids rise and sink in a circular path
front	a boundary between two air masses
rain gauge	a tool that measures how much rain has fallen

Changing Weather

by Jennifer Coates-Conroy

Moving Air

It is a beautiful, sunny day. The air is warm, and there are no clouds anywhere in the sky. But the weather report you saw on TV said it would rain this afternoon. Sure enough, a few hours later it is raining heavily. How did such a big change happen? And how did the weather reporter on TV know about it? Weather can be quite complicated, and it is always changing. But scientists have special tools and methods that allow them to predict the weather.

Many scientists believe that air pollution is making Earth's climate warmer.

Changing Climates

Many things can cause a climate to change. Some of them are natural, and some of them are caused by humans. Climates can cool because of asteroids hitting Earth or volcanic eruptions. These rare events can send lots of dust into the atmosphere, which blocks the Sun, cooling Earth. It is also possible that the Sun produced less heat in the past.

You may have heard of global warming. Climates can become warmer if there is more carbon dioxide, methane, or water vapor in the air. These gases are produced by volcanoes, the water cycle, and decaying matter. They are also produced when humans burn things such as coal or gasoline.

The weather and climate are always changing. But if you know what to look for, you can predict what might happen. The next time you see a weather map, try to figure out what the changing weather will bring.

Past Climates

Although climates change very slowly, they do change. Sometimes the changes are very big. For example, thousands of years ago, an ice age began. This was the result of Earth's climate cooling off. During this ice age, part of what is now the United States was buried under a huge sheet of ice!

No one wrote down what the climate was like during the ice age. But scientists know it happened because of the clues it left behind. As the ice slowly slid across the land, it pushed dirt and rocks into certain types of hills and lakes. Scientists can tell how the ice moved by mapping these features.

Scientists can also look at fossils for clues about past climates. For example, a fossil of a lizard might be found in a very cold area. We know that lizards cannot live where it is very cold. The fossil shows that the climate in this place must have been warmer long ago for the lizard to survive.

The white areas on this map show how much of Earth was covered by glaciers during the last ice age.

Layers of Air

The Earth is surrounded by a blanket of gases called the atmosphere. Our atmosphere is different from the atmospheres of all the other planets in our solar system. It is full of air, a mix of gases that allows life to exist on Earth. Air is about $\frac{8}{10}$ nitrogen and about $\frac{2}{10}$ oxygen. A tiny fraction of air is made up of carbon dioxide, water vapor, and other gases.

The atmosphere is divided into layers. The bottom layer, called the troposphere, is where most of our weather happens. The different layers have different temperatures and air pressures. Air pressure is caused by the weight of air above pushing down. As you go higher into the atmosphere, there is less and less air above you. This causes air pressure to decrease the higher you go. Air particles high in the atmosphere are farther apart than they are at the Earth's surface.

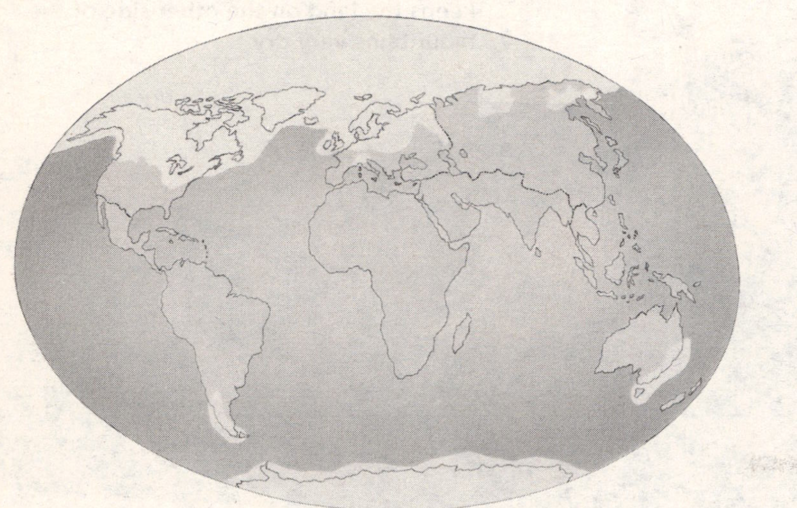

Convection Currents

Have you ever gone to the ocean on a hot summer day? If so, you may have noticed a cool breeze blowing in off the water. These sea breezes are caused by a difference in temperature between the land and the water. During the day, the Sun heats the land faster than the ocean. This causes the air over the land to be warmer than the air over the water. The warm air rises, and cool air sinks, rushing in under the warm air. When the cool air flows in from over the ocean, you feel a sea breeze. This type of air movement is called a **convection current.**

The convection current near the ocean is the opposite at night. At night, the land cools quickly. But the ocean, which has been heating up in the Sun all day, cools much more slowly. The air over the warm ocean water rises, and the cool air from the land flows in underneath it. The result is a land breeze, which blows from the land toward the water.

Sea breezes occur during the day.

Land breezes occur at night.

Oceans and Climate

Ocean temperatures rise and fall more slowly than land temperatures. Because of this, an ocean can have an effect on climates by the shore. In the winter, oceans hold heat, so areas on the coast usually do not get as cold as inland areas. During the summer, an ocean stays cool, so land on the coast usually stays cool as well.

Ocean currents can affect climates too. Sometimes they bring warm weather to areas that would usually be cold or cold weather to areas that would usually be warm. For example, the Hawaiian Islands have a very mild climate, even though they are located in the tropics. This is because ocean currents bring cool air to the islands.

Climate

Weather or climate?

As you have learned, weather changes fairly quickly. It is a description of what conditions are like in one place at a single moment. Climate is different from weather. The **climate** of a place is its average weather conditions over a long time, usually thirty years. While the weather in an area might change every day, climates usually do not change for a very long time.

Landforms and Climate

Sometimes the shape of the land can have an effect on the climate. For example, mountains along the coast often have a different climate from one side to the other. In California, storms often come in from the Pacific Ocean, bringing rain with them. When they get to the coast, they run into a long mountain range. As the storm clouds move up one side of the mountains, the temperature drops. This causes moisture to fall from the clouds as precipitation. Most of the moisture leaves the clouds before they reach the other side of the mountains. This makes the climate on the ocean side very wet, while the climate on the other side is much drier.

The convection currents that create sea and land breezes are small compared to some others in the Earth's atmosphere. There are six huge convection currents that help to cause weather. They are caused in part because the surface of the Earth is warmer near the equator than at other places. These currents, combined with the spinning of the Earth, create winds over huge areas. For example, in the United States, winds usually blow from west to east because of convection currents.

If you watch a TV weather report, you will probably hear about the jet stream. This is a band of very fast-moving wind that forms between the huge convection currents. Even though jet streams are very high in the atmosphere, they have a big effect on our weather.

Air Masses

Air moves across the surface of the Earth in huge bodies called air masses. An **air mass** has similar temperatures and amounts of water vapor all through it. Air masses take on the properties of the areas where they form. For example, an air mass that forms over a cold ocean will be cold and wet. One that forms over a hot desert will be hot and dry. Air masses keep these properties for a while as they move to new areas, bringing their temperature and moisture level with them.

Continental polar air: The cold, dry land near the poles creates cold, dry air masses.

Maritime polar air: The cold oceans near the poles create cold, moist air masses.

Continental tropical air: These air masses form over hot deserts and have warm, dry air.

Maritime tropical air: Warm, moist air masses form over tropical oceans.

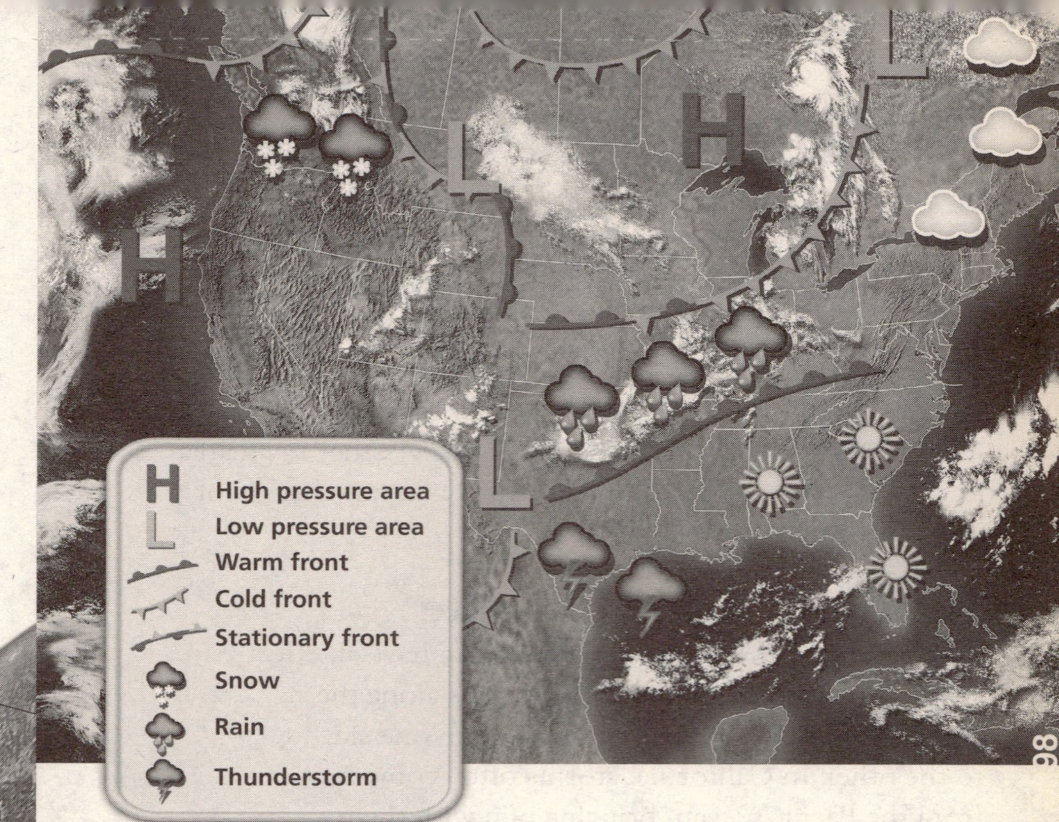

Weather maps show current weather conditions. They also show predictions. Although there are many different kinds of weather maps, most of them have the same types of colors and symbols. Fronts are shown with lines. These lines have triangles on them to show a cold front or half circles to show a warm front. The shapes point in the direction the front is moving. High pressure areas are shown with an H, while low pressure areas have an L. Clouds and precipitation are shown with little pictures. Look at the map and legend above to learn more about these symbols.

Weather Forecasts

Weather may be complicated, but it does follow patterns. You have probably noticed some of these patterns where you live. Your area might have a lot of storms during the fall. Or you might notice that the weather starts to become drier at the end of spring. Scientists can use these patterns to predict what the weather will do in the future.

Weather forecasters gather information about weather patterns. Then they try to figure out how air, land, and water interact with each other to make these patterns. They use their inferences to predict what will happen in the future.

Weather usually acts like similar weather has in the past. If current weather matches past weather very closely, forecasters can be more sure of how it will change. Forecasters can make better predictions if they have more information about the current weather.

The weather is usually controlled by the type of air mass in the area. The four main types of air masses are shown in the diagram below. They are continental tropical air, continental polar air, maritime tropical air, and maritime polar air.

Air masses are moved around by winds. These may be winds close to the ground, or they may be jet streams. An area may experience storms as the edge of an air mass passes through.

New York City experiences snow during the winter.

Summers in New York City are often hot.

Fronts

The boundary between two air masses is called a
front. When a front arrives, it often brings a change
of weather. A warm, wet air mass might be sitting over
your area. Then a cold, dry air mass might move in,
bringing colder, drier weather with it. Some fronts do
not move, or they move back and forth over the same
area. These are called stationary fronts.

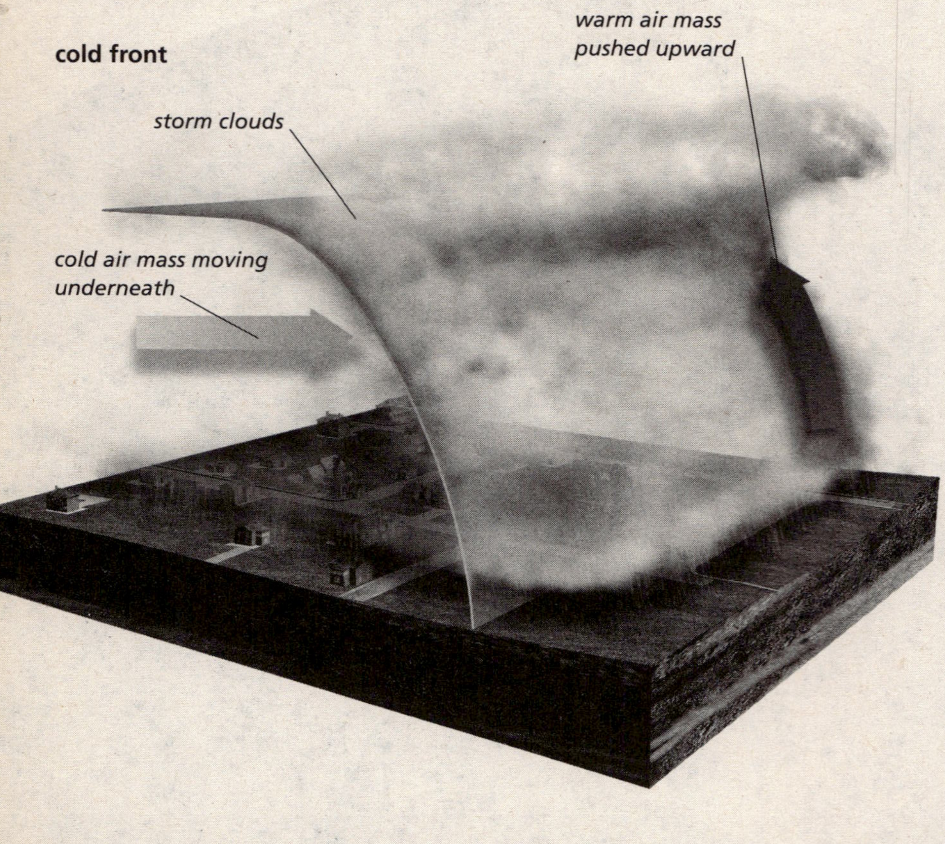

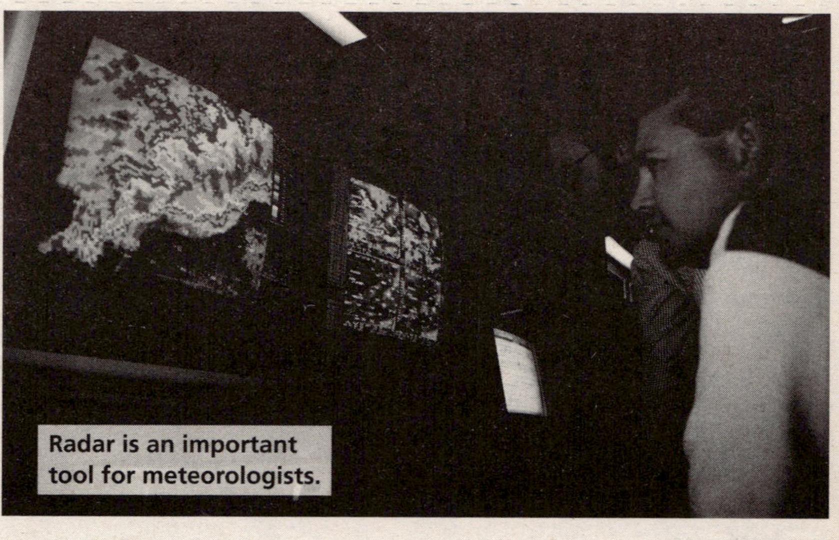

An **anemometer** is a tool for measuring wind speed. It
has several cups that spin when wind blows across them.
The faster the wind blows, the faster the cups spin.

A hygrometer measures the air's moisture. Some
hygrometers use a piece of horsehair to do this. When
the air is dry, the hair gets shorter. When it is moist, the
hair gets longer. This movement turns a pointer that
shows the humidity.

A **rain gauge** is a tall, thin, clear container that measures
how much rain has fallen. As rain falls, it fills the gauge.
Sometimes the top of the rain gauge is wider than the
bottom. This makes it easier to catch and measure small
amounts of rain.

Scientists use radar for measuring wind and precipitation
in a storm. It sends out invisible waves of energy, similar to
those that come from a radio station. Some of the energy
bounces off raindrops in the storm. Scientists can measure
the energy that bounces back to tell what the storm is doing.

Forecasting the Weather

Data Collection

Weather is a combination of temperature, moisture, clouds, precipitation, wind speed, air pressure, and wind direction. To measure each of these things, scientists use different tools. Some of them are very advanced and expensive. Some are very simple. In fact, you probably have one of them at home. Most houses have a thermometer, the tool used to measure air temperature.

Another common weather tool is a barometer. A **barometer** measures air pressure. Many barometers use a small, sealed container with a dial attached. When air pressure squeezes the container, it moves the dial to show the pressure. Some barometers are tubes full of mercury. The level of the mercury rises or falls with changes in pressure.

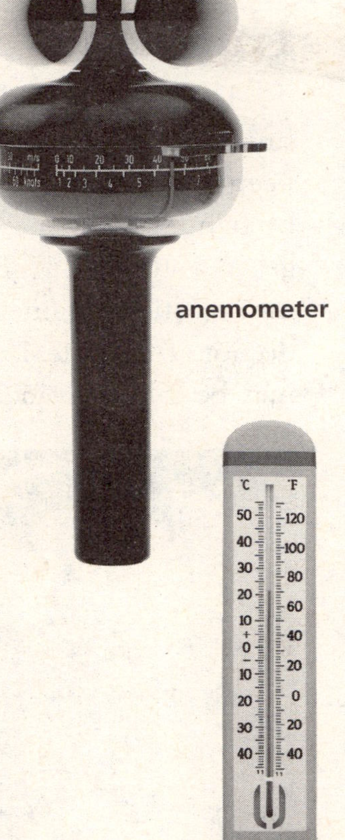
anemometer

thermometer

barometer

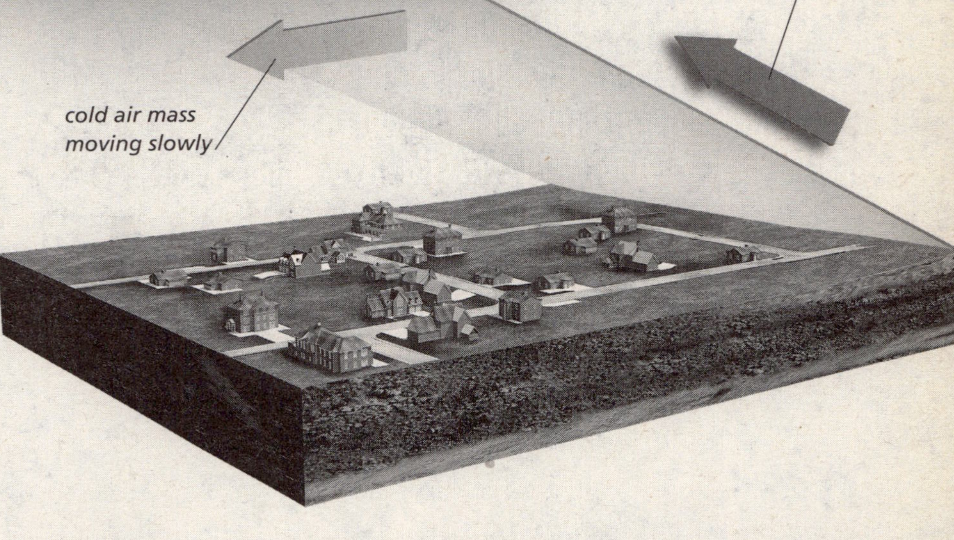

When a cool air mass moves into a warm air mass, it is called a cold front. The cold air pushes the less dense, warm air up. As this air rises, it cools, causing any moisture in it to fall as rain. A line of clouds often forms at a cold front.

A warm front forms when a fast-moving mass of warm air runs into a slower-moving, cooler air mass. The warm air rides up over the cool air, causing high-altitude clouds. Warm fronts move more slowly than cold fronts and cause steady, long-lasting precipitation.

Severe Weather

Thunderstorms

Sometimes storms can be violent and even dangerous. Thunderstorms are one of the most common forms of dangerous weather.

Thunderstorms usually form when moist air moves upward quickly. As the moisture climbs higher, it cools and forms clouds of ice and water vapor.

Eventually, water begins to fall back to Earth, dragging some air with it. This creates downward currents, which happen at the same time as the storm's upward currents.

Finally there is no more rising air. All the storm's currents are moving downward. The clouds shrink as their water vapor falls to the ground.

Hurricane Safety

There are a few things you can do to stay safe if a hurricane strikes. You should board up your windows to keep them from being smashed. Keep extra food and water on hand, in case the water supply is cut off or you cannot get to a store. Put things that could be ruined by floodwater into plastic containers. When the hurricane comes through, do not go outside. If a hurricane is dangerous enough, you may be told to evacuate. If this happens, leave right away.

Windows should be boarded up before a hurricane to keep them from being smashed.

Signs such as this are found in areas where hurricanes are common.

Hurricanes

A hurricane is another very dangerous type of storm. Hurricanes form over the ocean when the water is warm. Water vapor from the ocean moves into the air and condenses, forming clouds. When it condenses, it releases energy that can turn into the powerful winds of a hurricane. A storm must have winds of more than 120 kilometers per hour to be called a hurricane. Very strong hurricanes can have winds of more than 240 kilometers per hour.

Although hurricane winds are strong, they are not nearly as strong as a tornado's winds. Even so, hurricanes do much more damage than tornadoes. There are several reasons for this. First, hurricanes are huge. A tornado might be a few hundred meters across, but a hurricane can be hundreds of kilometers across. This means they damage a much wider area. Second, hurricanes last for days and travel long distances, possibly hitting several communities. Third, hurricanes cause huge waves and flooding that can do as much damage as their winds.

Lightning is one of the most impressive features of a thunderstorm. Lightning bolts are actually very powerful sparks of electricity. They can heat the air to a temperature of 30,000°C in less than a second. This causes the air to vibrate, making the sound we call thunder. Lightning bolts move from areas with one type of electrical charge to areas with an opposite electrical charge. When a charge builds up in a thunderstorm cloud and another builds up on the ground below, lightning can strike the ground. Lightning strikes tall objects first, such as trees or buildings. Try to stay away from these objects during a thunderstorm. The safest place to be is inside. If you cannot get inside, try to stay low, but do not lie on the ground.

Lightning bolts are actually huge electric sparks.

12

Tornadoes

A tornado is a very dangerous part of some storms. Tornadoes can flatten everything they touch, leaving a path of destruction hundreds of meters wide and many kilometers long. Winds inside a tornado can blow at hundreds of kilometers per hour, destroying houses, picking up cars, and even ripping the bark off trees! Despite the damage they cause, most tornadoes last only a few minutes.

Conditions have to be just right for a tornado to form. First, a storm must have layers of wind blowing at different speeds and in different directions. This causes a tube of wind to form between the layers. It rolls horizontally like a log, until upward and downward air currents tip it on its end. The tube is now a vertical column of spinning air called a funnel cloud. When the lower end of the funnel cloud touches the ground, it is called a tornado.

13

Tornadoes are one of the most destructive types of weather. When a tornado is approaching, there are often sirens and TV announcements to warn people. If you hear one of these warnings, you should go to a safe place as soon as possible. A basement is the best place to go. A room in the center of a building is the next best place. Wherever you go, you should try to stay away from windows, since the glass can break and fly around the room, causing injuries.

Tornadoes can do amazing amounts of damage in a very short time.

104

OUR CHANGING EARTH

by Mary Miller

Genre	Comprehension Skill	Text Features	Science Content
Nonfiction	Summarize	• Labels • Captions • Diagrams • Glossary	Earth's Surface

Scott Foresman Science 5.9

PEARSON

Scott Foresman

scottforesman.com

ISBN 0-328-13941-6

9 780328 139415

90000

What did you learn?

1. What are the three basic types of rock?

2. What are the two kinds of crust on Earth's surface?

3. What is the name of the process that breaks down rock by physical forces such as ice or gravity?

4. **Writing** in Science Erosion is the movement of particles away from a place. Write about the various ways that water causes erosion. Include details from the book to support your answer.

5. **Summarize** Explain how colliding plates can form volcanoes.

Vocabulary

chemical weathering
core
crust
igneous
mantle
mechanical weathering
metamorphic
plate
sedimentary

Picture Credits
Every effort has been made to secure permission and provide appropriate credit for photographic material. The publisher deeply regrets any omission and pledges to correct errors called to its attention in subsequent editions.

Photo locators denoted as follows: Top (T), Center (C), Bottom (B), Left (L), Right (R), Background (Bkgd).

Opener: ML Sinibaldi/Corbis; 6 (TR) Yann Arthus-Bertrand/Corbis, (CR) Brand X Pictures; 9 (CR) Roger Ressmeyer/Corbis, (B) Corbis; 10 (TL) ML Sinibaldi/Corbis, (TR, R) Digital Stock; 11 Jacques Descloitres/MODIS Rapid Response Team/NASA/GSFC; 12 Joel W. Rogers/Corbis; 16 (T) Corbis, (B) Digital Vision; 17 Digital Stock; 18 Digital Vision; 19 (T) Three Lions/Getty Images, (B) Digital Vision.

Scott Foresman/Dorling Kindersley would also like to thank: 12 (BR) Natural History Museum, London/DK Images; 20 (TR, CL) Natural History Museum, London/DK Images; 21 (CB, BL) Natural History Museum, London/DK Images, (L) National Trust/DK Images.

Unless otherwise acknowledged, all photographs are the copyright © of Dorling Kindersley, a division of Pearson.

ISBN: 0-328-13941-6

Copyright © Pearson Education, Inc.

Glossary

chemical weathering — the breaking down of rock by chemical processes

core — the center part of Earth

crust — the outermost and thinnest layer of Earth

igneous — rock formed when melted rock cools and hardens

mantle — a layer of nearly solid rock between Earth's crust and core

mechanical weathering — the breaking down of rock by physical forces

metamorphic — rock formed when other rocks are changed by heat and pressure

plate — a section of the crust that floats on Earth's mantle

sedimentary — rock formed when layers of minerals and rock particles harden into solid rock

OUR CHANGING EARTH

by Mary Miller

The Structure of Earth

Earth is made up of layers. The layers are called the crust, the mantle, the outer core, and the inner core. Each layer has different properties.

The Crust

The **crust** is Earth's top layer. It is also the thinnest layer. When you stand outside on the ground, you are standing on Earth's crust. There are two kinds of crust: continental crust and oceanic crust.

Continental crust makes up all of Earth's land. It can be as thick as seventy-five kilometers. The thickest continental crust is in mountain areas. Most continental crust is made of granite.

Oceanic crust lies beneath most of the ocean floor. It is made mostly of basalt. This type of rock is dark green or black. The oceanic crust has a thickness of about six to eleven kilometers.

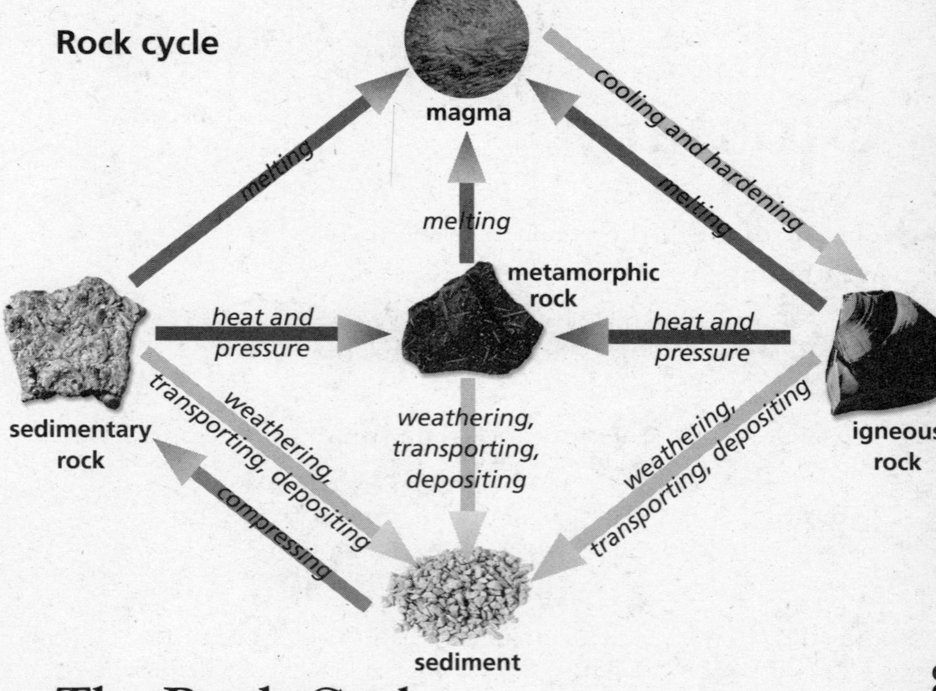

The Rock Cycle

Rocks are constantly being formed, destroyed, or changed from one type to another. Pressure, heat, erosion, and weathering help to drive this process, which is called the rock cycle. The rock cycle doesn't always follow the same order.

The Age of Rock Layers

The layers of rock at Earth's surface are younger than the layers of rock underneath, because the lower layers were formed first. Over time, events such as earthquakes and volcanoes can cause these layers to shift or even turn over.

If the layers are bent or tilted, scientists assume that something happened to move the layers after they were made. Scientists can tell the ages of fossils by studying the layers in which they are found.

Sedimentary Rocks

Sedimentary rocks form when layers of minerals and rock particles harden into solid rock. Sometimes the particles are cemented together by natural chemicals.

The type of sedimentary rock that forms depends on what was in the sediment. Some sedimentary rocks are formed from the remains of animals and plants.

Most fossils are found in sedimentary rocks. Scientists study the rock surrounding the fossil to learn more about the environment that existed when the organism was living.

Metamorphic Rocks

Metamorphic rocks are formed when other rocks are changed by heat and pressure. The mineral crystals in the rock can change in size or shape.

Sometimes the mineral crystals in metamorphic rock settle in layers. Under high pressure, the rock particles form rough layers. When the pressure is lower, the layers are fine and thin.

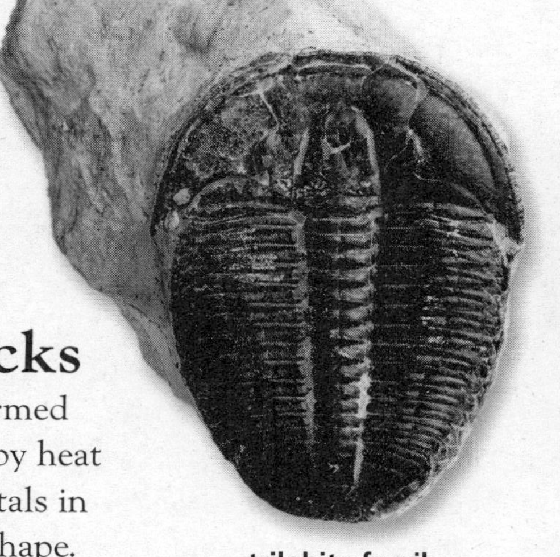

trilobite fossil

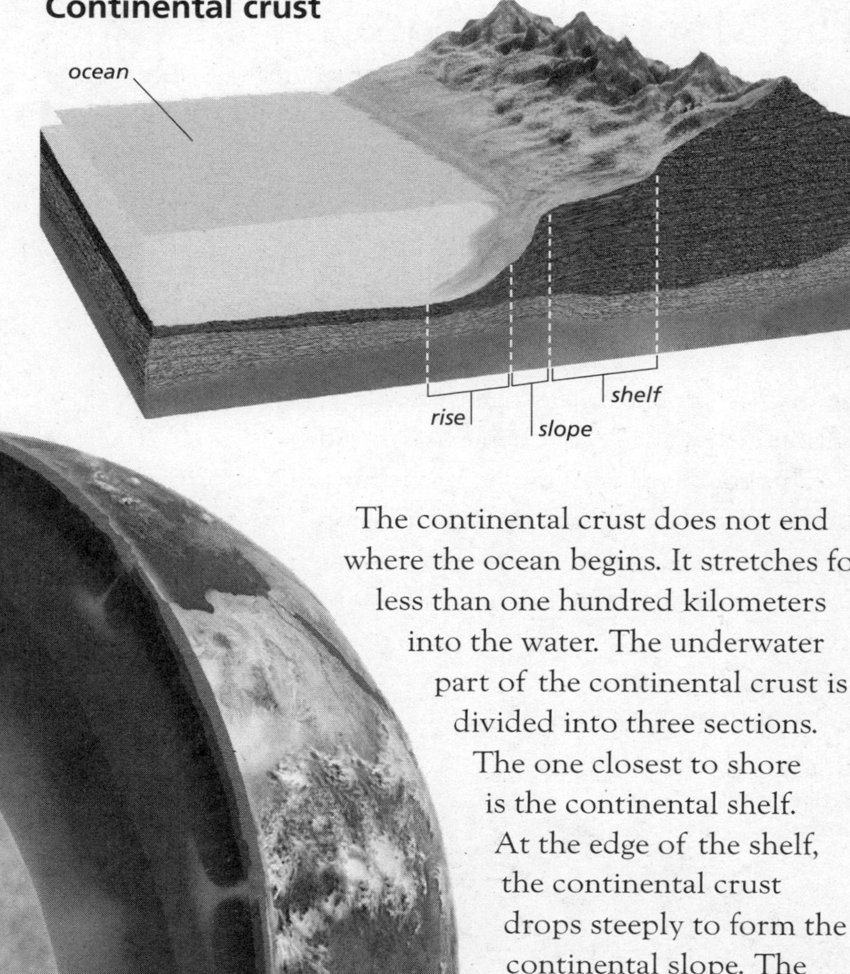

This metamorphic rock has formed in layers.

Continental crust

The continental crust does not end where the ocean begins. It stretches for less than one hundred kilometers into the water. The underwater part of the continental crust is divided into three sections.

The one closest to shore is the continental shelf.

At the edge of the shelf, the continental crust drops steeply to form the continental slope. The bottom of the slope levels off to form the continental rise. This area is the starting place of the oceanic crust.

The Mantle and Core

Underneath Earth's crust is a layer of nearly solid rock called the **mantle.** It extends from the base of the crust to an average depth of 2,900 kilometers, making up most of Earth's material. The top part of the mantle and the crust above it form the lithosphere.

Deep within Earth, the mantle is under very high pressure and heat. The temperature ranges from 360°C to 2,500°C. Under these extreme temperatures and pressures, the mantle's rocks do strange things. Even though the rocks are solid, they move and bend like liquid.

This rock is always moving. It is moved by convection currents. These currents occur when cool rock sinks and hot rock rises, creating a circular motion. The lithosphere floats on top of the mantle's convection currents.

Convection currents

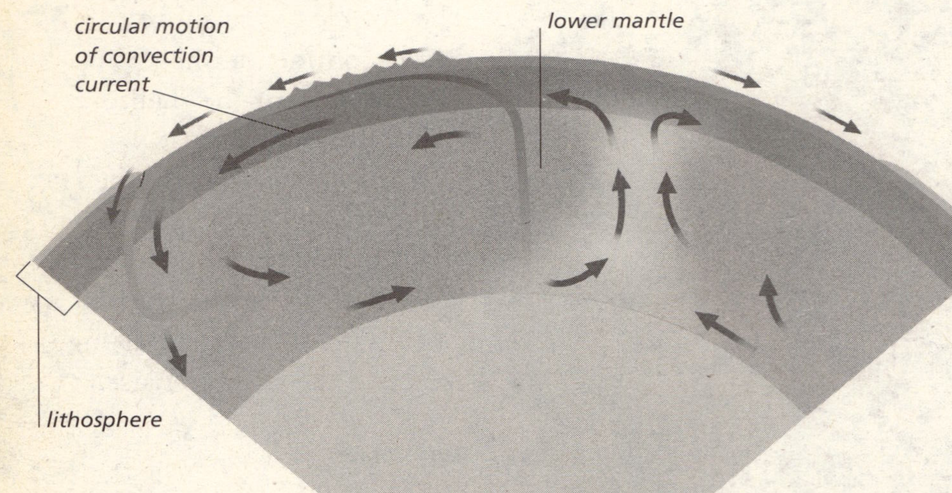

Rocks

There are three basic types of rock, each formed in a different way.

Igneous Rocks

Igneous rocks form when melted rock cools and hardens. As the hot, liquid rock cools, mineral crystals form. Melted rock that cools slowly makes igneous rocks with large crystals. Rock that cools quickly forms small crystals. When magma cools slowly underground, rocks with large crystals, such as granite, are formed. Basalt forms when lava is quickly cooled underwater. It has small mineral crystals.

The Giant's Causeway in Ireland is formed from basalt.

Minerals

Scientists can tell minerals apart by their color, hardness, and other characteristics.

Mineral properties

Color
Minerals come in all colors from clear to pink, red, blue, green, and black.

Hardness
Hardness is measured on Mohs' scale. Minerals are graded from one to ten.

Luster
Minerals can be shiny or dull. Some allow light through them, but others do not.

Streak
Streak is the name for the color a mineral leaves behind when scraped across a tile.

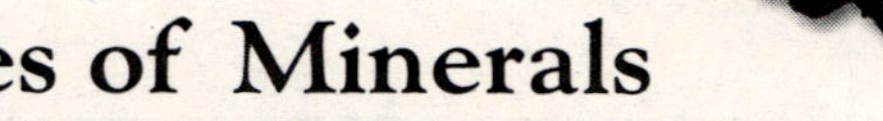

Properties of Minerals

Minerals are the natural materials that make up rocks. All particles of one mineral are arranged in the same way. Although there are thousands of different minerals, only a small number make up most of the rocks on Earth.

Minerals can be identified by their physical properties. These properties include color, hardness, luster, and streak.

At the very center of Earth is the **core.** The distance from the surface of Earth to the center of its core is about 6,400 kilometers.

The core is made of iron and nickel. There is a solid inner core and a liquid outer core. Temperatures at the core are very hot, reaching 7,000°C. The liquid in the outer core is always moving. Its currents make Earth's magnetic field.

Scientists cannot go to the core or mantle to study them. Earth's layers are so thick that they have not even been able to drill through the crust. Scientists have found other ways to study Earth's layers.

Sometimes material from the mantle pushes up through cracks in Earth's crust. Scientists can study this material to learn about the mantle. Another way to study Earth's layers is to measure the vibrations caused by earthquakes with an instrument called a seismograph. Scientists can also study the mantle in laboratory experiments. They re-create the heat and pressure of the mantle and then see what these conditions do to different kinds of rock.

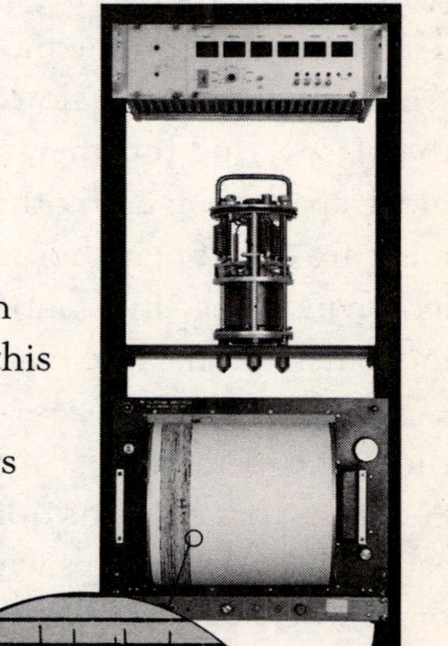

seismogram

seismograph

Earthquakes and Volcanoes

Earth's Plates

The lithosphere covers Earth in a thin layer. This layer is split into sections called **plates.** Some plates are huge, covering areas larger than continents. The plates float on the molten rock of the mantle.

Earth's plates are slowly moving. Sometimes the plates grind together, and sometimes the plates move apart from each other. The places where plates meet are called plate boundaries. The plates move less than twenty-five centimeters a year. These small movements can cause big changes on Earth's surface.

Some of the changes occur slowly over a long time. The formation of mountains is a slow change. A change that happens quickly can cause an earthquake. The places where plates meet are often where earthquakes strike, mountains form, and volcanoes erupt.

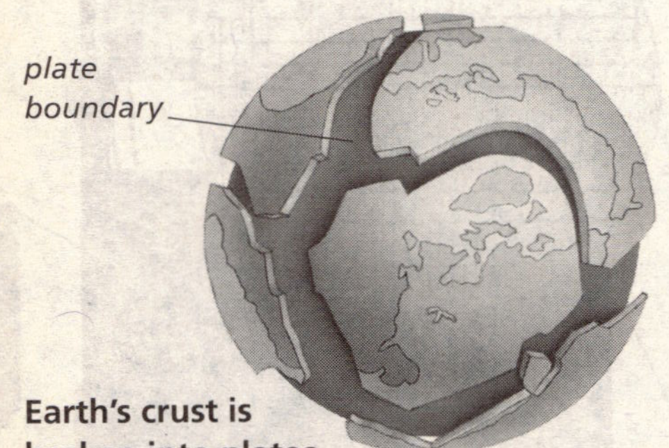

Earth's crust is broken into plates.

The San Andreas Fault is a sliding plate boundary.

In the 1930s in the Midwest, overfarming turned the soil to dust.

Field Erosion

Wind erosion can be a serious problem on farms. If fields become too dry and there are no plants to hold the soil in place, wind can blow the topsoil away. This is a problem for farmers because topsoil is necessary for growing crops.

To slow wind erosion, farmers often plant trees along the edges of their fields. The trees block some of the wind from reaching the fields.

Trees along the edge of this field protect the crops and soil from the wind.

Sand Dunes

Sand dunes are large hills of sand often found in the desert. These huge features are made by wind erosion. The size and shape of dunes depend on the amount of sand, the number of plants in the area, and the strength of the winds.

Winds can also blow sand dunes across the desert. The wind picks up sand from one side of the dune and deposits the sand on the other side. When the wind blows in the same direction most of the time, it can cause the dune to move in the direction of the wind. For example, dunes in southern Egypt sometimes move twenty to one hundred meters in a year.

The side of a sand dune that is away from the wind is always steeper than the side that faces the wind. Wind pushes sand up one side of the dune. After the sand is pushed over the top of the dune, the wind can no longer reach it. The sand falls straight down, forming a steep slope.

These sand dunes have formed in the Sahara desert.

East African Rift Valley

Plates move because convection currents in the mantle push and pull them in different directions. Gravity also forces plates to move. When gravity pulls the edge of a plate down into the mantle, the rest of the plate gets dragged along with it. There are three different kinds of plate boundaries: converging, spreading, and sliding.

At a converging boundary, two plates crash into each other. This can push up the edges of the plates, forming a mountain range.

A spreading boundary forms when plates move away from each other. New crust forms between the plates. The low area between the plates is called a rift valley. An example is the East African Rift Valley.

At a sliding boundary, two plates move past each other in opposite directions. The sliding of the plates can cause cracks in the crust, called faults. When the plates rub together at a fault, their motion can cause earthquakes. The San Andreas Fault in California has caused many serious earthquakes.

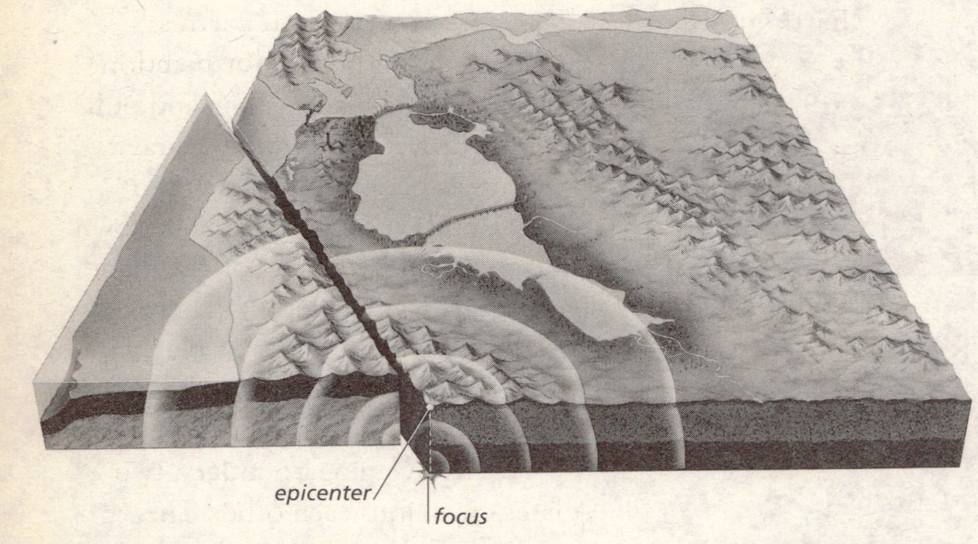

Earthquakes

Sometimes the forces that change Earth's surface are constructive. These forces can build mountains. At other times, forces are destructive. Earthquakes and volcanoes are examples of destructive forces.

Earthquakes occur at faults. Faults are cracks in Earth's surface where the surrounding rock has moved or shifted. Faults can occur anywhere on Earth, but the ones that cause earthquakes are usually at plate boundaries.

When plates slide past one another, they often get stuck together instead of sliding smoothly. Eventually the plates unlock and move with a sudden jerk. This movement causes the vibrations of an earthquake.

Such plate movements happen deep below Earth's surface. The place underground where the plates stick and then slip is called a focus. The place on Earth's surface above the focus is called the epicenter.

Monument Valley in Arizona

Wind Erosion

When strong winds blow sand or dirt against a rock, tiny bits of the rock can break off. These tiny pieces of rock are then carried away by the wind. This form of erosion can make amazing rock arches and towers. For example, wind erosion helped to carve the massive rock formations of Monument Valley in Arizona.

Wave Erosion

Ocean storms, tides, and currents erode the shoreline. As waves crash against rocks, the force can break the rocks into smaller pieces. The sand and gravel in the waves wear down the rock even more. Eventually, these bits of rock are broken down into grains of sand, which can easily be moved. Waves hit the beach at an angle, pushing the sand down the coast.

Not every part of a shoreline erodes at the same rate. For example, a cave forms when part of a cliff erodes more quickly than the rest of the cliff.

The powerful force of waves erodes rocks and shorelines.

Earthquakes can cause great destruction on Earth's surface. Sometimes the side of a hill will slide down and bury an entire neighborhood. This is called a landslide.

Many injuries can occur during earthquakes when buildings are destroyed. The city of San Francisco was struck by major earthquakes in 1906 and 1989. The earthquake of 1906 destroyed many more buildings than the 1989 earthquake. This is because modern buildings are designed to flex with an earthquake's motion, instead of falling down.

Earthquakes that occur under the ocean can cause tsunamis. These giant waves sometimes cause great destruction when they crash into a coastline. At other times a tsunami will go unnoticed.

the 1989 San Francisco earthquake

the 1906 San Francisco earthquake

Crater Lake in Oregon

Volcanoes

Most volcanoes occur near converging plate boundaries. As one plate moves below another plate, rock partially melts and makes magma. The magma can be forced through any weak spots in the crust.

Magma that reaches Earth's surface is called lava. The lava flows out of a hole in the volcano called a vent. The top of a volcano's main vent is called a crater. If a volcano is not active, the crater can fill with rainwater and form a lake. For example, Crater Lake in Oregon formed in an inactive volcano. It is the deepest lake in the United States.

Moving Sediment

Erosion and Deposition

Erosion is the movement of materials away from one place. Deposition puts sediments in new places. Together, erosion and deposition work to create sand dunes, valleys, and river deltas.

Gravity is the main force that powers erosion. For example, as gravity pulls glaciers down mountains, the rocks underneath are crushed into sediment. The sediment is carried downhill by the glacier. Sharp peaks and jagged ridges are left behind on the mountain.

Flowing rivers also cause erosion. As rivers flow downhill, the moving water picks up and carries away bits of sediment. Fast-flowing rivers may erode the land to form deep canyons.

Rivers flow more slowly as they near the ocean. A slow-moving river cannot carry as much sediment. Some of the sediment sinks to the bottom of the river, forming a delta. Deltas, such as the Mississippi Delta in Louisiana, have fertile soil.

Soil

Soil is a mix of sediments from different sources. Sediments can come from decayed plant and animal remains. They can also come from bits of weathered rock.

The color of soil can range from red to black to gray. Sediments in the soil determine its color. The size of the bits of sediment determines a soil's texture and ability to hold water. Sandy soils have coarse grains. They are rough to the touch and allow water to pass through easily.

Topsoil is the top layer of soil. Because of the high amount of decayed materials from plants and animals, plants grow well in it. Beneath the topsoil is the subsoil. It contains many minerals but less decayed matter. Solid bedrock lies beneath the subsoil.

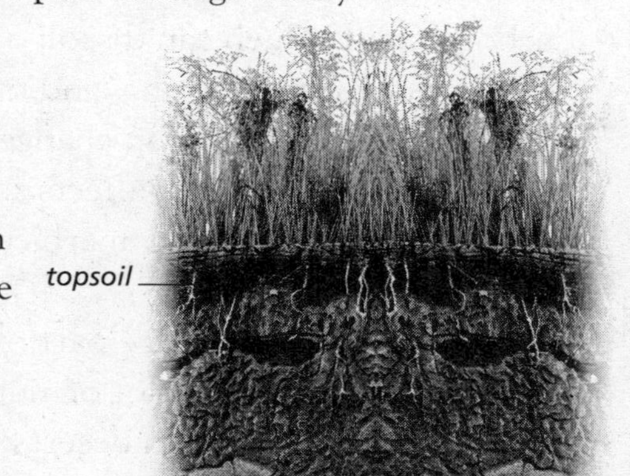

sandy soil

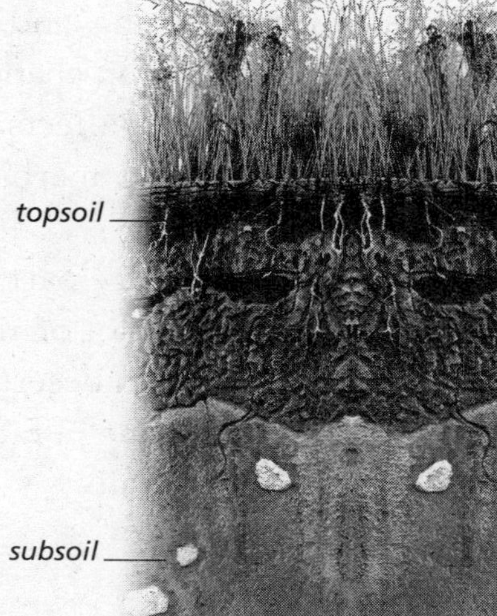

soil layers

Gases, such as carbon dioxide and water vapor, are often mixed with the lava. Trapped gases can blow a hole through the side of a volcano or push lava high in the air as it erupts from the vent. After the lava erupts from the volcano, it sometimes cools and turns into ash or solid rock before hitting the ground.

Volcanoes sometimes form on the ocean floor. An island forms when a volcano reaches the water's surface. The state of Hawaii is a string of islands that are actually volcanoes. This is a way in which volcanoes are constructive instead of destructive.

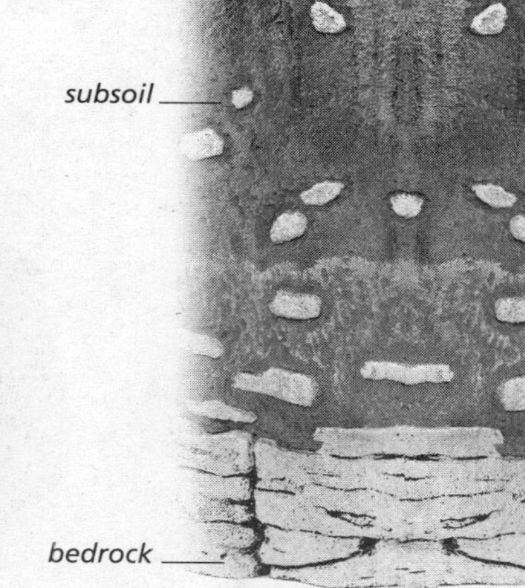

Hawaiian Islands

How Weathering Works

There are many ways Earth's surface can change. Weathering is a slow, destructive process that breaks rocks into smaller pieces. These pieces are called sediment.

Mechanical Weathering

Mechanical weathering is the breaking down of rock by physical forces such as gravity, ice, and plant roots. When rocks that have been buried come to the surface, the change in pressure can cause cracks in them. Rainwater can move into these cracks and freeze. When the rainwater freezes, it expands and causes the rock to split. This is called ice wedging.

The materials in a rock and its environment control the rate of weathering. For example, plant roots can grow into cracks in a rock. As the roots grow larger, they can push the rock apart. This type of weathering is more likely to occur in warm, moist climates where plants thrive, rather than in a desert. Plant roots can split soft rocks, such as sandstone, faster than hard rocks, such as granite.

A tree's roots can split rock.

Chemical Weathering

Chemical weathering is the changing of the materials in a rock by chemical forces. Raindrops absorb carbon dioxide from the air. This makes a chemical called carbonic acid, which can dissolve some kinds of rocks. Fungi and other organisms can give off chemicals that can change some types of rock.

Chemical weathering affects some rocks faster than others. For example, marble weathers more quickly than slate.

Because water is a large part of chemical weathering, areas with a lot of rain have more chemical weathering than deserts. For example, statues made of limestone in rainy London are often damaged by acid rain.

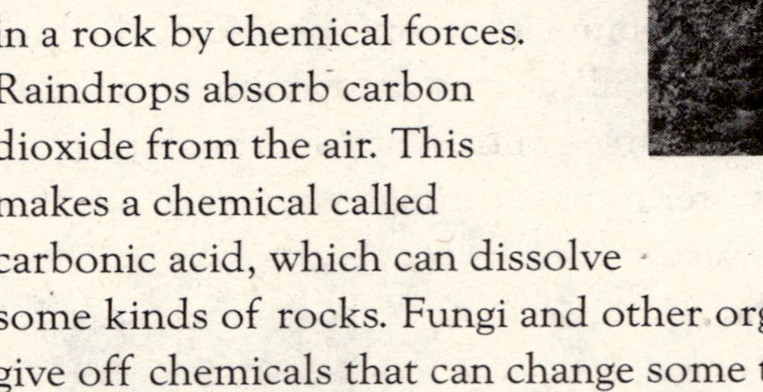

eroded statue

marble

slate

Earth's Natural Resources

by Natalie Goldstein

Genre	Comprehension Skill	Text Features	Science Content
Nonfiction	Main Idea and Details	• Labels • Captions • Diagrams • Glossary	Protecting Resources

Scott Foresman Science 5.10

What did you learn?

1. Why are fossil fuels considered to be nonrenewable resources?

2. What are three kinds of renewable resources that can be used to generate electricity?

3. What is recycling, and how does it help people save natural resources?

4. **Writing** in Science Water, soil, and air are necessary for nearly all living things. Write to explain how these vital resources are sometimes polluted. Include details from the reading to support your answer.

5. **Main Idea and Details** Explain the problems with our heavy use of fossil fuels for energy. Use details from the reading to support your answer.

Vocabulary

biomass
fossil fuel
geothermal
hydroelectric
nonrenewable resource
renewable resource
resource
solar energy

Picture Credits
Every effort has been made to secure permission and provide appropriate credit for photographic material.
The publisher deeply regrets any omission and pledges to correct errors called to its attention in subsequent editions.

Photo locators denoted as follows: Top (T), Center (C), Bottom (B), Left (L), Right (R), Background (Bkgd).

Illustration
10, 14 Tony Randazzo.

Photographs
5 Getty Images; 12 ©Vince Streano/Corbis; 15 Getty Images; 17 ©Jonathan Blair/Corbis; 19 (R, TL) Getty Images;
20 Getty Images; 22 (TC) Getty Images; 23 ©Bill Bachmann/Alamy Images.

Scott Foresman/Dorling Kindersley would also like to thank: 2 (CR), 3 (BR) Natural History Museum, London/DK Images;
16 (TR) Stephen Oliver/DK Images.

Unless otherwise acknowledged, all photographs are the copyright © of Dorling Kindersley, a division of Pearson.

ISBN: 0-328-13944-0

Glossary

biomass	any material that was recently alive, such as food waste or paper
fossil fuel	a material used as a fuel that comes from the remains of long-dead organisms
geothermal	using the heat inside Earth to generate electrical power
hydroelectric	using the power of flowing water to generate electricity
nonrenewable resource	a resource that cannot be replaced at all or cannot be replaced as fast as people use it
renewable resource	a resource that can be replaced
resource	something that meets a need for materials or energy
solar energy	energy from sunlight

Earth's Natural Resources

by Natalie Goldstein

Nonrenewable Energy Resources

Two Types of Resources

A **resource** is a supply of something that will meet a need for materials or for energy. Earth produces some resources faster than they are used. These are called **renewable resources.** A **nonrenewable resource** cannot be replaced or made as fast as people use it. Sometimes it cannot be replaced at all.

Green plants take in energy from the Sun.

Dead plants form peat.

You can help save resources by recycling. Collect paper, aluminum cans, plastic, and glass at school and at home. Find out if your town picks up recycled materials from your house. Or take them to your area's recycling center.

Recycling is just one way you can help conserve resources. Think of all the different types of resources you've read about in this book. Can you think of a way to conserve each of them? By reducing, reusing, and recycling resources, you are helping improve and protect your environment. You are helping Earth's environment too!

Recycling is one of the best-known ways of conserving resources.

Recycling

Do you put your plastic bottles in a different waste container than your regular trash? If so, you're probably recycling. Recycling means to treat a material so it can be used again. Glass can be recycled. It is ground up, melted, and reformed into new products. Plastic is recycled in a similar way. Paper can also be recycled. First it is soaked to make a soft pulp. The pulp is screened, washed, and then pressed into new paper.

There are many reasons to recycle. Recycling saves natural resources. It also saves energy. For example, it takes lots of energy to mine aluminum to make cans. It takes less energy to recycle used aluminum cans to make new cans.

Coal is a nonrenewable resource that takes millions of years to form. It forms when dead plants build up on the bottom of swamps. Layers of dead plants are pressed into a material called peat. Eventually, the peat turns into coal. Coal is an important fuel that people use to generate electricity. The plants that form coal take in energy from the Sun. This energy is stored in the coal and is released when it is burned.

Oil and natural gas are also formed when the remains of organisms are buried and changed. Oil, which is also called petroleum, forms from the remains of tiny sea organisms. Coal, oil, and natural gas are all called **fossil fuels** because they come from the remains of ancient organisms.

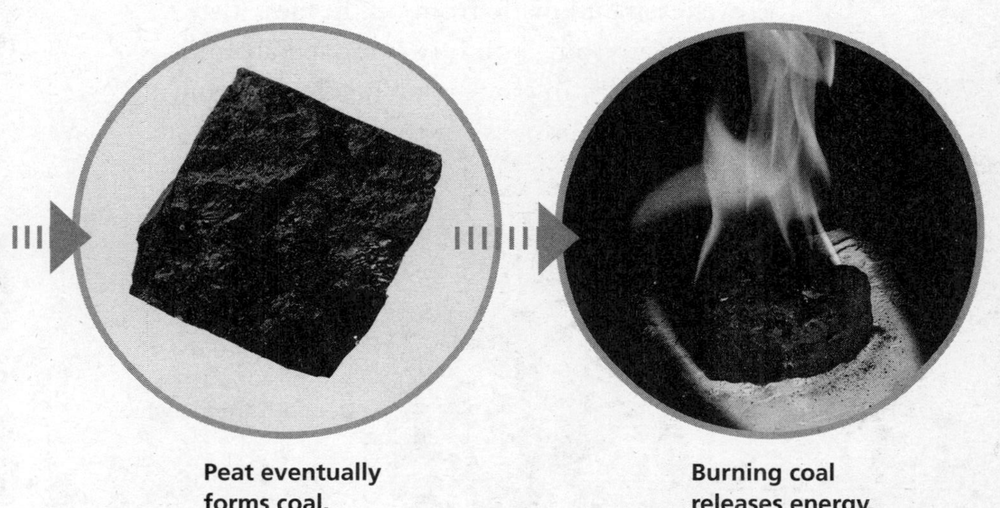

Peat eventually forms coal.

Burning coal releases energy.

Oil and Natural Gas

Oil and natural gas are buried deep within Earth, beneath land or underwater. Drilling rigs are used to make holes in Earth to reach these resources. When oil or natural gas are beneath the ocean, special rigs such as the one shown below must be used. The rigs are either towers that reach the ocean floor or platforms that float on the surface. Natural gas and oil are often found together. They are both pumped out of the ground and stored in large tanks until they are needed.

Oil is used in just about everything we do. Gasoline and diesel fuel for our vehicles are made from crude oil. If you ride to school in a bus, a car, or a train, you are using oil. Tractors running on gasoline help farmers grow the food you eat. Plastics, greases, and waxes are all made from oil. In fact, just about anything you buy is moved around the country in trucks that need oil to run. It is almost impossible to do anything that doesn't involve oil in some way.

Oil rigs, such as this one, are used to drill for oil beneath the ocean.

Conservation Laws

Today, there are many laws that protect natural resources. These conservation laws help people save natural resources by using them wisely. Some laws make factories and power plants control their pollution. Other laws make mining safer for the environment. Laws also set aside beautiful, natural areas for protection. Following the laws is often expensive, but doing this will make the world a better, healthier place to live.

Using Less and Reusing

The best way to conserve natural resources is to use less of them. For example, people can turn down the heat in winter to save electricity. Reusing things is another way of saving resources. This can be as simple as using an old plastic juice bottle as a water bottle, or covering your schoolbooks with the paper bags you used to carry groceries.

Can resources
be conserved?

Repairing Soil, Water, and Air

In Europe during the 1700s, people began doing things in new ways. Machines were used to do work that people used to do. This was called the Industrial Revolution. Since then, the machines people use have caused pollution. Factories, cars, and power plants pollute the air, the water, and the soil.

Scientists have tools that measure the amount of pollution in the air, water, and soil. By measuring how much pollution there is, scientists can make sure that pollution does not get too bad. If there is a lot of pollution, people can clean it up. Measuring tools also help scientists trace pollution to its source.

Oil spills can be very dangerous to ocean plants and animals.

Advantages and Disadvantages of Fossil Fuels

Fossil fuels have some advantages over other energy sources. For example, coal and oil are easy to store and move from place to place. It is easier to get energy from fossil fuel than from many other energy sources.

But there are many problems with fossil fuels. All fossil fuels are nonrenewable resources. One day we will run out of fossil fuels. Also, burning coal and oil causes a lot of air pollution, which is bad for people, animals, buildings, and plants. Oil spills are a pollution problem too. When ships that carry oil leak or sink, oil spills into the water. This is very dangerous for plants and animals living in the ocean.

People are looking for ways to make the collection, transportation, and use of fossil fuels safer. Better ships are being built that are less likely to spill oil. Cars are being designed to burn less fuel and make less pollution.

Other Energy Resources

Solar Energy

Scientists are trying to develop new energy sources that are renewable and make less pollution. One of the resources people have started using is solar energy. **Solar energy,** the energy in sunlight, is a renewable resource. For as long as the Sun shines on our planet, we will have solar energy.

There are two main ways people use solar energy. One way is to use devices called solar cells that turn sunlight into electricity. Many spacecraft get their electricity from solar cells. Another way is to use sunlight for heating materials. For example, sunlight is used to heat water for homes. Solar energy may be used to heat the space inside a home too.

Air is necessary for life. Nearly all living things breathe the oxygen in air. Cars, factories, and power plants often pollute the air. Polluted air can harm you. It also harms plants and animals.

Soil gives plants the minerals they need to grow. Animals rely on the plants for food. Soil may be polluted with chemicals. It may be damaged if too many crops are grown on it. Wind and water also erode soil.

All living things need water. Water is used by people for growing crops. Factories need water to make things we use every day. Water is polluted when people dump waste into it. Rain washes air pollution into water, causing chemical pollution that harms plants and animals.

Power plants cause pollution.

Polluted water harms fish and other animals.

Water, Soil, and Air

Water, soil, and air are very important resources. Without them, life could not exist.

In a way, water, air, and soil are renewable resources. Water is recycled through the water cycle. Clean air is renewable because, over time, pollution washes out of it. Soil is very slowly but constantly forming, through the weathering of rocks. However, renewing these resources takes a very long time, so we must use them carefully.

Advantages and Disadvantages

Solar energy has some great advantages. We will have sunlight for billions of years, so it is a renewable resource. Also, solar energy does not produce pollution.

But there are also some problems with solar energy. For example, it cannot produce power at night or on cloudy days. Solar energy systems are also expensive to make, and the factories that make solar cells can produce pollution.

Solar panels are made up of many solar cells. They make electricity for spacecraft.

Wind Energy

People have used wind energy for thousands of years. The wind was used to turn the blades of windmills. These blades were connected to huge stones inside mills. As the blades turned, the stones turned and ground grain into flour.

Beginning around 1800, small windmills were used on American farms. These windmills were attached to pumps that brought water up from beneath the ground.

Today, new windmills turn the wind's energy into electricity. A modern windmill's blades spin a generator that makes electricity. A gearbox inside the windmill lets the generator spin quickly, so it can still produce electricity even when there isn't much wind. The electricity can be sent through wires to power homes and factories.

Modern windmills are much more efficient than ancient ones.

Mining can be harmful to plant and animal habitats.

Minerals are nonrenewable resources. Earth contains a limited amount of them. Some minerals are much more common than others. Earth has much more iron than other minerals, such as copper, lead, or zinc. Because minerals are nonrenewable, people should use them wisely. Products made of minerals should be reused and recycled to make the minerals last longer.

Minerals are taken out of Earth by mining. Some mines are on the surface. Others are dug deep into the ground. Mining can harm the land. At the location of some mines, trees and plants are removed. The land is dug up and the plants and animals cannot live there any longer.

Mining also causes pollution. Mine dust can cause air pollution. Some minerals must be separated from rock with dangerous chemicals. The chemicals can cause air or water pollution. Often, chemicals and mine waste are kept in open pits or ponds. A storm or mudslide might cause the pit to leak, which would pollute nearby soil and water. Modern mining companies try to limit the harm caused by mining.

Other Types of Resources

Mineral Resources

Fuel for energy is not the only resource we get from Earth. We can also get mineral resources. Minerals are nonliving materials in Earth. Some common mineral resources are iron and salt. More rare minerals include gold, silver, and diamonds.

People use mineral resources in many ways. Gold is used in electronics and for jewelry. Iron is an extremely useful metal that is very common. Iron can be mixed with the element carbon to make steel. Steel is very strong and is used to make cars, tools, tall buildings, and many other useful things.

Gypsum and mica are also useful minerals. Gypsum is a white material that is used to make plaster and paint. Mica is a mineral also used in paint.

gold and diamonds

Gypsum and mica are minerals used in paint.

Many huge structures are built out of steel, which is made from the mineral iron.

Advantages and Disadvantages

Wind power has some of the same advantages as solar power. It is renewable. As long as there is weather on Earth, there will be wind. Wind energy does not cause any pollution.

Wind energy also has some of the same disadvantages as solar energy. Wind does not blow all the time. Many places in the world do not have winds that are strong enough to generate energy. Wind power also has some unique problems. Birds are sometimes killed when they fly into the tall windmills or the turning blades. Also, some people think that windmills are noisy and ugly. They do not want windmills near their homes.

Water Energy

Flowing water has been used for hundreds of years to do work for people. For example, factories were built along rivers. The flowing river water turned large paddle wheels. The energy of the moving wheels was used to cut wood, make cloth, or grind grain.

Today, moving water is used to generate electricity. This is called **hydroelectric** power. Hydroelectric power plants are built in dams, which block the normal flow of river water. The flow of water through the dam is controlled. The water flowing through the dam turns parts of large generators in the power plant. As they spin, the generators make electricity.

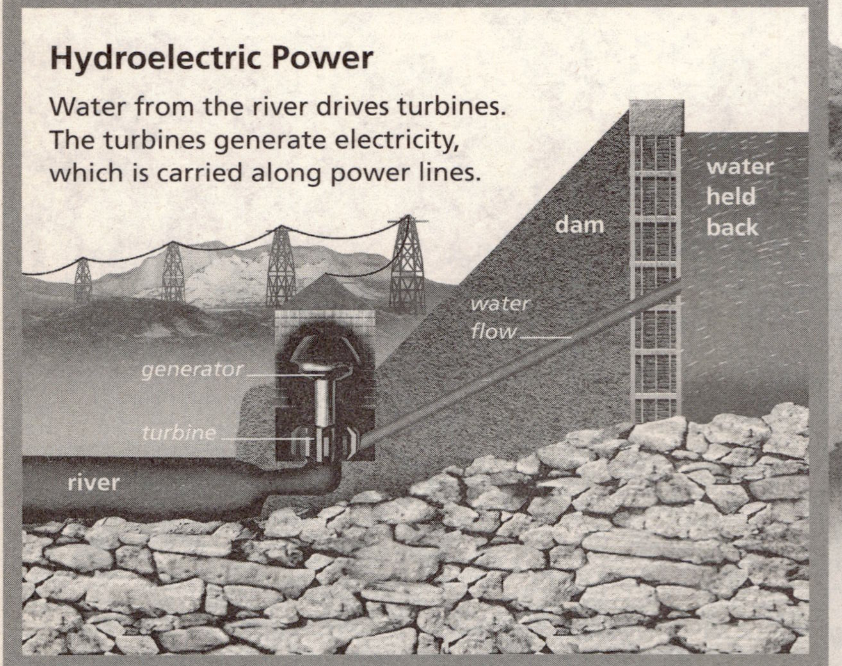

Hydroelectric Power

Water from the river drives turbines. The turbines generate electricity, which is carried along power lines.

Biomass Energy

Biomass is any material that was recently alive, including food waste, wood, paper, grasses, and leaves. Biomass can be burned in power plants to produce electricity.

Not all biomass is burned in power plants. Some is used to make fuel for cars and trucks. Chemicals added to some biomass change it into a liquid fuel that can be used like gasoline. Heating the liquid to high temperatures turns it into a gas. This can be used to heat homes in the same way as natural gas.

One of the best sources of biomass is garbage. It is a completely renewable resource because people are always making more garbage. Also, the more garbage we burn, the less we have to put into dumps and landfills. The biggest problem with burning biomass is that it produces air pollution.

Garbage can be used as fuel for a biomass power plant.

Geothermal Energy

Geothermal energy uses the heat inside Earth to generate electricity. This can be done in several ways. One way is to pour water down deep holes into extremely hot rock. There, the water gets very hot and may even boil and turn to steam. The hot water or steam rises to the surface. It enters a power plant where it is used to turn generators that make electricity.

Geothermal energy does not depend on changing weather conditions such as sunlight or wind. Although a few pollutants may be found in geothermal steam, it pollutes much less than fossil fuels. However, geothermal energy can be used only where there are very hot rocks or hot water close to Earth's surface. Places where this happens are not always close to where the power is needed.

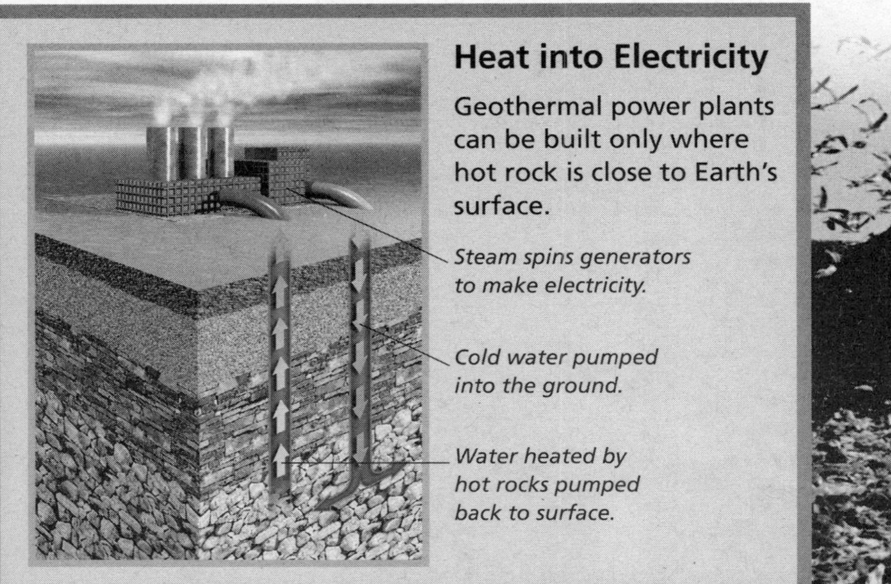

Advantages and Disadvantages

Hydroelectric power is another renewable source of electricity. As long as a river flows, a power plant in a dam can use the moving water to generate electricity. Another advantage is that it does not produce pollution.

But hydroelectric power has some disadvantages too. Hydroelectric power plants can be built only on large rivers with a lot of flowing water. When a dam is built, the land behind it is flooded. This destroys habitats for plants and animals. It may also destroy people's homes or entire towns. A dam may also harm river fish. Some fish need to swim up the river to lay eggs. The hydroelectric dam often blocks the river. The fish cannot swim past the dam. They cannot lay their eggs upriver, so the fish population may decline.

The flow of water through this dam generates electricity.

Nuclear Power

In a nuclear power plant, a rare metal called uranium is used to produce electricity. Atoms of uranium are split in a part of the plant called the reactor. This releases huge amounts of heat. The heat is used to make steam that drives generators. This is the same process that a fossil fuel plant uses, except the heat is generated by splitting uranium atoms instead of by the burning of oil or coal.

Nuclear power has some advantages over other power sources. Since so much energy is produced by splitting atoms of uranium, a nuclear plant needs only a tiny amount of fuel. Also, nuclear power produces no air pollution. Yet nuclear power has its disadvantages. Once the uranium has been used, it becomes a very dangerous waste product. This waste is very difficult and expensive to get rid of. Also, building a nuclear power plant is very expensive. Nuclear fuel is a nonrenewable resource. There is a limited amount of uranium on Earth. Someday all of it will be used up.

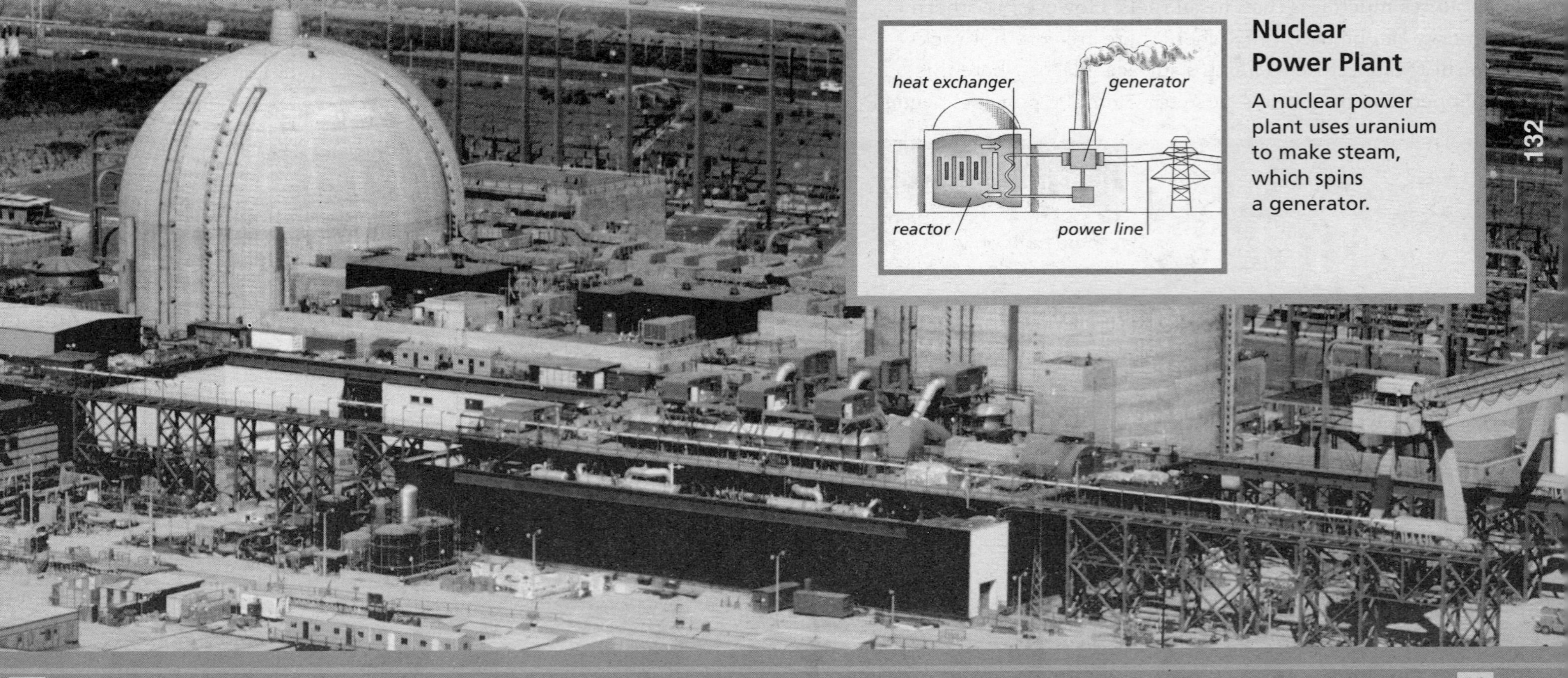

Nuclear Power Plant

A nuclear power plant uses uranium to make steam, which spins a generator.

Properties of Matter

by Emily Gray

Genre	Comprehension Skill	Text Features	Science Content
Nonfiction	Predict	• Labels • Captions • Diagrams • Glossary	Matter

Scott Foresman Science 5.11

PEARSON
Scott Foresman

scottforesman.com

ISBN 0-328-13947-5

90000

9 780328 139477

What did you learn?

1. Why are elements the "building blocks of matter"?

2. Mass, volume, and density are words used to describe three different properties of matter. Explain each term.

3. What are the particles that make up an atom? Name the charge each particle has.

4. **Writing** in Science Mixtures and solutions both combine materials. Write to explain how mixtures and solutions are different, and give an example from the text for each to support your answer.

5. **Predict** Weight is the pull of gravity on an object. What do you think would happen to an object's weight if there were no gravity at all?

Vocabulary

atom
compound
concentrated
dilute
electron
element
neutron
proton
saturated

Picture Credits
Every effort has been made to secure permission and provide appropriate credit for photographic material. The publisher deeply regrets any omission and pledges to correct errors called to its attention in subsequent editions.

Photo locators denoted as follows: Top (T), Center (C), Bottom (B), Left (L), Right (R), Background (Bkgd).

2 (C, BC) ©British Museum/DK Images; 11 (T) CDC/PHIL/Corbis; 15 (R) Digital Vision.

Scott Foresman/Dorling Kindersley would also like to thank: 2 (BR), 3 (BR), 9 (CB, CRB, BL, BR) Natural History Museum, London/DK Images; 10 (TR), 18 (BL, BR), 21 (C), 23 (BL, BR) Stephen Oliver/DK Images.

Unless otherwise acknowledged, all photographs are the copyright © of Dorling Kindersley, a division of Pearson.

ISBN: 0-328-13947-5

Glossary

atom	the smallest part of an element that has the properties of the element
compound	a substance created with two or more elements that has different properties than the elements
concentrated	a state in which a solvent contains a large amount of dissolved solute
dilute	a state in which a solvent contains a small amount of dissolved solute
electron	a negatively charged particle of an atom
element	matter that cannot be easily broken down into simpler substances
neutron	a particle of an atom with no charge
proton	a positively charged particle of an atom
saturated	a state in which a solvent contains all of the solute that can be dissolved in it

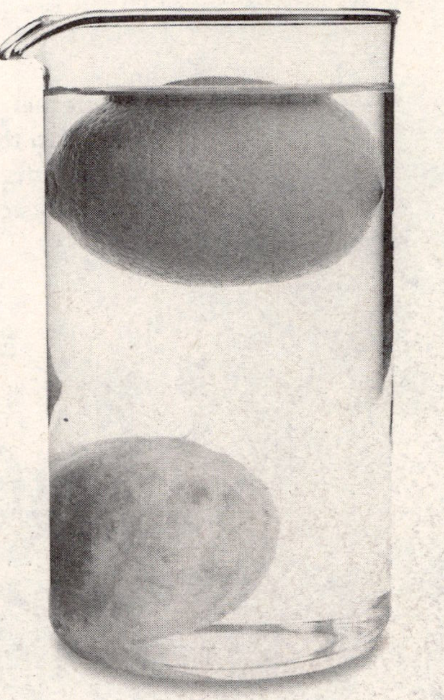

Properties of Matter

by Emily Gray

Properties of Matter

Elements

Elements are the building blocks of matter. More than one hundred elements exist. It is very difficult to break elements down into different materials.

Elements combine in many ways to make up all the different kinds of matter around us. Only a few elements are found in pure forms in nature. Living and nonliving things are made up of arrangements of different elements.

Each element has its own set of chemical and physical properties. Groups of elements with similar physical and chemical properties are known as families.

silver ore

The metals gold and silver belong to the same family of elements. Metals come from rocks called ores.

chunks of gold ore in quartz crystals

old silver coin

old gold coin

Solubility is the amount of a substance that can be dissolved by a solvent at a specific temperature. Solid solutes can be dissolved in solutions with higher temperatures.

Solutions can be described by how much solute is dissolved in the solvent. **Saturated** solutions contain all the solute that can be dissolved in the solution. If you add more solute to a saturated solution, it will not dissolve unless you raise the temperature. A solution is **concentrated** when it has so much solute that it is close to being saturated. A **dilute** solution contains only a small amount of solute.

Some materials will not dissolve in a liquid at all. Raising the temperature or changing the proportions of the solute to solvent will not help. Although salt will dissolve easily in water, salt cannot dissolve in oil.

Pour oil on top of water and add a droplet of food coloring. What happens when you stir the mixture?

When the mixture of chalk and water is heated, the chalk still does not dissolve in the water.

When the solution of sugar and water is heated, the remaining sugar crystals dissolve.

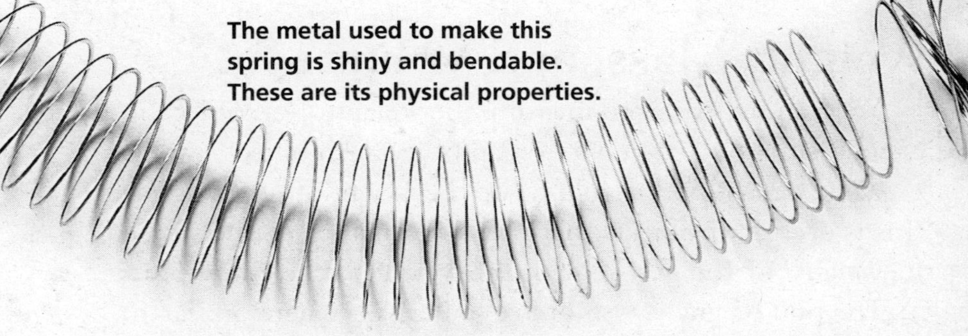

The metal used to make this spring is shiny and bendable. These are its physical properties.

Chemical properties are the ways that matter changes. For example, liquid water has the chemical property that it can be broken down by electricity into oxygen gas and hydrogen gas. Physical properties can be measured without changing the material. An object's color, mass, volume, odor, texture, and density are all physical properties. These properties can be measured using tools such as rulers, microscopes, thermometers, and scales.

Elements are classified as either metals or nonmetals. More than three-fourths of all elements are metals. Some physical properties of metals are that they are shiny, they are bendable, and they can conduct heat and electricity well.

Nonmetals are often gases and do not conduct electricity. They may be transparent and are usually fragile.

Heating a solution can also increase the rate at which liquids and solids dissolve in each other. When materials are heated, their particles spread out. This helps the solute dissolve faster in the solvent.

Not all solutions are composed of a solid and a liquid. Solutions can be made when liquids dissolve into other liquids. A gas can also dissolve into a liquid. Oceans contain dissolved salt, which is a solid. Oceans also contain dissolved oxygen and carbon dioxide, which are gases. These substances help the ocean to sustain plant and animal life.

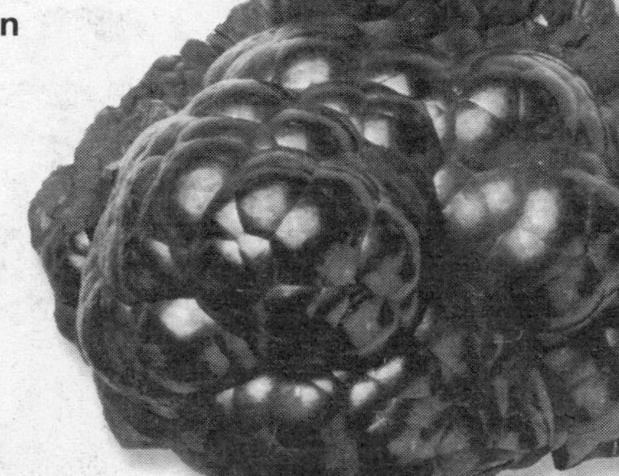

iron ore

The metal element iron is often mixed with the nonmetal carbon to produce steel.

steel screw

Weight, Mass, and Volume

You can use scales to measure the weight of an object. Weight is the pull of gravity on an object. An object's weight can also be measured by adding up the weight of all of its parts. This is useful for objects that won't fit on a scale. The sum of the weights of the parts equals the weight of the entire object.

The pull of gravity is not the same everywhere on Earth. The weight of an object may be different if it is measured in two different places. At higher altitudes on Earth, gravity is weaker. An object weighed at the top of a mountain would weigh less than if it were weighed at sea level.

Mass is the amount of matter in an object. An object's mass affects its weight, but weight and mass are two different things.

Weight changes as the force of gravity changes, but mass stays the same. The mass of an object is usually measured using a balance. The object you are measuring is placed on one side, and other objects with known masses are placed on the other side. When both sides balance, youadd the known masses. The object's mass is equal to the total of the known masses. For example, if five grams of mass balance an object, that object's mass is five grams.

Use a balance to measure the mass of objects.

Solvents can dissolve solutes only if the molecules of each substance have similar attractive forces. Water is called a universal solvent because it can act as a solvent in many different solutions. Sugar, starch, and salt all dissolve in water.

When a solute dissolves in a solvent, the individual particles of the solute separate and spread throughout the solvent. Solids can dissolve in a liquid more quickly if the pieces are smaller.

Salt water is a solution of salt dissolved in water. The two materials can be separated by evaporating the water.

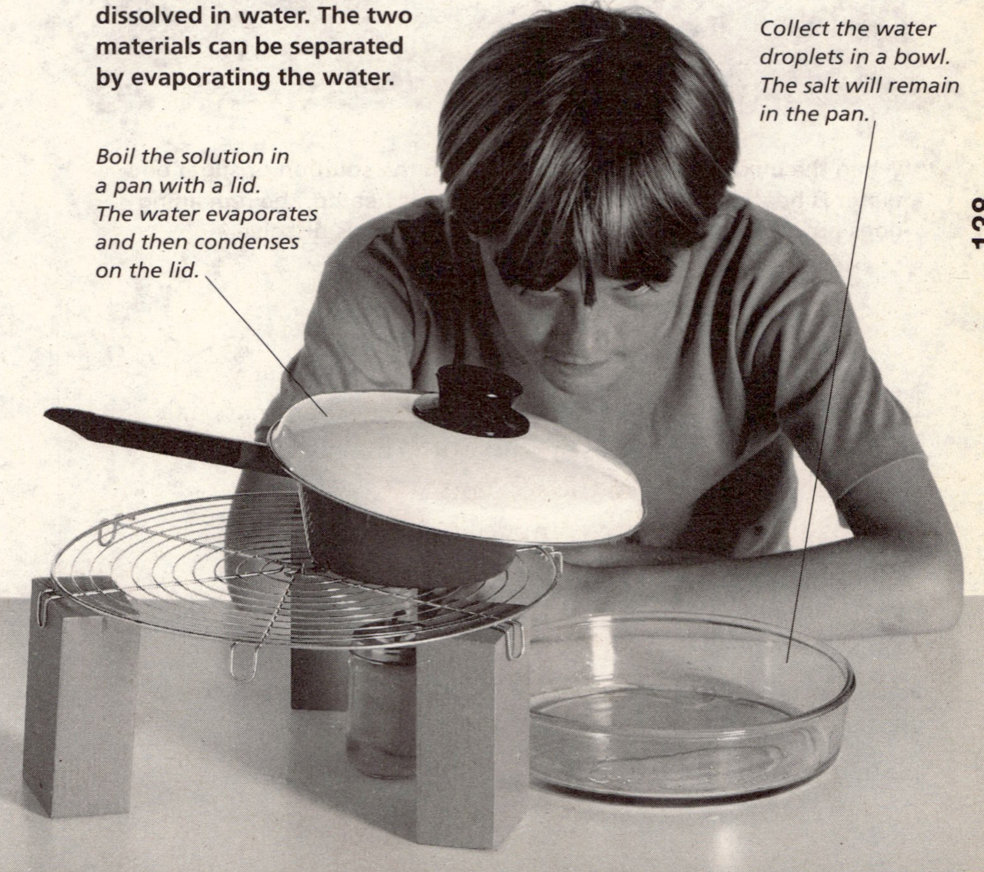

Boil the solution in a pan with a lid. The water evaporates and then condenses on the lid.

Collect the water droplets in a bowl. The salt will remain in the pan.

These pieces of chalk do not form a solution with water.

Sugar crystals do form a solution with water.

A few sugar crystals have not dissolved.

Solutions

Solutions are special mixtures of two or more substances. Solutions are different from mixtures. If you make a mixture of dirt and water, the dirt will eventually sink to the bottom. If you mix sugar and water, the sugar will dissolve in the water and will not sink to the bottom. This combination of sugar and water is an example of a solution. In a solution, substances are spread out evenly. They will not settle out as the dirt did in the water.

Solutions form when molecules have attractions for one another. These electrical charges hold molecules together and also allow liquids to dissolve other substances. The substance that dissolves in the liquid is known as a solute. The liquid in which a solute dissolves is known as a solvent.

You can measure the volume of a piece of clay by dropping it into a container full of water. The amount of water that spills out into a measuring jug is the clay's volume.

Volume is the amount of space occupied by an object. The volume of a solid is measured in cubic units. To find the volume of a box, you can use a simple mathematical formula. Multiply the length, width, and height to find the volume.

But what if an object has a strange shape that is hard to measure, such as a lumpy piece of clay? The volume of such an object can be measured with a graduated cylinder, as shown above. When the lump of clay is placed in the jug of water, some of the water spills out through the straw. The water is collected in the graduated cylinder. The volume of water shown on the cylinder's markings is the same as the volume of the clay.

Properties of Objects and Materials

The properties of an object are not always the same as the properties of a material. For example, shape is a property of an object, not a property of the material from which the object is made. The density, color, hardness, and texture are properties of materials, not objects.

Density and Buoyancy

Density is the amount of matter in a specific volume. If you have a golf ball and a table tennis ball that are the same volume, but one has more mass, their densities are different. The density of an object can be calculated by dividing the mass of the object by the volume of the object. This equation can be written as $D = \frac{M}{V}$.

Density is a physical property. The density of a material does not change even if the size of the object does. For example, the density of a tiny sliver of glass is the same as the density of a huge windowpane.

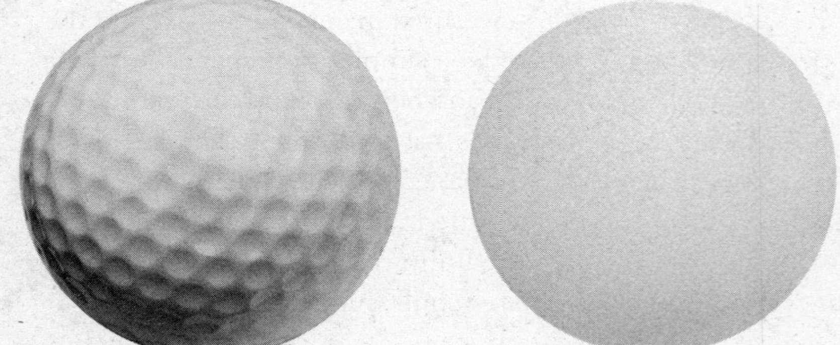

Golf balls and table tennis balls may have about the same volume, but their densities are different because the golf ball has more mass.

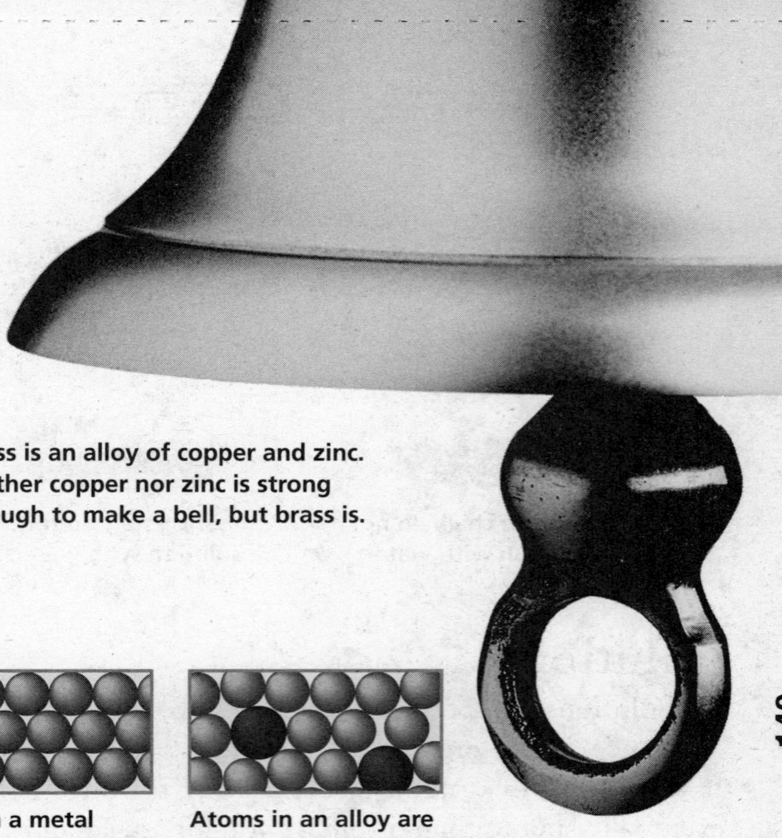

Brass is an alloy of copper and zinc. Neither copper nor zinc is strong enough to make a bell, but brass is.

Atoms in a metal element are arranged in a regular pattern.

Atoms in an alloy are arranged in an irregular pattern. This makes the metal stronger.

Some common metals are elements, while others are mixtures of elements. Gold, silver, copper, iron, and nickel are all examples of metals that are elements. Steel is a mixture of iron and carbon, while brass is a mixture of copper and zinc. Bronze is another example of a mixture. It is made up of tin, copper, and several other materials. All of these mixtures are known as alloys. The properties of an alloy are usually different than the properties of the materials used to make the alloy.

Mixtures and Solutions

Mixtures

When different materials are put together but do not form compounds, a mixture is formed. Usually, the materials keep their distinct properties. For example, if you mix lettuce, tomatoes, and peppers together in a salad, the colors and flavors of each vegetable do not change.

Materials in simple mixtures can be separated if they have different physical properties. For example, iron filings and sand can be separated easily with a magnet. The iron filings are attracted to the magnet, while the grains of sand are not. Moving a magnet over this mixture will pick up the iron filings, leaving the sand behind.

A mixture of iron filings and sand can be separated easily with a magnet. The iron sticks to the magnet, leaving the sand behind.

If an object can float, it is buoyant. Objects with different buoyancies are used for different things. For example, life jackets and balloons are buoyant. They are designed to float. Anchors and lead weights are not buoyant. They are designed to sink. Certain materials are used for each purpose.

Buoyancy is the density of an object compared to the density of the material around it. For example, wood is less dense than water, so it floats in water. Wood is more dense than air, so it does not float in air.

A lemon floats in water, but if you peel the lemon, it will sink.

An unpeeled lemon is less dense than the surrounding water, so it floats.

A peeled lemon is more dense than water, so it sinks.

How do atoms combine?

Atoms

An **atom** is the smallest part of an element that has the chemical properties of that element. When two or more atoms combine, a molecule is formed. The atoms of elements can react with one another. They can combine to form chemical compounds in many different ways. The properties of an atom determine how atoms react and combine with one another. These properties also determine how elements react with other elements.

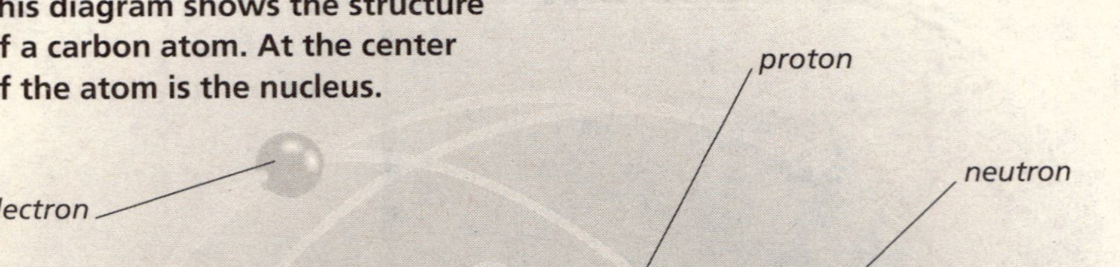

This diagram shows the structure of a carbon atom. At the center of the atom is the nucleus.

The boiling point is not always a fixed temperature. The boiling point of a substance is sensitive to changes in pressure. If you boiled water at sea level, the boiling point would be slightly higher than if you were to boil the same water on a high mountain. This temperature difference is not large but has been recorded by scientists.

Condensation occurs when a gas turns back into a liquid. If gas particles touch a cold surface, their temperature drops. As they cool, they slow down and become trapped on the surface. If enough atoms are trapped, a liquid drop is formed. The clouds we see in the sky form by condensation of water.

When water condenses in the atmosphere, it forms clouds.

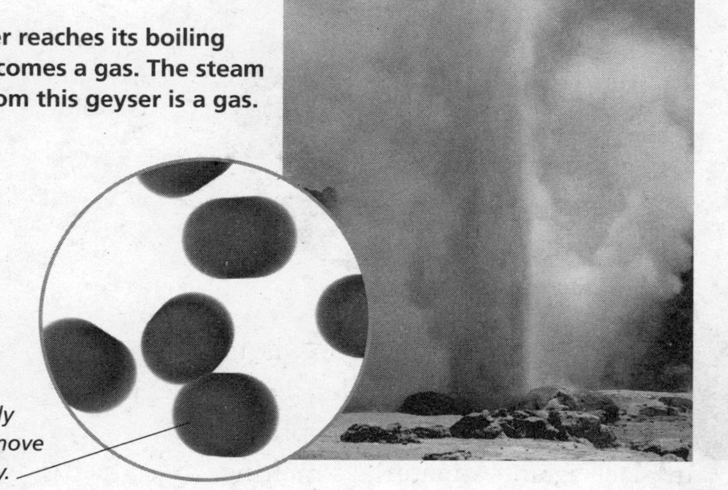
When water reaches its boiling point, it becomes a gas. The steam erupting from this geyser is a gas.

Gases

Gas particles are very far apart compared to the particles of solids or liquids. A gas does not have a fixed shape or volume. Gas particles spread out evenly to fill a container. Gas particles usually do not affect each other unless they collide, because they are far apart.

Evaporation happens when liquids turn into gas. Particles at the surface of a liquid evaporate if they move upward with enough speed.

If the temperature of a liquid is high enough, particles will evaporate throughout the liquid. This is called boiling. The bubbles in boiling water are gas that has evaporated below the surface and is rising to the top.

. Different types of matter have different melting points. The same holds true for the boiling point of a substance. The boiling point is the temperature at which a liquid changes to a gas. Different liquids have different boiling points. The boiling point of a liquid is a physical property. Nothing is added to or subtracted from a substance when it boils.

Atoms are made up of particles called electrons, protons, and neutrons. The nucleus, or center, of an atom consists of protons and neutrons. Each element has a unique number of protons. For example, an atom of carbon has six protons. No other element has this number of protons in its atoms. The nucleus is surrounded by electrons. Some particles have a property known as an electrical charge.

Neutrons have no electrical charge. **Electrons** have a negative charge, while **protons** have a positive charge. These charges react with one another as a magnet would: the negative charge and positive chargé attract one another. This attraction holds the atom together. An atom usually has an equal number of protons and electrons. This makes the atom electrically neutral, which means that the negative and positive charges are equal.

All elements are recorded in a chart known as the periodic table. Every element has a box in the table that shows the name of the element and its symbol. The symbol has one, two, or three letters. The first letter of the symbol is capitalized. The box also contains the atomic number, which is the number of protons in the nucleus.

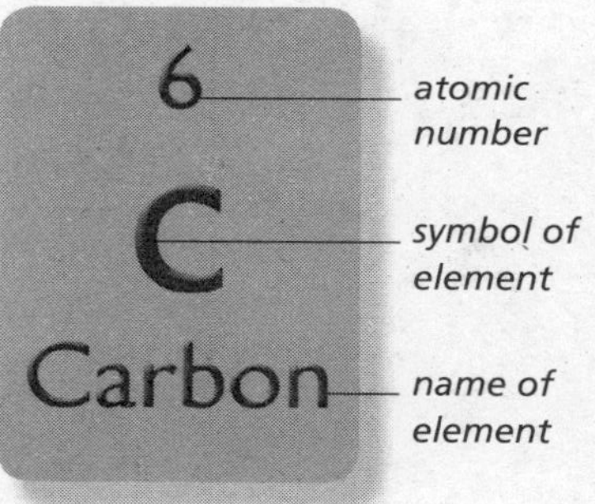

Coal contains a large amount of carbon.

Compounds

A **compound** is a type of matter made up of two or more elements. Compounds act differently than the elements they are made up of. For example, water is a compound made up of hydrogen and oxygen. Both of these elements are gases at room temperature. But water is a liquid.

Some compounds hold together because they share electrons. The electrons go around two atoms, bonding the atoms together.

Each compound can be described using a formula. The formula tells how many atoms of each element are in the compound. The formula for water is H_2O. The 2 after the H means that there are two hydrogen atoms in one molecule of water. There is no number after the O. This means there is only one oxygen atom per water molecule. A molecule is the smallest particle of a compound.

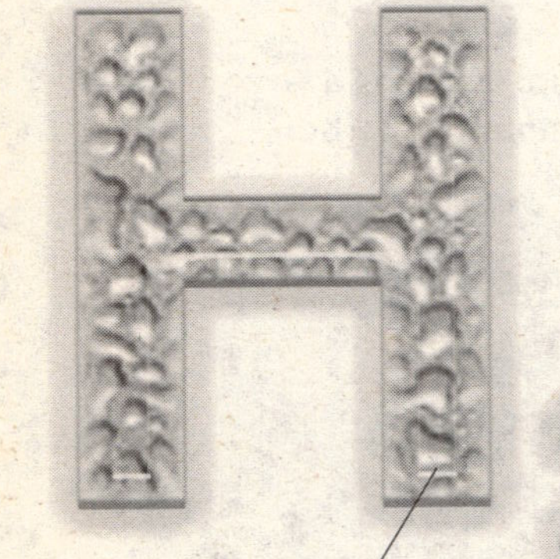
A water molecule is made up of two atoms of hydrogen and one atom of oxygen.

formula for water

Particles in a liquid have space to move around.

As the temperature drops, liquids eventually freeze. The molecules and atoms slow down and vibrate in place again. A material's melting temperature is always the same as its freezing temperature. For example, when the temperature of water in liquid form cools below 0° Celsius, it freezes into ice. When the temperature of ice rises above 0° Celsius, it turns from a solid to a liquid. The temperature at which this change occurs is known as the melting point or the freezing point.

The freezing point is not the same for all materials. You can determine what a material is by its freezing point, because different materials have different freezing points.

The freezing point of a material is a physical property, because nothing is added to or subtracted from the material during the change. Only the temperature of the material changes.

Water is in a liquid state at room temperature.

144

Phase Changes

Solids and Liquids

There are three phases, or states, of matter. Matter may be a solid, a liquid, or a gas. The motions and arrangements of atoms and molecules, along with the temperature of the material, determine the state of the material. For example, water is in a solid state when it freezes and becomes ice. We can drink water in its liquid state, at room temperature. When water is found in the air, it is a gas. These states are considered physical properties and do not depend on chemical reactions.

Solids have a fixed shape and volume. Their particles vibrate in place. Strong forces hold the particles together.

When the temperature rises, molecules can gain enough energy to move away from their positions. Then the solid melts and turns into a liquid. Molecules in a liquid are still held together, but they are not in a fixed position. They can move past and around one another. Although liquids do not have a definite shape, they still have a fixed volume.

Ice is water in a solid state.

Particles in a solid are tightly packed.

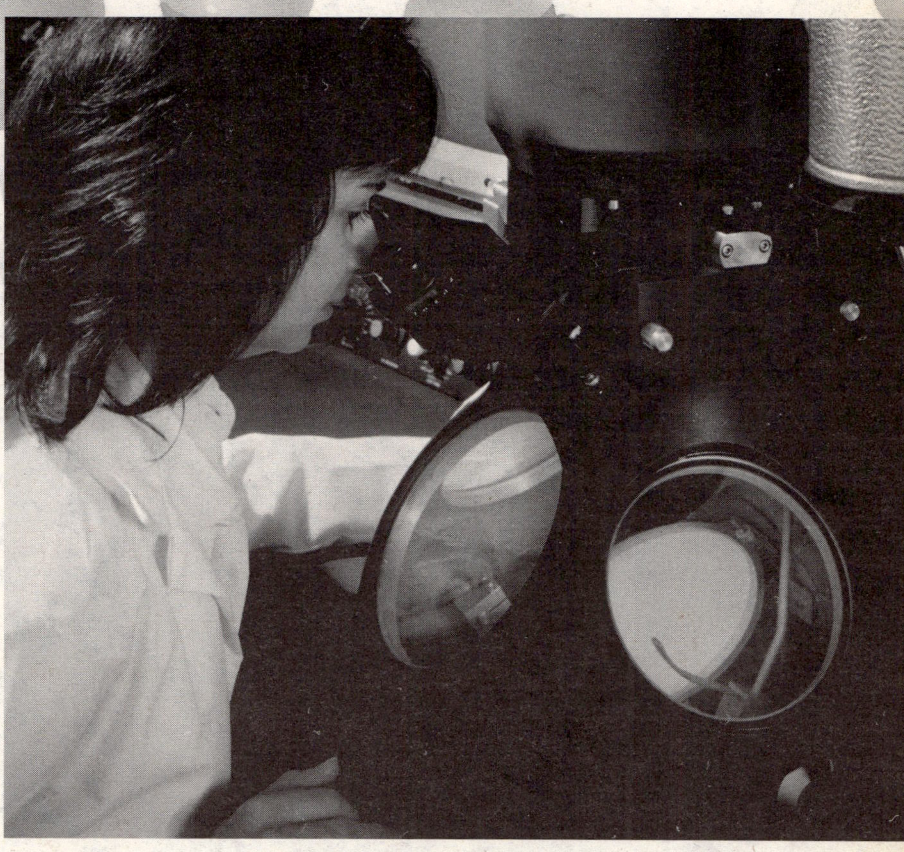

This machine helps scientists to see things that are too small to be seen with a regular microscope.

Seeing Molecules

Molecules and atoms are too small to be seen. Even the most powerful microscope cannot help you see an atom or molecule. In order to make images of atoms and molecules, special technology is needed. Scientists use powerful equipment to detect the shape of an atom or a molecule. Then the shape is shown on a computer screen.

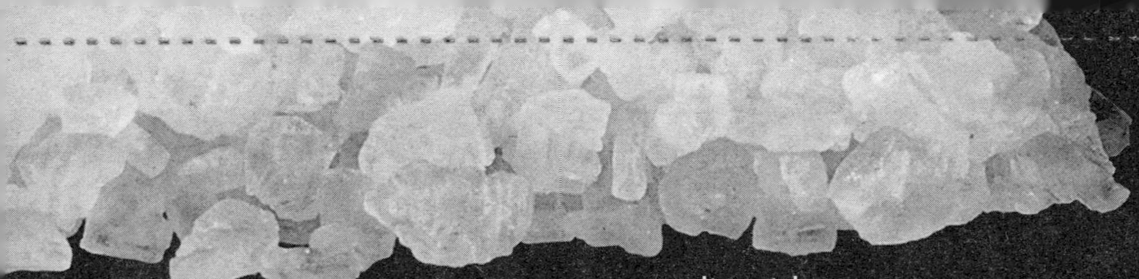
salt crystals

Salts

Salts are compounds that bond in a certain way. The elements in salts are held together by opposite charges, like magnets. If an atom has more electrons than protons, it has a negative charge. An atom with more protons than electrons has a positive charge.

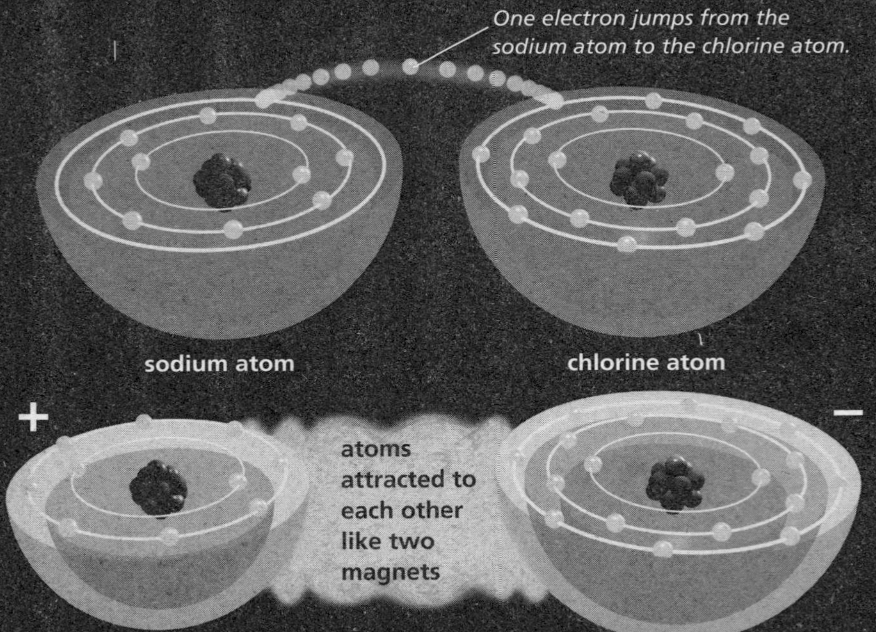

The sodium atom now has more protons than electrons. This gives the atom a positive charge.

The chlorine atom now has more electrons than protons. This gives the atom a negative charge.

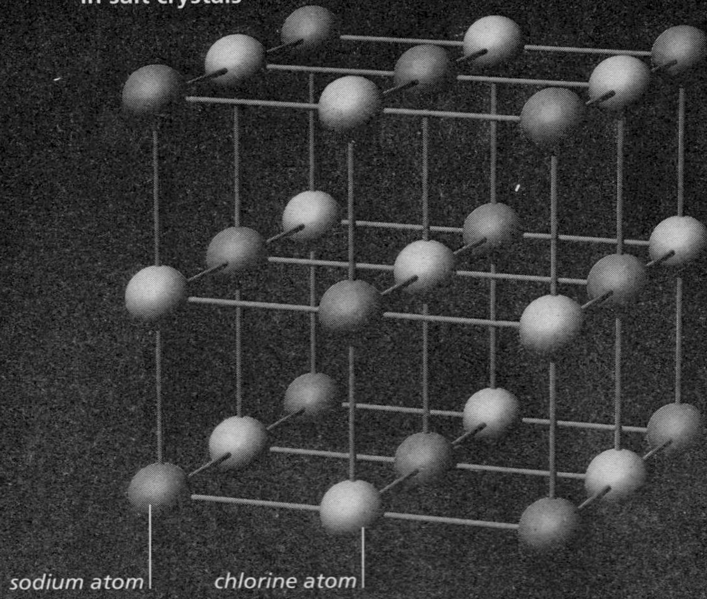

a regular pattern of atoms in salt crystals

Salts are made up of one metal element and one nonmetal element. All salts form crystals. This means that their molecules are arranged in a repeating pattern. Crystals are usually brittle, and they have high melting points. Other crystals include sand, sugar, and diamonds.

As you learned, compounds are very different from the elements that combine to make them. Salt is no exception. One molecule of table salt is made up of one atom of sodium (Na) and one atom of chlorine (Cl). The formula for table salt is written as NaCl. Pure sodium is a metal that is soft and silver. Pure chlorine is a gas that is poisonous. Separately, these elements can be harmful, but together, they form a compound that is safe to eat.

Changing Matter

by Mary Miller

Genre	Comprehension Skill	Text Features	Science Content
Nonfiction	Draw Conclusions	• Labels • Captions • Charts • Glossary	Changes in Matter

Scott Foresman Science 5.12

PEARSON

Scott Foresman

scottforesman.com

ISBN 0-328-13950-5

9 780328 139507

90000

What did you learn?

1. What is the difference between a physical change and a chemical change?

2. Explain decomposition, combination, and replacement chemical reactions.

3. If the total mass of the reactants in a chemical equation is ten grams, what will the total mass of the products be? What rule tells you the answer?

4. **Writing** in Science Chemicals have improved modern life in many ways. Write to explain how chemicals have improved modern health, agriculture, and transportation. Use details from the books to support your answer.

5. **Draw Conclusions** Warning labels on some household chemicals tell you to open a window for fresh air. Why do you think they tell you this?

Vocabulary

chemical change
chemical equation
combustion
physical change
polymer
product
reactant

Picture Credits
Every effort has been made to secure permission and provide appropriate credit for photographic material. The publisher deeply regrets any omission and pledges to correct errors called to its attention in subsequent editions.

Photo locators denoted as follows: Top (T), Center (C), Bottom (B), Left (L), Right (R), Background (Bkgd).

Opener: Getty Images; 2 Cory Sorensen/Corbis; 3 Getty Images; 4 (B) ©Angus Beare/DK Images, (TR) ©British Museum/ DK Images; 8 Wes Thompson/Corbis; 11 D.I.Y. Photo Library; 12 (B) Charles E. Rotkin/Corbis; 16 (TR) Bettmann/Corbis, (BR) Lester V. Bergman/Corbis; 17 (BL) Corbis; 21 Getty Images; 22 (BR) Leslie Garland Picture Library/Alamy Images.

Unless otherwise acknowledged, all photographs are the copyright © of Dorling Kindersley, a division of Pearson.

ISBN: 0-328-13950-5

Changing Matter

by Mary Miller

Glossary

chemical change	a change in which matter is changed into a completely different kind of matter
chemical equation	a way of writing what happens during a chemical reaction
combustion	a chemical reaction in which heat and light are given off
physical change	a change that does not alter the chemical composition of matter
polymer	a large molecule made of many identical smaller units connected together
product	a substance made during a chemical reaction
reactant	a substance used in a chemical reaction

Chemical Changes

Two Types of Changes

Matter can go through physical and chemical changes. When a **physical change** occurs, the object still keeps its chemical makeup. A physical change can be a change in position, size, or shape. Other physical changes can alter an object's volume or phase of matter. For example, cut a log in half and it looks different physically. But both smaller pieces of the log are still made of wood.

Cutting a log results in a physical change rather than a chemical change.

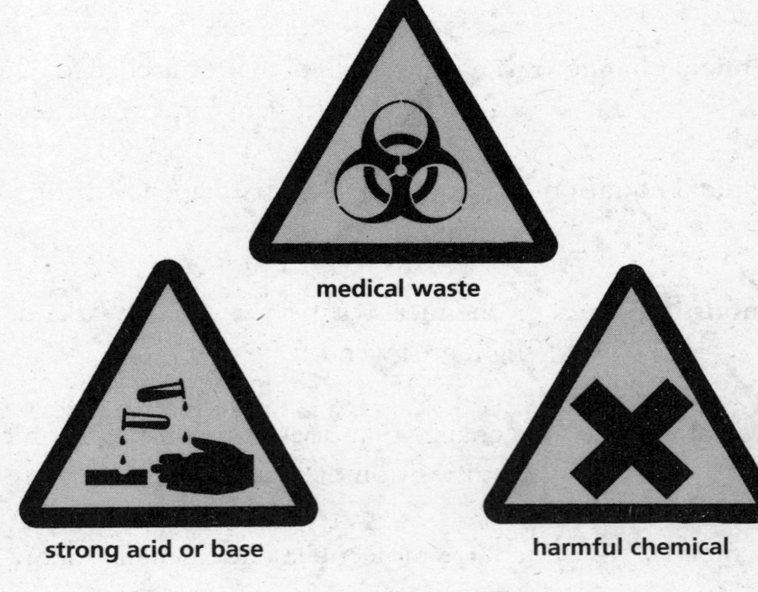

Warning labels are used to warn people if a product contains something that could be harmful.

Many dangerous chemicals are found under your kitchen sink. The chemicals in cleaning supplies such as bleach, ammonia, and drain opener can be very dangerous. It is important to read the directions before using any of these products. The label might tell you to wear gloves or safety goggles. Many labels tell you to keep a window open for fresh air. Cleaners should never be mixed together. Mixing cleaners together can create dangerous chemical reactions.

Chemical changes are a big part of our everyday lives. They give us energy and special materials, and they even keep us healthy. In fact the book you are reading right now would not be here if it weren't for chemicals.

Safety

Some chemicals have made life safer. The chemicals in disinfectants kill germs that can cause disease. Chemicals in medicines cure people of many illnesses.

For all the good chemicals have done, there are some dangers. If chemicals are used improperly, they can be hazardous. Manufacturers put warning labels on products that are dangerous to people, pets, or the environment.

household bleach

Cleaning products may contain chemicals that can be dangerous.

A chemical change occurs when an object changes into a completely different type of matter. For example, if you toss the cut-up log into a campfire and it burns, the wood becomes a new material. It changes into ash and gas. These new materials have different chemical and physical properties than the log did.

Burning wood causes a chemical change to happen.

151

Evidence of Chemical Changes

During a chemical change, atoms are rearranged in a way that cannot be undone easily. They form different kinds of matter. A chemical change might show as a change in color. The formation of a gas or solid can also be evidence of a chemical change.

Oxygen triggers many chemical reactions. When oxygen reacts with iron, rust forms. The gray metal turns reddish brown. The new color is evidence of the chemical change. A chemical change can also happen to a sliced apple. The sugars in the fruit react to oxygen in the air. The apple turns brown.

If vinegar is added to a bowl of baking soda, a lot of bubbles will form. These bubbles are carbon dioxide gas. Neither the vinegar nor the baking soda contains this gas. It is formed by a chemical change.

rusted horseshoe

Oil refineries separate the different compounds that make up petroleum.

Rust can occur when metal is left outside for long periods of time. A chemical change causes the metal to change color.

In the 1800s chemists fixed these problems. By heating it and adding sulfur, the rubber became usable year-round. In the mid-1900s chemists discovered how to make artificial rubber.

In the United States many people get around in automobiles. These vehicles need fuel to run. Petroleum, or crude oil, fuels our transportation system. Petroleum is a mixture of many different compounds. These compounds are separated at large oil refineries.

Transportation

Imagine riding a bicycle on a brick sidewalk. Now imagine that your bicycle's tires are made of wood. That would be a bumpy ride! Until the 1800s all wheels were made of wood or metal. Thanks to chemistry, our bikes, cars, buses, and even our shoes are more comfortable. It's all because of a material called rubber. Rubber has been around for a long time. It is a natural material that comes from plants. It is waterproof and flexible. But it melts in hot weather and becomes brittle in cold weather.

Bicycle tires are made of rubber.

Rubber is made from a liquid collected from trees.

Chemical Changes and Energy

Some chemical changes cause the bonds between atoms or molecules to break. Other chemical changes can form new bonds. The forming or breaking of bonds always involves energy. As materials react with each other, they either take in energy or give it off.

Some energy changes can be observed as they occur. For example, logs burning in a campfire undergo the chemical process of **combustion.** During combustion, the burning logs give off energy. The energy can be observed as the heat and light of the fire.

An apple turns brown when it is exposed to air.

A chemical change occurs when you mix baking soda with vinegar.

Types of Chemical Reactions

Chemical Equations

During a chemical reaction, one or more substances change into different substances. These new materials have different chemical and physical properties from the original materials. A substance used in a reaction is called a **reactant.** A reactant goes through a chemical change to form a new substance called a **product.** A product has a different arrangement of atoms than the reactant it comes from.

A **chemical equation** is a special kind of "sentence" that shows what happens during a chemical reaction. The reactants are written on the left side of the chemical equation. The products are written on the right side. An arrow is drawn from the reactants to the products. It works a bit like an equal sign in a math equation.

Mercury oxide is an orange powder. When it is heated, mercury oxide breaks down into its elements. These elements are mercury metal and oxygen gas. Heat is the energy source that breaks the bonds between the atoms of these elements. The chemical equation for this reaction is:

$$2HgO \longrightarrow 2Hg + O_2.$$

Mercury oxide is heated to form beads of mercury and oxygen gas.

Nylon is a polymer. A **polymer** is a large molecule made of many identical smaller units connected together. In nylon each unit is made of six carbon atoms, eleven hydrogen atoms, one nitrogen atom, and one oxygen atom. A polymer can have thousands or even millions of units in a single chain.

Plastics are another kind of polymer created by scientists. There are many different kinds of plastic. Many plastics are made with chemicals found in petroleum. Plastics are used in many everyday things. Some of them are very light and strong. Plastics are also inexpensive to make.

Nylon is drawn out as a thread from a beaker.

New Materials

Many materials used every day come from nature. For example, corn is a tasty vegetable. But it has many nonfood uses. Corn helps to make paper plates, makeup, and even crayons. Wood is a natural material used to make many things, including houses, paper, sports equipment, musical instruments, and furniture. But many common materials are not found in nature. They were invented by scientists. For example, the plastics used to make things such as toys, cups, and food containers are human-made materials.

In the 1800s scientists began trying to make a fiber to replace silk. Silk is soft and strong. It is a popular fabric for clothing. Silk comes from the cocoons of silkworms. The silk threads must be removed from each cocoon by hand. This difficult work makes silk very expensive. Early attempts by scientists to make silk were failures. Some human-made silks easily burst into flames. Others stretched out of shape. In the 1930s an American chemist had success. His silklike fabric was called nylon.

Natural silk is made from the cocoons of silkworms.

Matter Is Conserved

Chemical reactions follow certain rules. One rule is that matter cannot be created or destroyed. Matter is only changed from one form into another. This rule is called the Law of the Conservation of Mass. It means that the total mass of the reactants must equal the total mass of the products. The mass you start with equals the mass you end up with.

For example, wood reacts with oxygen in the air to burn. The mass of the wood and the oxygen will equal the products of ash, smoke, and gases.

wood

When wood burns, no mass is lost. The mass of the wood plus the oxygen used is the same as the mass of the ash plus the smoke and gas released.

fire

ash

Three Kinds of Reactions

There are many kinds of chemical reactions. Sometimes, compounds split apart to form smaller compounds or elements. This kind of reaction is called a decomposition reaction. In this type of reaction, two elements separate from each other, just as one train car might unhitch from another. Remember the earlier example of mercury oxide being heated to form mercury metal and oxygen gas. That chemical reaction is an example of decomposition.

Other times, elements or compounds come together to form new compounds. This kind of reaction is called a combination reaction. To picture a combination reaction, think of one train car connecting with another. This kind of reaction occurs when zinc and sulfur are mixed together. They form a compound called zinc sulfide.

The elements in a compound can be thought of as the cars in a train. They can connect, disconnect, and switch positions.

Fresh fruit and vegetables contain vitamins that help keep us healthy.

Years ago, some people suffered from a disease called scurvy. It made people pale and weak. Scientists discovered that if people ate certain foods, such as oranges and lemons, they would not become ill. Scientists identified chemicals called vitamins in these foods that prevented diseases. Today vitamins are added to many foods. Many people also take daily vitamin tablets. Diseases caused by lack of vitamins are now rare in the United States.

Fertilizers are chemicals that farmers add to the soil. These chemicals increase the amount of food that will grow. Nutrient-rich soil also helps plants grow stronger and healthier. In the 1900s chemists found ways to make large amounts of fertilizers in factories. Farmers used these fertilizers to grow more food than they had before. Larger harvests lowered the cost of many foods. More people could afford to buy fresh fruits and vegetables, which made them healthier.

Farmers use fertilizers to produce larger harvests of crops.

156

Uses of Chemical Technology

Health

Chemists have made important discoveries that have improved our lives in many ways. For example, many years ago, people often died from simple cuts. Bacteria infected the cut. The infection spread through the person's blood. There was no medicine to cure it. Often, the person died from the infection.

Alexander Fleming

In 1928 a British scientist made an accidental discovery. The scientist's name was Alexander Fleming. His discovery led to the creation of powerful medicines to treat infections. Fleming had been growing bacteria in special dishes. One of his dishes became contaminated with mold. Fleming saw that the bacteria near the mold died. The mold had produced a substance that killed the bacteria. Fleming called this substance penicillin, after the name of the mold. By the 1940s this chemical had become a lifesaving medicine. Today many medicines can kill bacteria. These medicines are called antibiotics.

penicillin mold

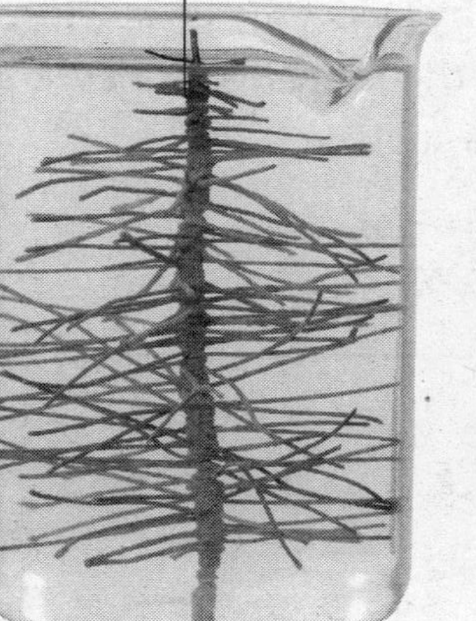

The third kind of reaction is called a replacement reaction. One or more compounds split apart, and the parts switch places. Think of two trains switching their cars.

An example is dipping a copper strip into a silver nitrate solution. The copper displaces the silver atoms. The products are copper nitrate and silver metal crystals. In some replacement reactions, two compounds switch places. For example, the compounds silver nitrate and sodium chloride can be combined. These compounds break apart and switch places. The new compounds formed are silver chloride and sodium nitrate. The sodium and silver switched places.

Uses of Chemical Properties

Separating Mixtures

Physical methods can separate substances in some mixtures. If corks and glass marbles are mixed together, they can be separated easily. This is because cork and glass have different physical properties. If you place the mixture in water, the marbles will sink and the corks will float to the surface.

A mixture of corks and marbles can be separated by placing it in water.

Metal	Flame color
barium	light green
calcium	brick red
copper	blue/green
lead	blue/white
manganese	violet
nickel	brown
potassium	lilac
sodium	yellow

Acids and bases can be identified by their chemical properties. Acids and bases react with chemicals in a special kind of paper. This paper is called universal indicator paper. These reactions cause the paper's color to change. Strong acids turn the paper red. Strong bases turn the paper purple. Weaker acids or bases produce different colors.

Universal indicator paper is not used alone to identify a substance. Many different acids turn the paper red. And many different bases can turn the paper purple. The paper is a good start, but other tests must be performed to identify an acid or base correctly.

Scientists also use flame tests to identify substances. In a flame test, a material is heated to a high temperature by a flame. Different substances turn the flame different colors. For example, potassium turns the flame light purple. The flame color of the metal copper is bluish green. Scientists use special laboratory equipment to study the colors of the flames.

Identifying Substances

Scientists use physical properties to identify substances. Magnetism is an example of a physical property. Substances can also be identified by their chemical properties. Acids and bases are two common types of substances.

Lemons are acidic.

Orange juice and soft drinks contain acids. Soap and ammonia contain bases. Strong acids or bases react more violently with materials than weak acids or bases do.

hydrochloric acid

vinegar

pure water

liquid soap

household cleaner

Soap contains bases.

Special paper is used to measure acids and bases.

A chemical reaction occurs when paint-stripping chemicals come into contact with paint.

Substances with different chemical properties can also be separated from each other. Paint can be removed from wood by using the different chemical properties of the two materials. Paint-stripping chemicals are specially made to dissolve paint. When they come in contact with paint, a chemical reaction occurs. The paint becomes soft, so it can easily be scraped off a surface. Wood is not affected by the chemicals. The paint can be removed without damaging the wood underneath.

Removing Metal from Ore

Ores are rocks from which we get metal. Ores are metals mixed with other elements. For example, zinc ore contains zinc oxide, a compound of zinc and oxygen. The zinc ore is heated in a hot furnace with solid carbon. The heat makes the oxygen separate from the zinc and attach to the carbon. The result is pure zinc and carbon dioxide. This process works because oxygen bonds more strongly to carbon than to zinc. This chemical property of oxygen allows people to separate zinc from zinc ore.

A smelting furnace separates zinc from the zinc ore.

When the colorless lead nitrate solution is added to a colorless solution of potassium iodide, a product of yellow lead iodide is formed.

Chemical properties can also be used to separate elements from solutions. For example, lead can be taken out of a liquid solution. In this experiment, there are two clear liquids. The first liquid is a solution of lead nitrate. The second is a solution of potassium iodide. The solution of lead nitrate is poured into the solution of potassium iodide. As soon as the solutions mix, the lead reacts with the iodine. These two elements form a new compound. This new compound is called lead iodide. It is a yellow solid. The lead iodide can be filtered out of the liquid to remove the lead from the solution.

Objects on the Move

by Mary F. Blehl

Genre	Comprehension Skill	Text Features	Science Content
Nonfiction	Cause and Effect	• Labels • Captions • Diagrams • Glossary	Forces and Motion

Scott Foresman Science 5.13

PEARSON
Scott Foresman

DK

scottforesman.com

ISBN 0-328-13953-X

90000

9 780328 139538

What did you learn?

1. What is the difference between work and power?

2. If two forces push on an object from opposite directions with exactly the same force, what is the net force?

3. If you roll a ball across a flat parking lot and it doesn't hit anything, it will slow down and stop eventually. What force causes this?

4. **Writing** in Science Gravity, electricity, and magnetism are three types of force. Write to explain the similarities and differences among them.

5. **Cause and Effect** Imagine lifting a box with a pulley system. The pulleys let you lift ten kilograms with a force of only five kilograms. However, you are still doing the same amount of work. Why is this?

Vocabulary

acceleration
equilibrium
force
inertia
machine
power
velocity
work

Picture Credits
Every effort has been made to secure permission and provide appropriate credit for photographic material. The publisher deeply regrets any omission and pledges to correct errors called to its attention in subsequent editions.

Photo locators denoted as follows: Top (T), Center (C), Bottom (B), Left (L), Right (R), Background (Bkgd).

Opener: Digital Vision; 4 Museum of Flight/Corbis; 8 Joe Sohm/Corbis; 10 Digital Vision; 11 Kelvin Murray/Getty Images; 14 Brand X Pictures; 21 (B) David Young-Wolff/PhotoEdit.

Scott Foresman/Dorling Kindersley would also like to thank: 7, 17 NASA/DK Images.

Unless otherwise acknowledged, all photographs are the copyright © of Dorling Kindersley, a division of Pearson.

ISBN: 0-328-13953-X

Copyright © Pearson Education, Inc.

by Mary F. Blehl

Glossary

acceleration	the rate at which the velocity of an object changes over time
equilibrium	when all the forces acting on an object are in balance with each other
force	a push or pull that acts on an object
inertia	the tendency of an object to resist a change in motion
machine	a device that changes the direction or the amount of force needed to do work
power	the rate at which work is done
velocity	the speed and direction of an object's motion
work	the energy used when a force moves an object

163

Describing Motion

Different Kinds of Motion

Motion is everywhere. The planets are in motion around the Sun. Cars are in motion as they are driven down the street. There's even motion inside your body. Blood moves through your veins and arteries to keep you alive.

We have names for different kinds of motion. The Moon is in constant, or steady, motion as it revolves around Earth. As you walk through your day, you have variable motion. You speed up, slow down, and change direction. When you are on a swing you have periodic motion, because you go back and forth at a steady rate. The strings on a guitar move with vibrational motion when they are plucked. The wheels on a bicycle turn in circular motion.

The forces you have learned about are working all the time. Picture yourself sitting quietly in your living room reading. Can you think of any forces at work? Gravity holds you down. Friction keeps you from slipping out of your seat. Electricity provides the light that lets you read. If the weather is nice, you might get up, walk to the door, turn the knob, and go outside. Can you name the simple machine you just used?

Complex Machines

Sometimes simple machines are combined into more complex ones. For example, a car contains many simple machines. It uses wheels and axles, pulleys, and levers.

Bicycles are complex machines too. The rider uses levers to work the brakes. The gears on the rear wheels are a system of wheels and axles. Even the bolts used to hold the bike together are simple machines. They are inclined planes wrapped around metal rods.

On a swing you have periodic motion as you travel back and forth.

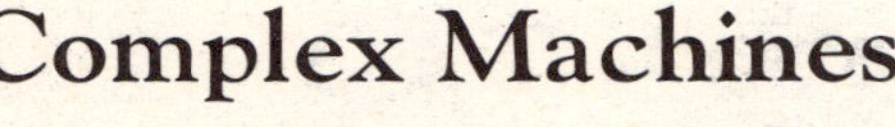

Speed and Velocity

Average speed is how far something moves in a certain amount of time. Average speed can be found using this equation:

$$\frac{\text{distance}}{\text{time}} = \text{average speed}$$

For example, if you run 100 meters in 10 seconds, your average speed would be 10 meters per second.

$$\frac{100\text{m}}{10\text{s}} = 10\ \frac{\text{m}}{\text{s}}$$

The Inclined Plane

Picture yourself trying to get a piano up some stairs. It would be very difficult. If you could push the piano up a ramp, the job would be much easier. A ramp is an inclined plane. It is also a simple machine.

An inclined plane is a flat surface with one end higher than the other. Inclined planes are used for all sorts of jobs.

A screw is made of an inclined plane twisted around a metal rod.

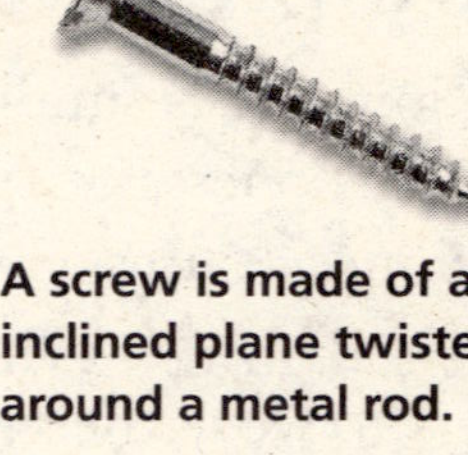

A doorstop is a type of inclined plane called a wedge.

It is easier to roll a wheelchair up a ramp than it is to lift it up stairs.

The Lever

A lever has two parts: a bar and a fulcrum. The fulcrum is a fixed point that the bar can pivot around. A force on one end of the lever will move a load on the other end. A seesaw is an example of a lever that changes the direction of a force. If you push down on one end, the other end goes up.

Moving a lever's fulcrum changes the amount of force needed to lift a weight. If you move the fulcrum closer to the weight, you can push down on the lever with less force and lift the weight more easily. But the closer the fulcrum is to the weight, the longer the distance you must push the lever. Even though less force is needed, the same amount of work must still be done.

A seesaw and a wheelbarrow are examples of two different types of levers.

Motion is always measured in relation to a location, or point of reference. If you are sitting very still on board a fast-moving airplane, you might think you are not moving. If your point of reference is the airplane, this is true. But if your point of reference is a building on the ground below, you are moving because you are moving along with the plane.

Speed can change with a different point of reference. As you walk down the plane's aisle, you might be walking at 1 or 2 meters per second. But from a point of reference on the ground, you are moving at hundreds of meters per second.

Velocity is an object's speed and direction. An airplane might have a speed of 225 meters per second and a velocity of 225 meters per second west.

From the point of reference of someone on the ground, this plane is moving at hundreds of meters per second.

Forces

Pushing and Pulling

A **force** is any push or pull that acts on an object. When you put a force on a moving object, you can cause it to speed up, slow down, or change direction.

The strength of a force is called magnitude. The unit used to measure magnitude is the newton, which is represented by the symbol N. All forces also have a direction. For example, when you run, your feet create a force down toward the ground.

As this boy runs, his feet exert a downward force on the ground.

The Wheel and Axle

All wheels and axles work the same way. There is a rod, or axle, that goes into the center of the wheel. When the wheel turns, the axle also turns. If a rope is tied to the axle and the wheel is turned, the rope wraps around the axle. If a weight is attached to the other end of the rope, it can be lifted more easily than by simply pulling on the rope.

The wheel and axle is used to make all kinds of work easier. Doorknobs and steering wheels are two examples. Cranes use a wheel and axle to lift heavy loads. Even the reel on a fishing rod is a wheel and axle!

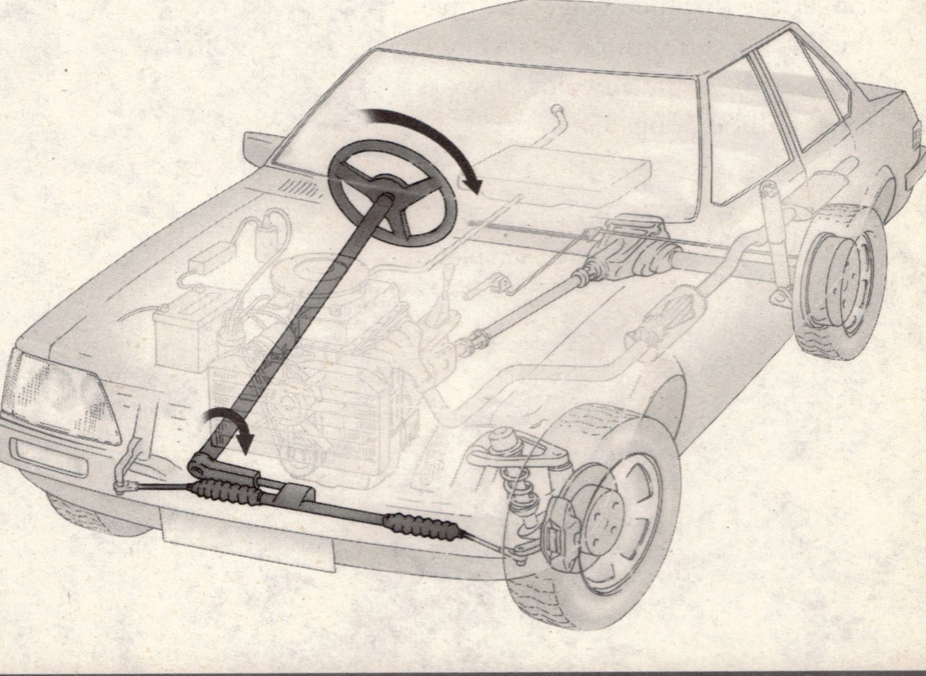

A steering wheel reduces the force needed to turn the wheels of a car. The driver must turn the wheel farther to do the same amount of work, which reduces the force needed.

168

Simple Machines

Working with Machines

A **machine** is something we use to change the amount or the direction of the force needed to do work. Some simple machines are the pulley, the lever, the wheel and axle, and the inclined plane. Simple machines have very few parts. Sometimes they have only one.

Machines can make work easier, but they don't reduce the amount of work that needs to be done. Often, a machine lets you use less force to do work, but you have to use that force over a longer distance. The total amount of work stays the same.

The Pulley

A pulley is a simple machine made up of a rope that runs around a wheel. This lets you change the direction of the force. If you use a system of pulleys called a block and tackle, you can lift heavy objects without much force. However, you must pull the rope farther to do the same amount of work.

◀ This pulley changes the direction of the pull, but it doesn't decrease the force needed to lift the weight.

This block and tackle allows the weight to be lifted using half the force that would usually be needed. But the rope must be pulled twice as far. ▶

The Moon's gravity is weaker than Earth's gravity. This is because the Moon has less mass than Earth.

Gravity

Every object pulls other objects toward it because of the force of gravity. So why don't all objects stick together? It is because gravity depends on an object's mass. Objects with little mass have a very weak gravitational pull that you can't even feel. Huge objects, such as Earth, have a very strong force of gravity.

Mass is different from weight. Mass is the amount of matter an object contains. Weight is how gravity pulls on an object's mass. Objects with more mass weigh more. While an object's mass always stays the same, its weight can change if the strength of gravity changes. For example, gravity gets weaker as you move farther from the center of Earth. So if you were to climb a very high mountain, your weight would be less than it would be if you were by the ocean. If you traveled to the Moon, which has less gravity than Earth, your weight would also be less.

Magnetic and Electric Forces

Magnetism is the force exerted by magnets. It attracts objects made of iron, cobalt, nickel, and gadolinium. Magnets have two poles: a north and a south. If you put two magnets together, the north pole attracts the south. The south pole attracts the north. If you try to put two north poles or two south poles together, they will push each other away.

Electricity is a different kind of force. It occurs between objects with different electrical charges. Atoms have protons, which are positively charged. They also have electrons, which are negatively charged. If an object gains electrons, it will have a negative charge. If it loses electrons, it will have a positive charge.

This large magnet is powerful enough to lift a car.

Newton's Third Law

Newton's third law says that for every force there is an equal and opposite force. Imagine sitting at a desk in a chair with wheels on the bottom. If you push hard on the desk, you roll backward. Why is this? You pushed forward, but you rolled backward. It's because when you push on the desk, it pushes back on you! The force is equal, meaning that you move away from the desk with the same amount of force you used to push. It is also opposite, meaning you move in the direction opposite to the one in which you pushed.

You may not know it, but you are experiencing Newton's third law right now. As you sit and read this book, your body's weight pushes down on your chair, and the chair pushes you back up with equal force. If the force of the chair pushing up were any weaker, you would fall through it.

Newton's third law explains how a rocket can move. When the rocket's fuel is burned, the exhaust gases create a downward force. This creates an opposite force that pushes the rocket upward.

The downward force of this rocket's engines creates an equal upward force. This pushes the rocket into the sky.

One way to generate an electric charge is to rub two objects together. If you rub an inflated balloon on a piece of cloth, electrons move from the balloon to the cloth. The balloon then has a positive charge.

Charged objects exert forces on other charged objects. If you hold the charged balloon over your head, it will make your hair stand up. The positively charged balloon attracts your negatively charged hair. In this way, charges work just like the poles of a magnet. If you pushed two positively charged balloons together, they would repel each other.

Charged balloons stick to your clothes and hair.

Gravity, Electricity, and Magnetism

Gravity, electricity, and magnetism are similar in some ways. All three forces can act between objects that don't touch each other. And all three get stronger as objects get closer together. There are differences between these forces as well. Placing certain materials between objects can block electricity and magnetism. But gravity cannot be blocked. Gravity can only pull on objects. Electricity and magnetism can push or pull.

171

Friction

Did you ever wonder why cars slide on icy roads, but not on dry ones? The answer is friction. Friction is the force that occurs when two materials rub against each other. Friction slows down moving objects and keeps still objects from starting to move.

Friction changes depending on the shape, speed, and texture of the objects involved. For example, cars slide on icy roads because the smooth surface of ice doesn't create much friction.

Air and water also have friction. The shape of an object going through air or water can affect the amount of that friction. So we make things in certain shapes to reduce friction. Cars, airplanes, and submarines all have smooth curves to let them slip easily through air or water.

This skier's clothes decrease friction with the air. His skis have little friction with the snow.

Newton's Second Law

Acceleration is the rate at which velocity changes over time. In his second law, Newton said that force is equal to mass multiplied by acceleration. This formula is often written:

$$F = m \times a$$

According to this law, if a strong force acts on a small amount of mass, the mass will accelerate quickly. If the same force acts on an object with more mass, it will accelerate more slowly.

The formula for the second law of motion can be written differently to find different information. If you need to find an object's acceleration, the formula is:

$$a = \frac{F}{m}$$

If you need to find the mass of an object, the formula is written:

$$m = \frac{F}{a}$$

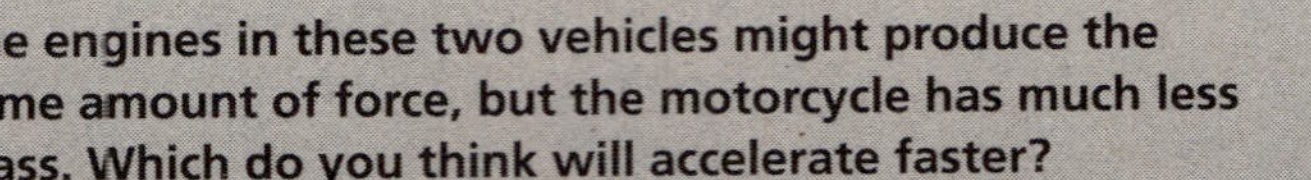

The engines in these two vehicles might produce the same amount of force, but the motorcycle has much less mass. Which do you think will accelerate faster?

172

Newton's First Law of Motion

Newton's first law of motion says that moving objects will keep moving unless a net force acts to stop them. It also says that nonmoving objects will remain still unless a net force moves them.

This resistance to changes in motion is called inertia. Objects with more mass have more inertia. If you tried to roll a soccer ball across the ground using just one finger, it would be easy. If you tried the same thing with a bowling ball, it would be much more difficult. This is because the bowling ball has more mass and inertia. The large mass of the bowling ball resists the change in motion that you are trying to make with your finger.

The Moon is another example of Newton's first law and inertia. In space, there is no air, so there is very little friction. As the Moon travels around Earth, there is very little to slow it down. It has been moving for billions of years because of inertia.

There is very little force slowing the Moon so it keeps moving around Earth.

Work and Power

In science, **work** means the energy used when a force moves an object. To calculate work, multiply the force used by the distance the object was moved.

Work = Force x Distance

Work is measured in joules (J). A joule is the work done when one newton of force moves an object one meter. If the object is not moved at all, no work has been done even if energy was used. Imagine pushing a boulder that is too heavy for you to move. You may be putting a lot of force on the boulder, but if it does not move, no work gets done.

In science, **power** is how fast work can be done. The same amount of work gets done whether you run a kilometer or walk a kilometer. But running is faster, so it takes more power. If you do the same amount of work in half the time, you use twice as much power. Power is measured in watts (W). Watts can be calculated by dividing the amount of work in joules by the time in seconds.

Although a lot of energy is being used in this photo, no work is being done. Why not?

12

Newton's Laws of Motion

Sir Isaac Newton was an English scientist who lived from 1642 to 1727. He made many important contributions to science and mathematics. Newton is probably best known for his laws explaining motion.

Net Forces

There are usually several forces acting on an object at the same time. For example, if you hit a baseball into the air, there will be a force from the bat. There will be a force from gravity. And there will be a force from the friction with the air. All the forces acting together on an object are called the net forces. Sometimes equal forces act on an object from opposite directions, so the object does not move. When this happens, we say the forces are in **equilibrium.** Imagine a tug-of-war that no one is winning. If both teams pull with equal force, the rope does not move. The net force is zero, because the two pulling forces cancel each other out.

But what if one team did not pull as hard? The forces would be unbalanced. Then the net force would be in the direction of the stronger pull, and the rope would move in that direction.

If two forces act on an object in the same direction, they are added to find the net force.

If two forces act on an object in opposite directions, they are subtracted to find the net force. In this photo, the forces are equal so the box does not move.

In this photo, the force pushing the box to the left is stronger than the one pushing it to the right. The box moves to the left.

13

Science
Science

How Energy Changes

by Emily Gray

Genre	Comprehension Skill	Text Features	Science Content
Nonfiction	Predict	• Labels • Captions • Charts • Glossary	Forms of Energy

Scott Foresman Science 5.14

PEARSON
Scott Foresman

DK

ISBN 0-328-13956-4

90000

9 780328 139569

scottforesman.com

175

What did you learn?

1. What does the frequency of a sound measure?

2. What two factors determine how much kinetic energy an object has?

3. What are the three ways heat moves?

4. **Writing** in Science Light energy and sound energy have many similarities and differences. Write to describe what some of these similarities and differences are. Use details from the book to support your answer.

5. **Predict** Suppose a pendulum is swinging back and forth. The movement of the pendulum produces both potential and kinetic energy. Predict at what point the potential energy and kinetic energy will be greatest during the swing of the pendulum.

Vocabulary

conduction
convection
electromagnetic radiation
energy
kinetic energy
potential energy
thermal energy

Picture Credits
Every effort has been made to secure permission and provide appropriate credit for photographic material. The publisher deeply regrets any omission and pledges to correct errors called to its attention in subsequent editions.

Photo locators denoted as follows: Top (T), Center (C), Bottom (B), Left (L), Right (R), Background (Bkgd).

Opener: Tom Szuba/Masterfile Corporation; 2 Dean Siracusa/Alamy Images; 4 Aflo Foto/Alamy Images; 5 (T) Tom Szuba/Masterfile Corporation; 9 (BR) Getty Images; 11 (BR) Getty Images; 13 (T) M. Moellenberg/Masterfile Corporation; 15 (R) © Stockbyte; 16 ImageState/Alamy Images; 17 Rob Matheson/Corbis; 18 (B) Digital Vision; 21 (B) Dr. Arthur Tucker /Photo Researchers, Inc.; 22 (T) Victoria Pearson/Getty Images.

Scott Foresman/Dorling Kindersley would also like to thank: 13 (BR) Denoyer-Geppert International/DK Images; 20 (BR) Stephen Oliver/DK Images.

Unless otherwise acknowledged, all photographs are the copyright © of Dorling Kindersley, a division of Pearson.

ISBN: 0-328-13956-4

Glossary

conduction	the movement of heat between two objects that are touching
convection	the transfer of heat by a moving liquid or gas
electromagnetic radiation	the combination of electric and magnetic energy
energy	the ability to do work or cause a change
kinetic energy	energy that is produced by the motion of an object
potential energy	energy stored in an object
thermal energy	the total of all the kinetic and potential energy of the atoms of an object

How Energy Changes

by Emily Gray

Energy

The word energy can refer to many different things. In science, **energy** is the ability to do work or cause a change. Energy can change matter in several ways. An object's motion, color, shape, temperature, or other qualities can be changed by energy.

You are probably familiar with sound, light, electricity, and magnetism. But there are many forms of energy. Chemical energy is the form that holds molecules together. Nuclear energy holds the nucleus of an atom together. Mechanical energy is the energy of objects that are moving or may start to move. Thermal energy is the energy of heat.

Gasoline's chemical energy is converted to mechanical energy inside a car's engine.

The **convection** process transfers heat when liquids or gases move in a specific way. When a liquid or gas is heated, its particles move faster and spread apart. A hot liquid or gas is less dense than when it is cooler. It floats to the top. As it cools, the liquid or gas becomes denser and sinks, moving in a circular pattern.

Radiation is the transfer of heat by electromagnetic waves. Heat is usually transferred by infrared waves. Other types of electromagnetic waves can also transfer heat. As objects give off heat, their temperature decreases. Energy has many forms and moves in many ways. It is in sounds, heat, light, electricity, and moving objects. In fact, energy is all around you all the time. Whenever you walk down the street, hear a song, or even feel sunlight on your face, you are experiencing energy!

A metal pan conducts heat from the stove to the food. The wooden handle does not conduct heat well, so it protects your hand.

Conduction, Convection, And Radiation

If you sit in a warm car or touch a mug of hot cocoa, you feel warmth. Thermal energy moves between materials with different temperatures. Thermal energy normally flows from warmer substances to cooler substances. This energy flows between you and the things around you, making you feel warm or cool. This movement of thermal energy is what we usually call *heat*.

Heat moves in three ways: conduction, convection, and radiation. Thermal energy is transferred by **conduction** when two materials touch and their particles collide. The warmer object transfers some of its kinetic energy to the particles of the cooler object. The temperature of the warmer object decreases as energy flows to the cooler object. If the two objects are in contact for enough time, the kinetic energy will continue to flow until the temperatures of both objects are equal.

The heat rising from the mug is an example of convection.

The heat you feel from an electric heater is radiation.

Fluorescent light bulbs use energy more efficiently than standard light bulbs.

Energy cannot be created or destroyed. It can, however, change form or transfer from one object to another object. For example, the liquid gasoline in a car's gas tank has chemical energy. When it burns inside the engine, the chemical energy is converted to mechanical energy. The gasoline turns into a gas that expands rapidly, driving the engine and turning the car's wheels. Heat, light, and sound energy are also released by the exploding gas.

Many devices we use each day change the form of energy. An electric stove turns electric energy into thermal energy, which heats food. The stove also creates light energy, which can be seen in the glowing burners.

The amount of energy that moves or changes can be measured. People can then determine how energy-efficient devices are. For example, fluorescent light bulbs are more efficient than standard light bulbs. A fluorescent bulb uses less electricity to produce the same amount of light.

179

Kinetic Energy

Kinetic energy is produced by the motion of an object. The amount of kinetic energy an object has depends on its mass and speed.

An object's kinetic energy increases as its speed increases. If you hit a baseball with a bat slowly, the baseball will not travel very far. If you swing the bat quickly, the ball you hit will travel much farther. The bat will have more kinetic energy. The amount of kinetic energy the bat has will affect the distance the ball travels.

A fast-moving bat has more kinetic energy than one that moves slowly.

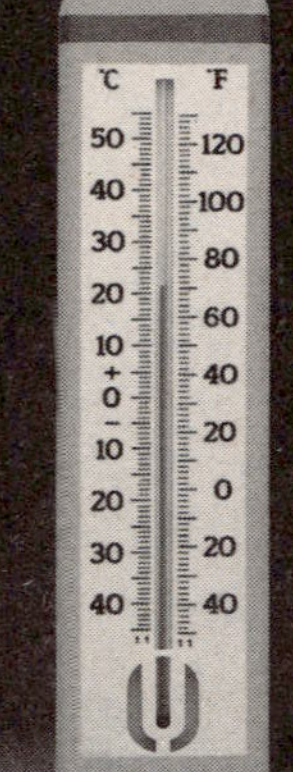

Materials with more thermal energy have high temperatures.

Temperature

Temperature is a measure of thermal energy. The temperature of a material is associated with the average kinetic energy of its particles. Objects are made up of many different particles, and some of those particles are usually faster, or hotter, than other particles.

Thermometers are commonly used to measure temperature. Most thermometers contain a liquid, such as mercury or alcohol, in an enclosed tube. As the temperature increases, the liquid expands. The amount that the liquid expands tells us the temperature of a substance.

This thermographic image shows which areas are hot and cold. Red areas are warmer than blue areas.

Thermal Energy

When you take a warm cake out of the oven, the cake has kinetic energy because it is moving. After the cake is put down, it still contains a form of kinetic energy. This is because the atoms inside the cake are moving, producing thermal energy. **Thermal energy** is the total of all the kinetic and potential energy of the atoms of an object.

Phase Changes

Matter can exist as a solid, a liquid, or a gas. Changes in these states are known as phase changes.

As the thermal energy of a material increases, the particles of the material move more quickly. If the thermal energy of a solid increases enough, the solid may melt into a liquid. The thermal energy of a liquid form of a substance is always higher than the solid form of a substance.

Another phase change can occur if the liquid continues to increase in heat. If the particles of a material heat up enough, the material will turn into a gas.

The atoms in the liquid water are moving faster than those in the ice. The atoms in the boiling water are moving faster than those in the liquid water.

A bowling ball's kinetic energy is the combination of its speed and its mass.

Kinetic energy is also affected by the mass of an object. For example, picture a bowling ball and a foam ball the same size. If you roll the bowling ball at some bowling pins, you can easily knock down the pins. If you use the foam ball, the pins probably won't move at all. Although the two objects are the same size, the bowling ball has more mass, and therefore has more kinetic energy.

Kinetic energy can also be changed into other forms of energy. When you clap your hands, they have kinetic energy. When they strike each other, the kinetic energy turns into sound energy. The harder your hands come together, the louder the sound.

Clapping changes kinetic energy into sound energy.

Potential Energy

Potential energy is energy that collects in an object. It is sometimes called stored energy. There are several types of potential energy. An object's position can affect the amount of potential energy it has.

Gravitational potential energy is one type of potential energy. If a roller coaster car sits at the top of a hill on the track, it has potential energy. It is not moving, but as it starts to roll down the hill, its potential energy becomes kinetic energy. An object's gravitational potential energy increases if it starts from a higher place. The roller coaster car rolling down a large hill will go faster than one rolling down a small hill. If the object has more mass, it also has more gravitational potential energy.

A roller coaster car has potential energy as it sits at the top of a hill. When it rolls down, the potential energy becomes kinetic energy.

When light is absorbed by your skin, it turns into thermal energy. This is why sunlight feels warm.

When there is a dense object in the path of light, a shadow is cast. Light bends at the edges of the object. The size of a shadow depends on the size of the object and its distance from the light source. Shadows are larger when the object is larger and closer to the light source.

When light is absorbed, light energy is transformed into thermal energy. That is why an object that is directly under the Sun is warmer than an object that is in the shade. Colored material absorbs some frequencies and wavelengths of light. It reflects other frequencies. The ones that are reflected produce the colors that we see.

White light is a mixture of wavelengths from different parts of the spectrum. A prism splits white light into its component colors.

Light also bends, or refracts, when it passes at an angle from one type of material into another type of material. Prisms are transparent objects that bend the different wavelengths of light and separate those wavelengths. When white light enters a prism, it exits as different colors. Rainbows appear because light reflects and refracts through water droplets in the air.

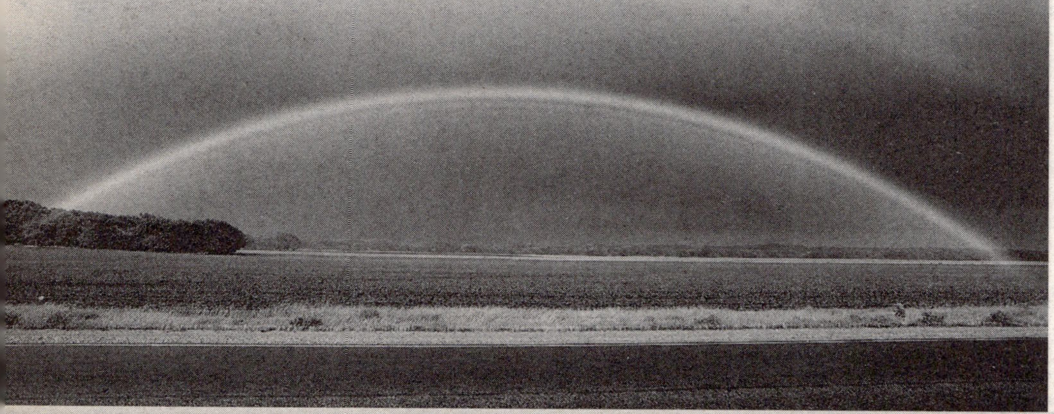

Raindrops can act as prisms, turning white sunlight into a rainbow.

Another type of potential energy can be explained by looking at the spring in a windup toy. As you wind up the key on the side of the toy, the spring is compressed, storing potential energy. The more you wind the key, the more potential energy is stored. When you let go of the toy, it starts to move. The potential energy stored in the spring is converted to kinetic energy.

Magnets can have a similar kind of potential energy. If you hold the north poles of two magnets together, they will push each other apart. It will feel as though you are squeezing a spring. When you let go of the magnets, this potential energy will turn into kinetic energy. The magnets will move away from each other.

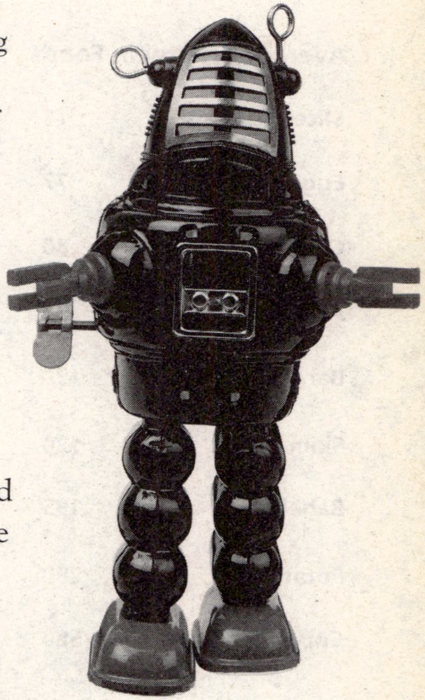

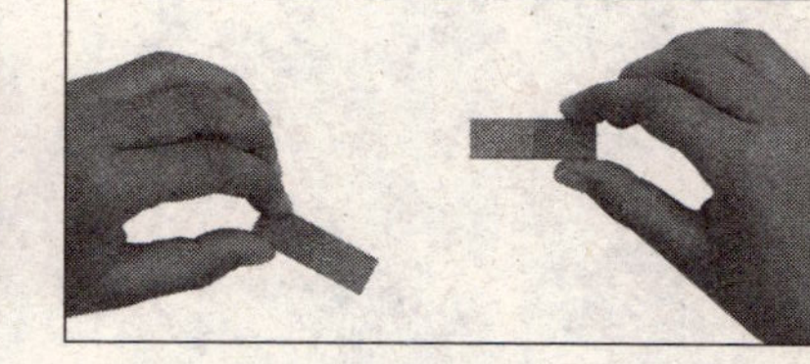

When this toy is wound up, it stores potential energy. When it is released, the potential energy becomes kinetic energy.

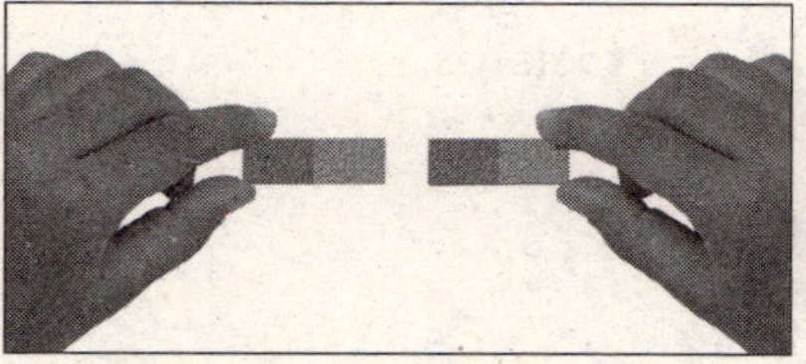

Unlike poles on a magnet will attract each other.

Like poles on a magnet will repel each other.

Chemical Energy

Average Energy in Foods	
Slice of Bread	71
Egg	77
Orange	80
Apple	90
Banana	120
Skim Milk	120
Bagel	195
Potato	280
Cup of Ice Cream	580

This chart shows the average energy values of some common foods.

Chemical energy is created when electrons form bonds between atoms in molecules. Bonds form when atoms share electrons or whenelectrons move from one atom to another. The more electrons included in a bond, the more chemical energy the bond has.

Fuels are a type of chemical energy. When you burn gasoline in a car or burn a log in a woodstove, you are using fuel. When fuels are burned, chemical energy is changed into other types of energy. Some types of fuels have more chemical energy than other types of fuels. A kilocalorie is one way to measure the heat energy given off by a burning fuel. One kilocalorie is the amount of energy needed to raise the temperature of one liter of water one degree Celsius.

When wood burns, chemical energy is changed into light energy and heat energy.

You see lightning before you hear thunder because light travels much faster than sound.

184

How Light Moves

Sometimes you can see that light travels in straight lines.

Sound waves are vibrations of particles. They cannot travel through a vacuum. Electromagnetic waves, however, are not vibrations of particles, so they can travel through a vacuum. Light travels the fastest in a vacuum. It moves at about 300 million meters per second in a vacuum. It doesn't travel as fast through materials such as air or water. Light travels much faster than sound.

Light moves in straight lines. Light waves move in the same way, even if they come from different objects. Light from the Sun, from light bulbs, or from a candle all move in the same manner.

The speed of light or the direction of light may change, depending on the type of material it passes through. Dense materials usually slow light down more than less dense materials.

Nuclear Energy

A neutron collides with an atom and the center of the uranium atom splits in half.

An atom is held together by energy. When an atom is split, some of this energy is released.

Potential energy can also be found in the structure of atoms. Atoms are made up of protons, neutrons, and electrons. The protons and neutrons of an atom are located in its nucleus. An atom's electrons surround the nucleus.

The nucleus of an atom contains a large amount of potential energy. Very strong forces hold the protons together. If the nucleus is split, energy is released.

Nuclear power plants produce energy that heats water, turning it into steam. The steam turns turbines connected to generators. The generators make electrical energy.

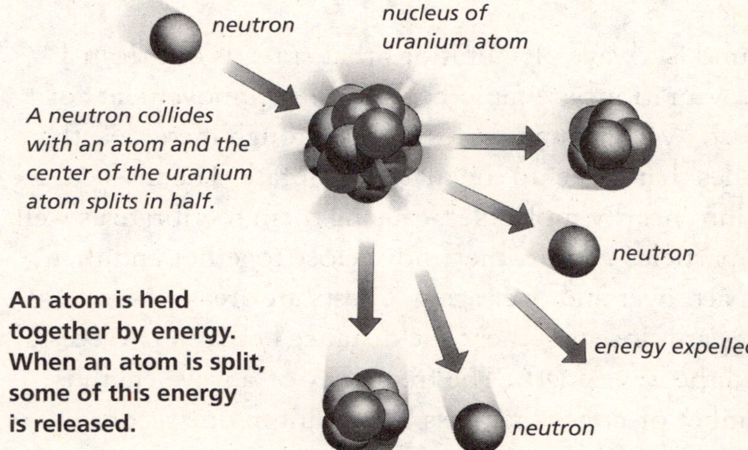

In a nuclear power plant, the bonds that hold atoms together are broken, releasing heat energy.

Sound Energy

Sound is a wave of vibrations that spreads out from a source. Vibrations are rapid back-and-forth movements of an object. When sound waves travel through materials, the molecules that make up the material vibrate. The molecules bump into nearby molecules, causing them to vibrate as well.

As particles vibrate, they move close together and then back apart, over and over again. Crests are areas where particles are close together. The distance between two crests is called the wavelength. The frequency of a wavelength is the number of crests that pass by a point in one second. Frequency also measures how fast particles are vibrating.

The electromagnetic spectrum consists of the entire range of light wavelengths. Humans can see only some of these wavelengths. Some wavelengths that are too long to be seen with the naked eye have low frequencies and low energy. Infrared waves, microwaves, and radio waves are types of long wavelengths. Many things that give off visible light also produce infrared waves.

Other wavelengths that are too short for us to see have high frequencies. Ultraviolet light, X-ray, and gamma ray radiation all have short wavelengths. These types of wavelengths have more energy than visible light.

The Sun is an example of a star, and all stars transmit visible light throughout the universe. The Sun and other stars also give off ultraviolet, infrared, X-ray, and other radiation. Stars also give off radio waves.

When a bow is rubbed across the strings of a violin, the strings vibrate, changing kinetic energy into sound energy.

Microwaves can be used to cook food.

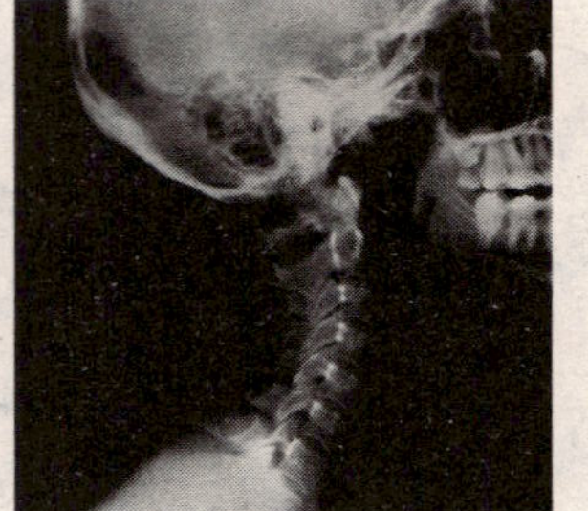

X rays carry more energy than visible light and can penetrate soft parts of our bodies.

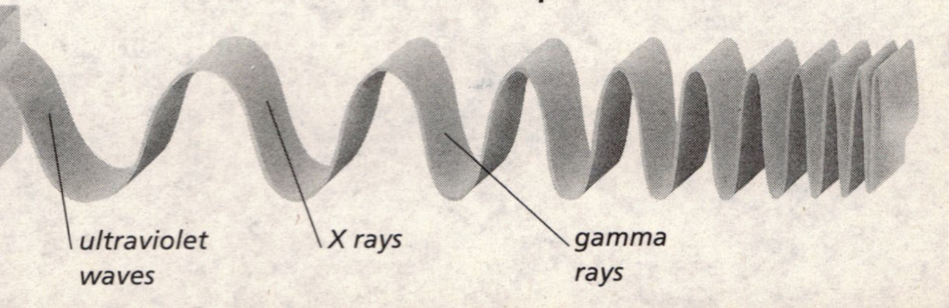

Light Energy

Like sound waves, light waves have certain wavelengths and frequencies. Light can also be reflected by, absorbed by, or pass through certain objects, just as sound can.

Light is different from sound in one major way: light is not a vibration of particles. Light is a form of **electromagnetic radiation,** which is a combination of electric and magnetic energy. The electrons in an object transmit, or give off, light.

Electromagnetic radiation makes up a spectrum, or range. Many different frequencies and wavelengths are included in this spectrum. Objects that you see every day transmit or reflect certain wavelengths of visible light. The light enters your eyes, and you see the different wavelengths as different colors.

Some sounds are louder than others. This is because an object that produces a loud sound vibrates more than an object that produces a quieter sound. If the source of a sound is vibrating more, the sound waves will have more energy. Units called decibels are used to measure the loudness of a sound. If the loudness of a sound increases by 10 decibels, the sound carries 10 times more energy.

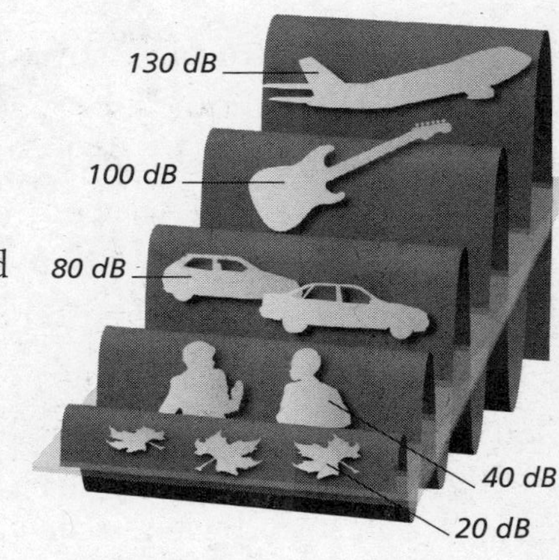

The decibel scale is used to measure the loudness of sounds.

The light we see is only part of the electromagnetic spectrum. It also includes X rays, radio waves, and microwaves.

Radios work using different bands of radio waves than TVs.

Your Voice

The vocal cords in your throat vibrate when you speak. Air rushes past the vocal cords, making the air particles around you vibrate. The vibrations travel through the air in all directions as sound waves, and other people can hear you talk.

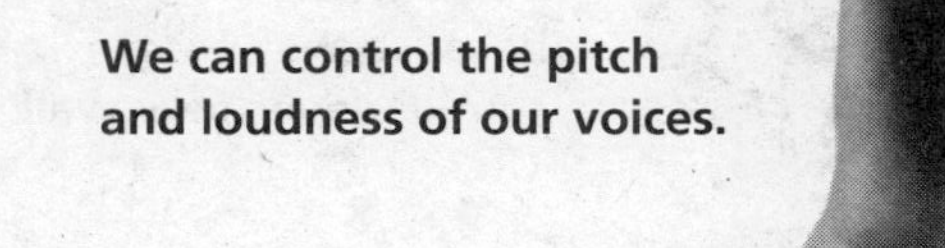

We can control the pitch and loudness of our voices.

12

How Sound Behaves

Sound can travel through solids, liquids, or gases. Sound cannot travel through a vacuum. A vacuum is an empty space that does not contain particles. Since there are no particles to vibrate and carry sound waves, there is no sound. This is why there is no sound in outer space.

When sound waves reach a different material, a few things can happen. The sound waves can bounce back from the border between the materials, the waves can pass, or they can be absorbed. Echoes are sound waves that bounce, or reflect, at the same angle at which they hit an object.

Sound waves travel at different speeds in different materials. Sound travels about 1,500 meters per second in the ocean. The speed that sound travels in air depends on the air's temperature. It travels about 330 meters per second in air that is 0°C.

Bats use echoes to help them find food.

Materials for musical instruments are chosen because they carry sound waves very well.

Sound Transfers Energy

Recording studios use special materials to absorb sound.

Sound cannot travel beyond the walls of this recording studio. Soundproofing materials are regularly used in rooms such as this to prevent sound from moving past a certain point. This means that the sound bounces around and inside the soundproofing material many times. The material absorbs sound energy and turns it into thermal energy. This causes the sound to be harder to hear outside the room.

When sound reaches your ear, your eardrum absorbs some of the energy. Your eardrum vibrates, and you hear the sound.

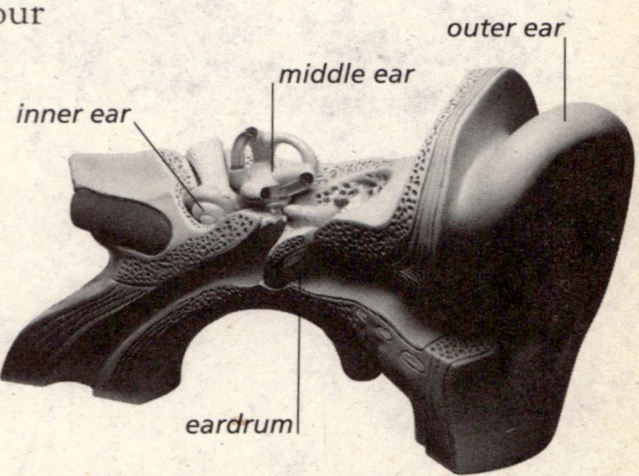

13

Electricity and Its Uses

by Sam Brelsfoard

Genre	Comprehension Skill	Text Features	Science Content
Nonfiction	Cause and Effect	• Labels • Captions • Diagrams • Glossary	Electricity

Scott Foresman Science 5.15

PEARSON

Scott Foresman

scottforesman.com

ISBN 0-328-13959-9

9 780328 139590

90000

What did you learn?

1. What materials are good conductors?
   What materials are good insulators?

2. What are some things a circuit diagram
   can tell you?

3. How is an electromagnet different from
   a regular magnet?

4. **Writing** in Science If two items are plugged
   into the same parallel circuit, and one is
   turned off, nothing happens to the other.
   Write to explain why this happens. Use details
   from the book to support your answer.

5. **Cause and Effect** If one light bulb on
   a string of lights in a series circuit blows out,
   what will happen to the other bulbs?

Picture Credits
Every effort has been made to secure permission and provide appropriate credit for photographic material.
The publisher deeply regrets any omission and pledges to correct errors called to its attention in subsequent editions.

Photo locators denoted as follows: Top (T), Center (C), Bottom (B), Left (L), Right (R), Background (Bkgd).

3 (CL) ©Comstock Inc.; 4 (TR) Getty Images; 5 (B) David Parker/IMI/Univ. Birmingham/Photo Researchers, Inc.

Unless otherwise acknowledged, all photographs are the copyright © of Dorling Kindersley, a division of Pearson.

ISBN: 0-328-13959-9

Copyright © Pearson Education, Inc.

All Rights Reserved. Printed in the United States of America. The blackline masters in this publication are designed for use with appropriate equipment to reproduce copies for classroom use only. Scott Foresman grants permission to classroom teachers to reproduce from these masters.

2 3 4 5 6 7 8 9 10 V004 13 12 11 10 09 08 07 06 05

Glossary

circuit diagram	a map of a circuit
conductor	a material through which an electrical charge can move easily
current	the flow of electrical charges through a material
electromagnet	an object that becomes magnetic when an electrical current passes through it
insulator	a material that can stop the flow of an electrical charge
resistor	a material that resists the flow of an electrical charge
volt	the measure of the electrical energy provided by an energy source

191

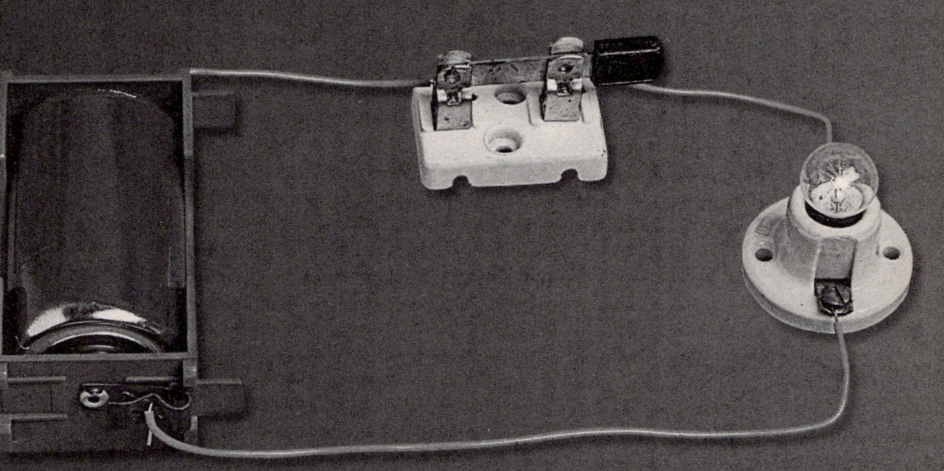

Electricity and Its Uses

by Sam Brelsfoard

Moving Charges

Electric Charges

Most atoms have a neutral charge. This means they have the same number of protons and electrons. Protons have a positive charge. Electrons have a negative charge. As long as there is an equal number of protons and electrons, these charges will cancel each other out, and the atom will remain neutral. The number of protons in an atom usually stays the same. But the number of electrons can change. Atoms can gain or lose electrons. If this happens, the atom no longer has a neutral charge.

You may have experienced charges moving from one object to another. Maybe you have walked across a carpet in your socks on a dry day. You reach for the doorknob to leave the room. Zap! A spark leaps from your finger to the metal knob.

Uses of Electromagnets

Electromagnets are found in many of the devices we use every day. They are found in motors, microphones, loudspeakers, and doorbells. In a speaker, patterns of electrical pulses are sent through a magnet. This causes the speaker to move, which produces vibrations. These vibrations are the sounds you hear when you listen to a compact disc or the radio. The pattern of electrical pulses controls what you hear.

From compact disc players to computers to light bulbs, electricity is a part of almost everything we do. What would your life be like without electricity?

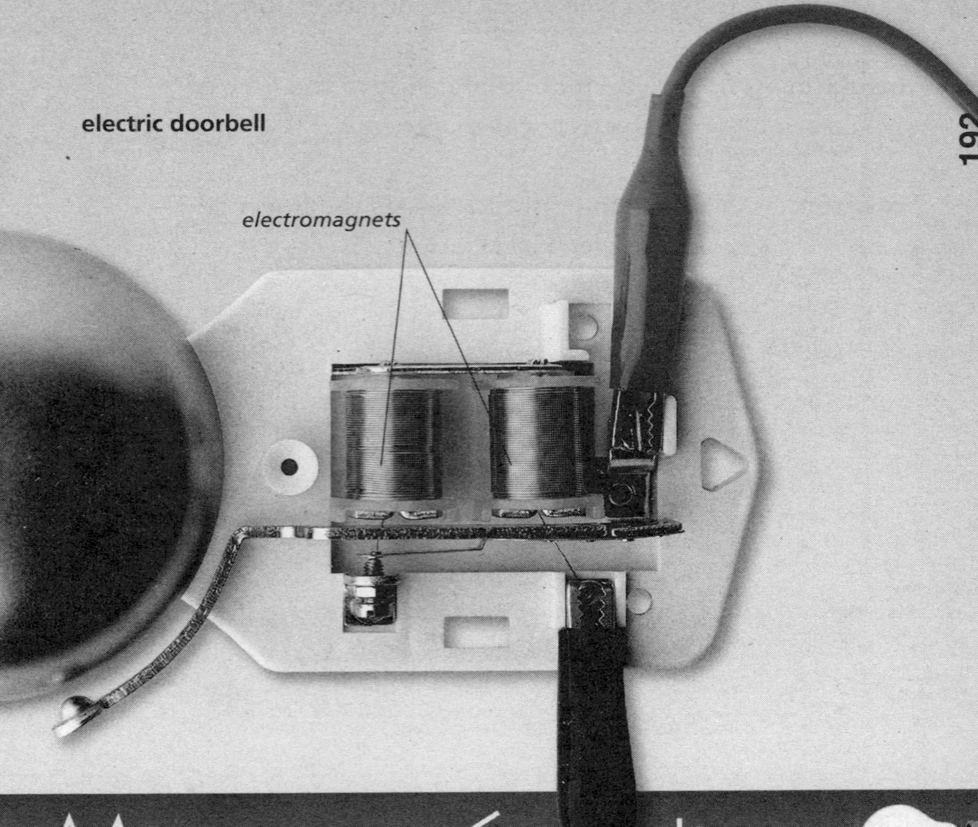

electric doorbell

Electromagnets

When you think of magnets, you probably think of the ones that hold papers onto your refrigerator. These small magnets are made of special materials that are attracted to certain metals. But magnets don't have to be made from special materials. In fact, they can be made from ordinary items found in any hardware store. If you wrap a piece of copper wire many times into a coil and then attach the two ends of the wire to the two poles of a battery, you will make a magnet.

The type of magnet described above is called an electromagnet. An **electromagnet** is a magnet that carries an electrical current. Every electrical current produces a magnetic force. You can make this force stronger by making more coils in the wire or by coiling the wire around a piece of metal.

Just like a regular magnet, an electromagnet has a north and a south pole. It is stronger at its poles than in the middle. But unlike a regular magnet, an electromagnet can be turned off by disconnecting it from its power source.

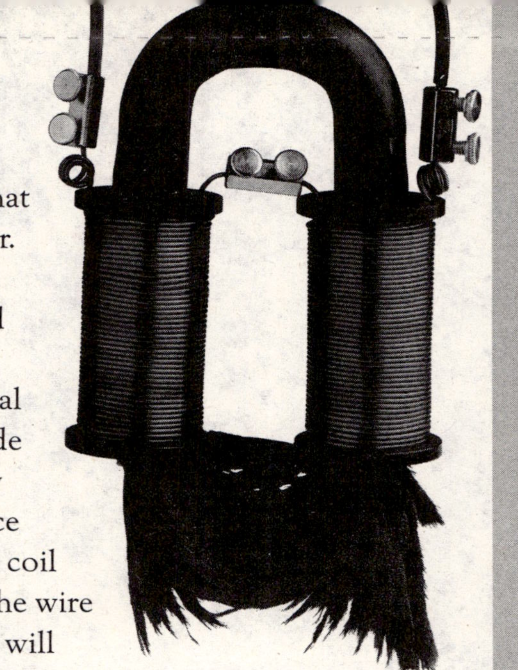

An electromagnet can lift iron filings.

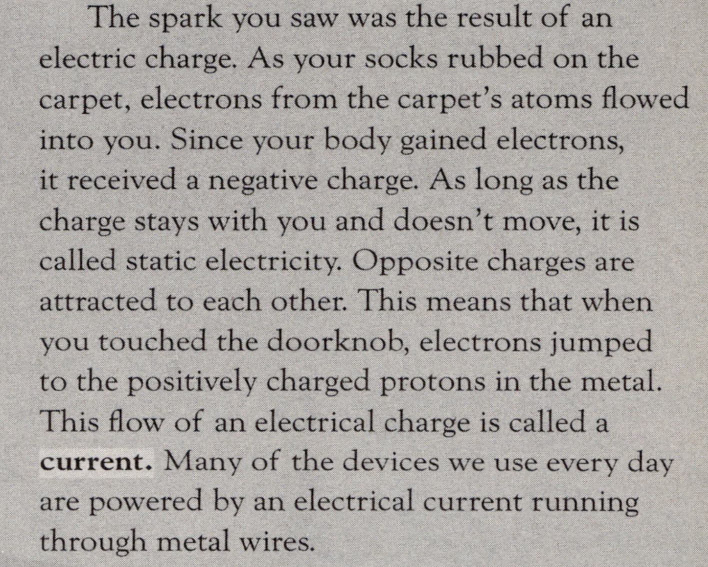

The spark you saw was the result of an electric charge. As your socks rubbed on the carpet, electrons from the carpet's atoms flowed into you. Since your body gained electrons, it received a negative charge. As long as the charge stays with you and doesn't move, it is called static electricity. Opposite charges are attracted to each other. This means that when you touched the doorknob, electrons jumped to the positively charged protons in the metal. This flow of an electrical charge is called a **current.** Many of the devices we use every day are powered by an electrical current running through metal wires.

Conductors

In some materials, electrons are not held tightly to their atoms. This allows electrical charges to move through them easily. Such a material is called a **conductor.** Good conductors include copper, gold, silver, and aluminum. Electrical wires and computer parts are often made from these metals. They conduct the best when they are not mixed with other metals. There are other good conductors that are not metals. Conductors may be solids, liquids, or gases.

Resistors are materials that resist the flow of an electrical charge. These materials cause some electrical energy to change into thermal energy. When electricity passes through the coils of a portable electric heater, electricity is converted into heat. **Insulators** are very strong resistors that stop most electrical currents. Plastic and rubber are good insulators. They are often used as an outer coating for electric wires, so that the wires may be handled safely.

This copper wire is a conductor. The plastic coating around it is an insulator.

electric heater

close-up of coils

computer chips

A parallel circuit has many branches. Each branch may contain one or more resistors. If there is a break in any of the branches, the current will continue to flow through the other branches. For example, in your living room, you may have a lamp and a television plugged in. Both of these things are on the same parallel circuit. What happens to the television when you turn off the lamp? Nothing! This is because the current keeps flowing through the television, even though the current has stopped flowing to the lamp.

Complex Circuits

Parallel Circuits

The circuits you saw on the last few pages were fairly simple. Electricity flows around them in one path. But the circuits in most of the electrical devices you use every day are more complicated. Many of them are parallel circuits. A parallel circuit has more than one path for electricity to follow. Some parallel circuits have thousands of paths, while some have as few as two. Computer chips have millions of paths in their circuits.

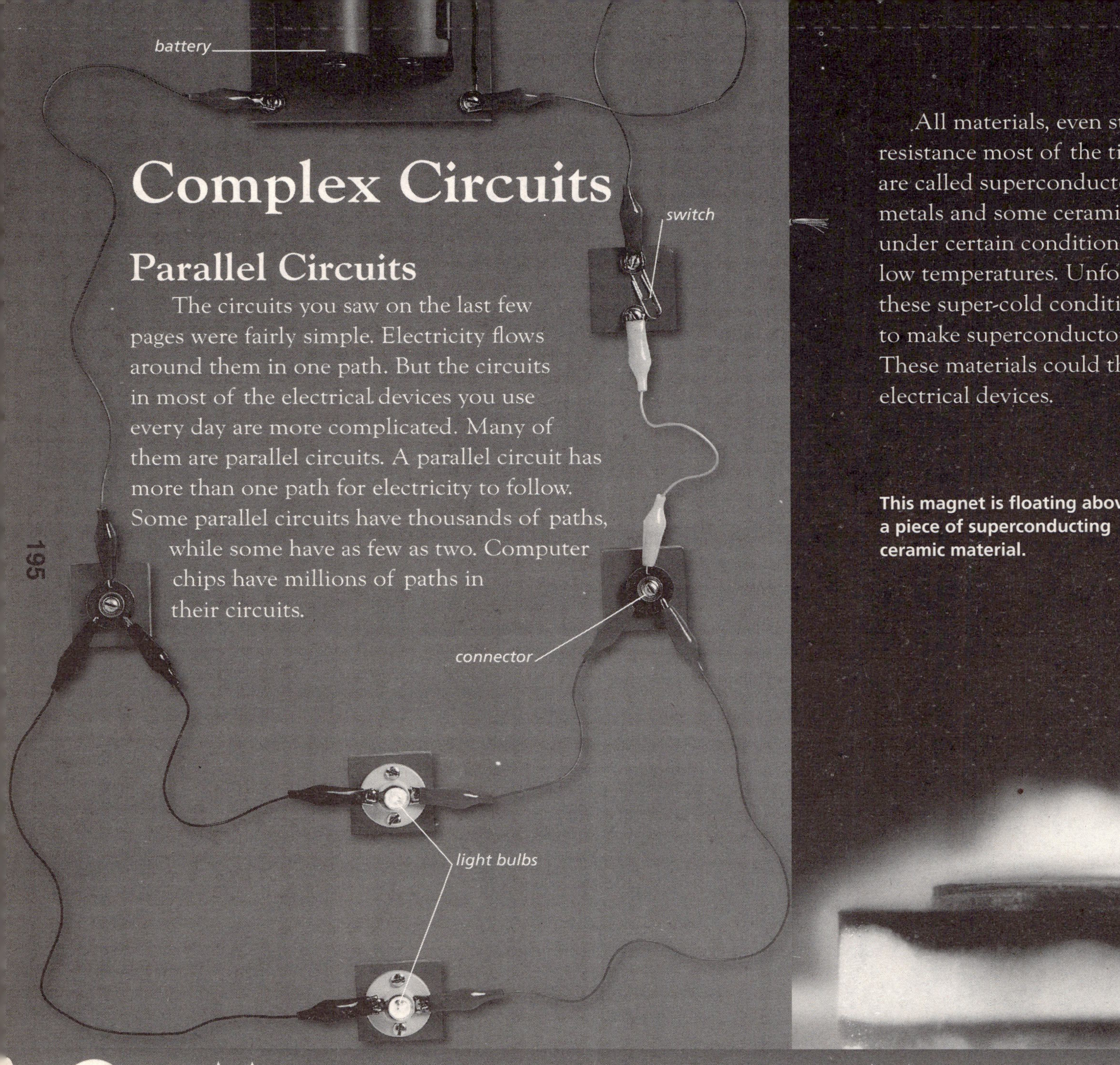

All materials, even strong conductors, have some resistance most of the time. Materials with no resistance are called superconductors. Some materials, including many metals and some ceramics, can become superconductors under certain conditions. This usually happens at very low temperatures. Unfortunately, it is difficult to produce these super-cold conditions. Scientists are looking for ways to make superconductors work at warmer temperatures. These materials could then be used to make very efficient electrical devices.

This magnet is floating above a piece of superconducting ceramic material.

Simple Circuits

Parts of a Circuit

A circuit is a looped path that carries an electrical charge. A circuit must have a source of electricity and at least one conductor. The conductor is usually a wire. There may be a gap in the conductor, which can be opened or closed with a switch. Opening the gap stops the flow of electricity. Circuits often have resistors as well. Circuits transfer electrical energy from one place to another. They can send this energy over very long distances.

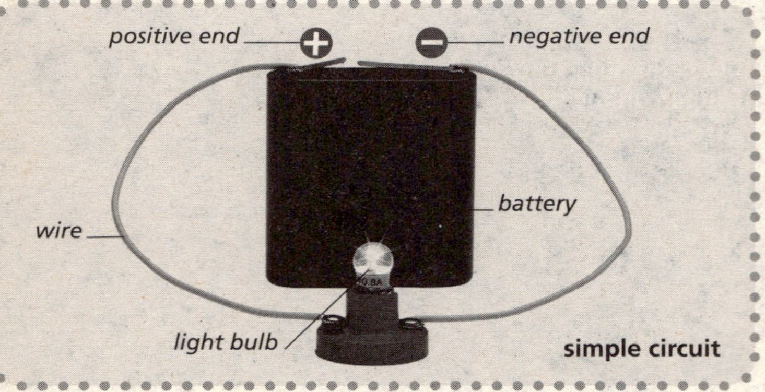

A battery is one type of energy source that can be used in a circuit. A battery has a negative end and a positive end. It has chemicals inside of it that react to produce a current. The current flows out from the negative end, around the circuit, and back to the positive end.

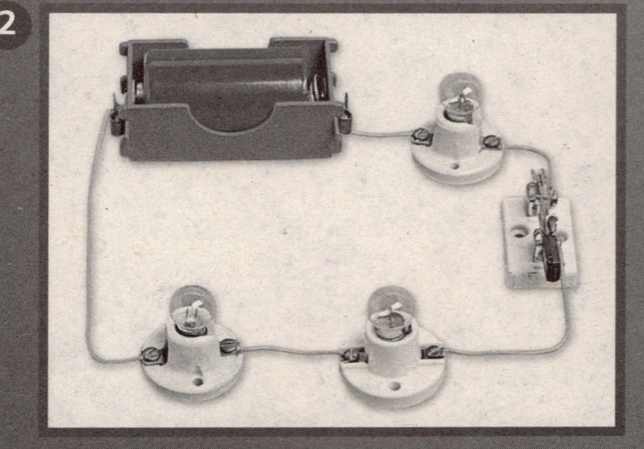

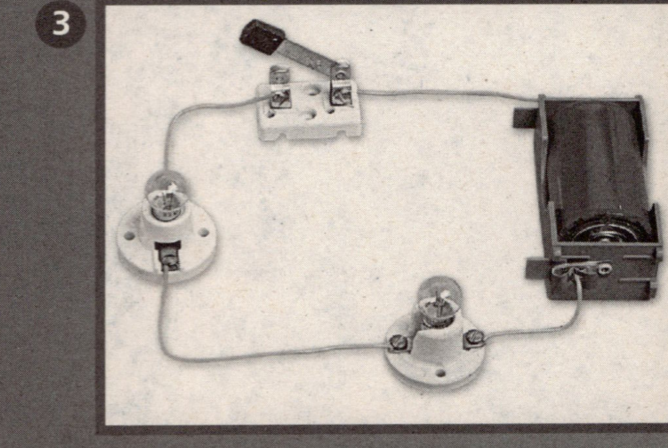

Series Circuits

Look at the circuit diagram below. Notice that it has more than one resistor on it. Circuits such as this one are known as series circuits.

Now look at the three circuits in the photographs on the opposite page. Look at the number of light bulbs on each circuit. Also notice where the light bulbs, the switches, and the battery are in relation to each other. Compare each picture with the circuit diagram. Which one matches it?

Series circuits can cause problems. Look at the circuits in the photos again. Suppose the switches were closed. What do you think would happen if one of the light bulbs blew out or was removed? It would stop the flow of electricity. This would turn off the other light bulbs.

circuit diagram

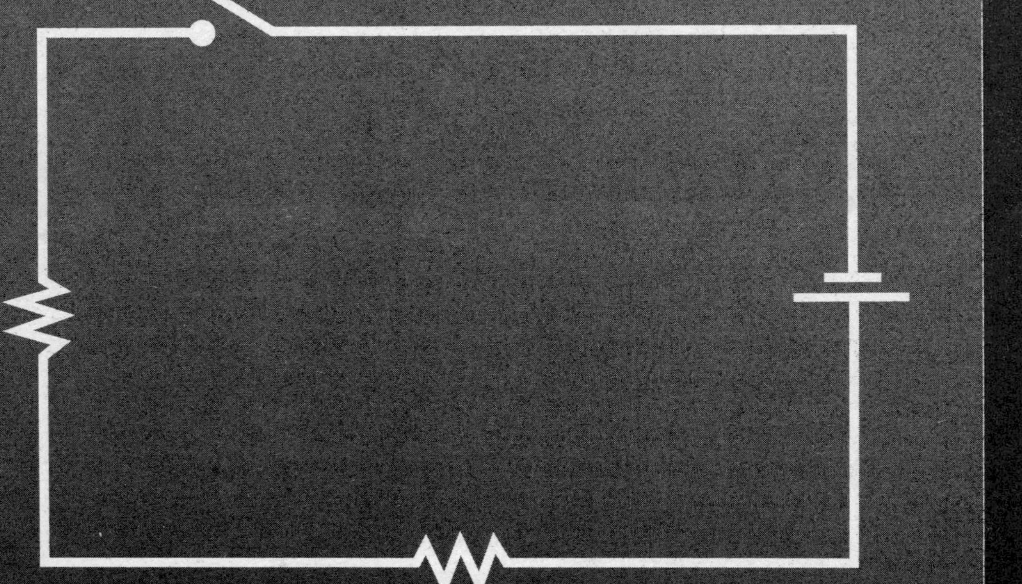

Some of the electrical energy in a circuit changes into heat as it passes through the conductor. Resistors can change electrical energy into other types of energy. Light bulbs, for example, are resistors that can change electrical energy into light and heat energy.

Circuit Diagrams

A road map can show you the streets you need to follow to get somewhere. It may also tell you what stores and restaurants can be found along the way. A **circuit diagram** is a map of a circuit. It shows the path that the current takes and any power sources, switches, or resistors along the way. There are symbols for each of these things.

A circuit diagram may also contain electrical measurements. It may show the amount of electrical energy provided by the power source. This is measured in a unit called a **volt.** Different types of batteries deliver different numbers of volts. The AAA, AA, C, and D batteries that we use in compact disc players and flashlights each deliver about 1.5 volts. Another common battery is the small rectangular type, which delivers about 9 volts.

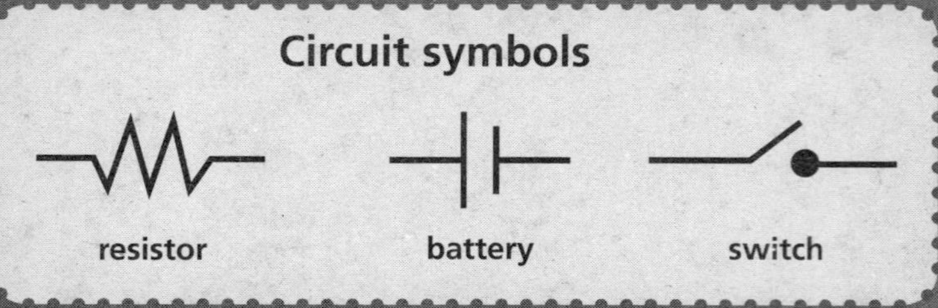

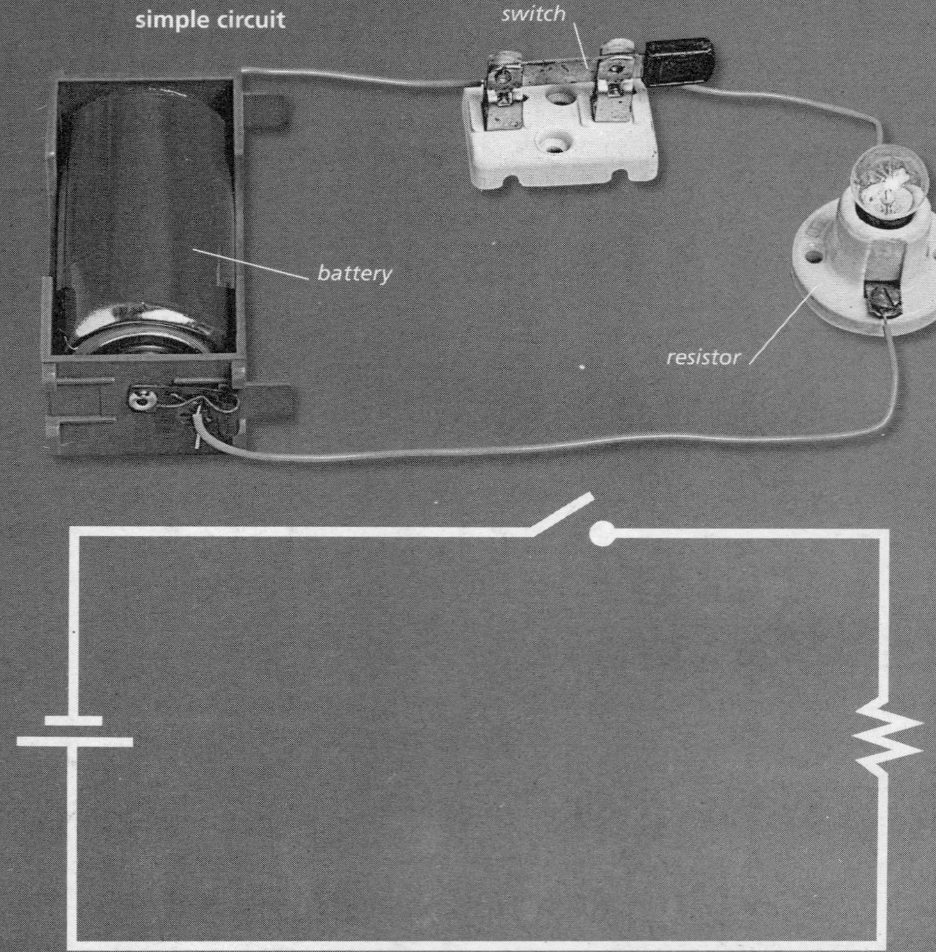

Resistance to electrical current is measured in units called ohms. A normal household light bulb has about 240 ohms of resistance.

Current is measured in units called amperes. The word *ampere* is usually abbreviated to *amp*. Amps tell the amount of charge moving past a given spot each second.

Exploring the Universe

by Anne Cambal

Genre	Comprehension Skill	Text Features	Science Content
Nonfiction	Summarize	• Labels • Captions • Diagrams • Glossary	Stars and Galaxies

Scott Foresman Science 5.16

PEARSON
Scott Foresman

DK

ISBN 0-328-13962-9
9 780328 139620
90000

scottforesman.com

What did you learn?

1. Why are modern telescopes built very large?

2. Some stars turn into black holes when they collapse, but others don't. Why is this?

3. What can astronomers learn from the color of a star?

4. **Writing** in Science Many constellations can only be seen during certain times of the year. Write to explain why this is. Include details from the book to support your answer.

5. **Summarize** Summarize how ancient leaders used eclipses to make themselves seem very powerful.

Picture Credits
Every effort has been made to secure permission and provide appropriate credit for photographic material.
The publisher deeply regrets any omission and pledges to correct errors called to its attention in subsequent editions.

Photo locators denoted as follows: Top (T), Center (C), Bottom (B), Left (L), Right (R), Background (Bkgd).

Opener David Nunuk/Photo Researchers, Inc.; 5 John Webb/The Art Archive; 9 David Nunuk/Photo Researchers, Inc.; 18 (TL) ©Anglo-Australian Observatory/DK Images, (B) Jet Propulsion Laboratory/NASA; 19 (BC) ©Anglo-Australian Observatory/DK Images; 22 (BR) John Chumack/Photo Researchers, Inc.; 23 Larry Landolfi/Photo Researchers, Inc.

Scott Foresman/Dorling Kindersley would also like to thank: 11, 15 NASA/DK Images.

Unless otherwise acknowledged, all photographs are the copyright © of Dorling Kindersley, a division of Pearson.

ISBN: 0-328-13962-9

Glossary

black hole a point in space where gravity is so strong that nothing can escape it

constellation an area of the sky and all the stars seen in that area

galaxy a huge system of planets, stars, dust, and gas held together by gravity

light-year the distance light travels in one year, about nine trillion kilometers

nebula a cloud of gas and dust in which stars may form

supernova a huge explosion that occurs when a very large star collapses

Exploring the Universe

by Anne Cambal

The History of Astronomy

Patterns in the Sky

It's a cold, rainy day at the end of winter. You are tired of this weather, and you want to know when it will be warm enough to go swimming. How will you find out when the seasons will change? You will probably look at a calendar. But what would you do if there were no calendars?

People solved this problem thousands of years ago by observing the night sky. Ancient people needed to know when the seasons would change so they would know when to plant their crops. They noticed that the Sun, the Moon, and the stars moved in regular patterns. The patterns were visible at the same time each year. Calendars were made based on these patterns.

Although the movement of the stars in the night sky is really caused by Earth's movement, the stars themselves also move. We don't notice the movement of the stars because they are so far away. But over hundreds of thousands of years, they move enough to change the patterns we see in the sky.

The night sky is a busy place. The Moon is spinning around Earth, just as Earth and planets are spinning around the Sun. The whole solar system is moving within our galaxy.

This time-lapse photograph shows how the stars appear to move across the sky.

As Earth moves around its orbit, constellations come into and out of view.

Stars in Motion

If you have ever spent a few hours watching the stars, you might have noticed that they seem to move. You might take a look at the sky just after sunset and see the constellation Canis Major, or the Great Dog. If you take a look a few hours later, you'll notice that the dog has moved! Or has it? Actually, Canis Major has stayed in place. The movement you notice is the rotation of Earth. Just as the Sun seems to rise and set because of Earth's spin, the stars seem to move across the sky. The stars seem to move from east to west, just as the Sun does.

The constellation Orion looks like a hunter. Three bright stars form the hunter's belt, making it easy to spot. But if you look for Orion during the summer, you won't be able to find it at all. This is because of Earth's orbit around the Sun. When it is nighttime during the summer, our side of Earth is facing away from Orion, so the constellation cannot be seen.

Orion as seen through a specialized telescope

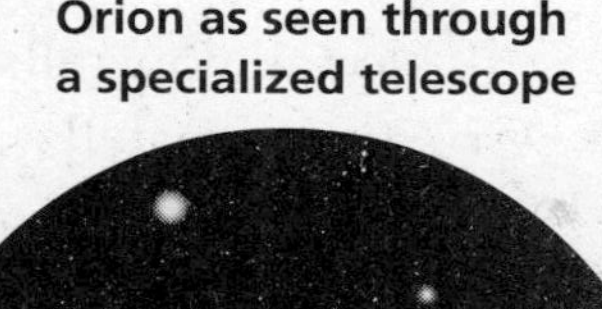

Eclipses

When ancient people saw something in the sky that did not fit into the normal patterns, they often became alarmed. For example, today we know that an eclipse is a rare but normal event. A solar eclipse happens when the Moon blocks our view of the Sun. A lunar eclipse happens when Earth casts a shadow on the Moon. Long ago, people did not understand eclipses. They thought these events meant that something very bad was going to happen.

But some ancient leaders learned that eclipses follow patterns. By observing the movements of the Sun and the Moon, they learned the patterns. They learned to predict when an eclipse was going to happen. People who could predict eclipses seemed very powerful.

Astronomy Everywhere

Ancient people from all over the world observed the stars. We know this because many of them built buildings and other structures to help them keep track of the patterns in the sky.

Long ago, people in North America built huge stone circles on the ground. These circles, called medicine wheels, were designed to show the positions of the Sun and other stars at certain times of the year. Some of the circles are more than two thousand years old. One of the most famous medicine wheels is located on top of Medicine Mountain near Sheridan, Wyoming.

This medicine wheel marks the positions of stars in the sky.

The flag of Australia features the Crux constellation.

Crux

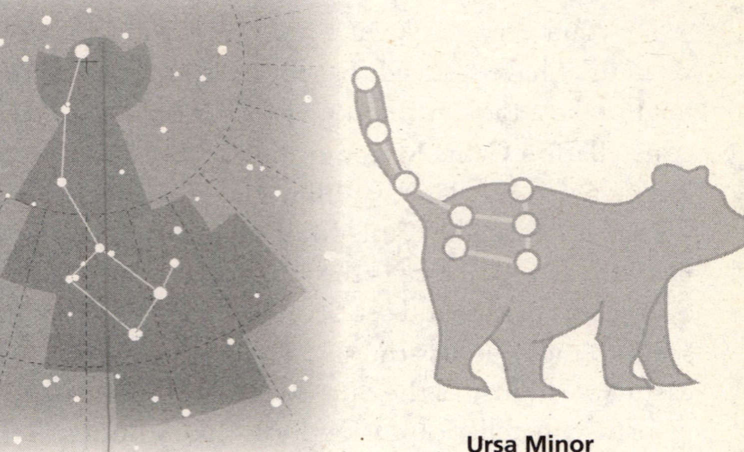

Ursa Minor

Not all constellations are visible everywhere on Earth. Crux is a constellation that is shaped like a cross. It is not visible in most places north of the equator. Crux is a very well-known constellation. It is pictured on the flags of several countries, including Australia.

Ursa Minor looks similar to Ursa Major. Its name means the Little Bear. This constellation is not visible in most places south of the equator.

204

Constellations

Have you ever seen a giant bear in the night sky? Ancient stargazers saw a pattern of stars in the sky that reminded them of a bear. They named this pattern Ursa Major, or the Great Bear. Such patterns of stars are called constellations. Today scientists define a **constellation** as an area of the sky and all the stars found within that area. They divide the sky into eighty-eight constellations. These constellations all have names. Many of these names are the same as the names of the ancient star shapes, such as Ursa Major or Orion.

These constellations make finding stars in the night sky easier. Knowing a star's constellation is a bit like knowing what city a person lives in. It's a lot easier to think about the locations of eighty-eight large constellations than the locations of thousands of stars.

Memorizing star groups as characters from stories helped sailors navigate across the sea.

The native people of some islands in the southern Pacific Ocean used the stars to navigate, or find their way, at sea. On land they made large, complicated maps that showed where the stars would appear in the sky. Sailors could not take these large maps to sea but instead used them as a learning tool to recognize the stars they would see. They would memorize patterns of stars. When they went to sea, they would use small maps to remind them of what they had memorized.

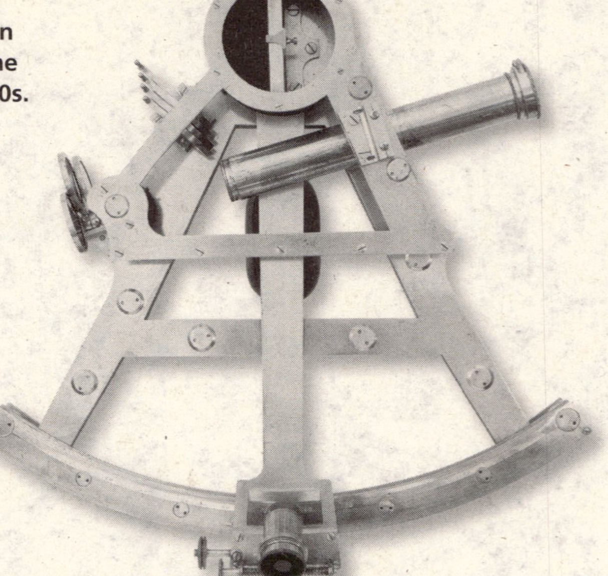

Star Tools

As time went on, people invented more advanced and convenient tools for observing the sky. The astrolabe came into use in Europe and the Middle East during the Middle Ages. It was a disc-shaped tool with a few moving parts. Astrolabes were used to measure the angle between the horizon and a star or the Sun. Sailors at sea could use this information to find out where they were and what time it was.

In the 1700s an instrument called a sextant replaced the astrolabe. A sextant works like an astrolabe, but it is easier to use. It has a metal frame that is shaped like a slice of pie. There are mirrors, a moving arm, and a small telescope attached to this frame. Using a sextant, sailors at sea can find our how far north or south they are on Earth. With the help of an accurate clock, they can also find out how far east or west they are. Sextants are accurate to within a few hundred meters.

elliptical galaxy

irregular galaxy

Another type of galaxy is an elliptical galaxy. These can be nearly round or oval-shaped. They might also have a shape similar to a football. Some elliptical galaxies are small, while others are very large. The largest known galaxies are elliptical.

Irregular galaxies have no real shape. They are probably young galaxies in which stars are still forming.

Grouping Stars

spiral galaxy

Galaxies

Earth and Sun are part of a large system of planets, dust, stars, and gas called a **galaxy.** Our galaxy is called the Milky Way. There are billions of galaxies in the universe, but only a few can be seen without a telescope. They appear as single points of light.

Astronomers have discovered that galaxies come in many shapes and sizes. Most are spiral galaxies, which look like pinwheels. They have thick middles and thin arms spreading out in all directions. Their stars rotate around the center of the galaxy. Some spiral galaxies may have black holes at their centers.

The Milky Way is a spiral galaxy. This is what it would look like from the side.

The First Telescopes

When we think of watching the stars, one of the first things that comes to mind is the telescope. But in the history of astronomy, the telescope is a rather new invention. The first telescope was built in the early 1600s. It was invented to make it easier to see faraway objects on Earth. The famous Italian scientist Galileo Galilei was the first person to use a telescope to study the stars and planets. He is most famous for discovering that Earth revolves around the Sun. In Galileo's time, people believed that everything in the sky revolved around Earth. It would be many years before Galileo's discovery was accepted by most people.

Sir Isaac Newton was an English scientist who invented an improved telescope. Newton's telescope used mirrors instead of lenses. This reflecting telescope allowed astronomers to see objects that were farther away and to see things in sharper detail. Many telescopes used today are based on Newton's telescope.

Newton's reflecting telescope

Galileo was an important early astronomer.

Modern Telescopes

Telescopes work by collecting lots of light and focusing it. Bigger telescopes collect more light and therefore produce brighter images. Telescopes have gotten bigger and bigger since they were invented. Newton's telescope had a mirror about five centimeters across. The largest modern reflecting telescopes, the Keck I and Keck II, have mirrors ten meters across!

Most objects in space produce types of electromagnetic radiation that humans cannot see. These include radio waves, infrared waves, ultraviolet waves, X rays, and gamma rays. Modern telescopes such as the Kecks can detect these types of radiation. They give astronomers much more information about the universe than Galileo and Newton had.

Images of space can look fuzzy because their light must pass through Earth's atmosphere. To solve this problem, the Hubble telescope has been launched into space. Because it is outside the atmosphere, it can take very clear pictures of the stars.

The Keck I and Keck II are two of the largest reflecting telescopes in the world.

Supernovas are much brighter than the stars from which they form.

When the Sun reaches this huge size, it will cool slightly and turn red. This type of star is known as a red giant. Since red giants have run out of hydrogen, they start using helium as fuel. When the helium runs out, the outer layers of the star simply float off into space. The core shrinks to a tiny fraction of the red giant's size. This type of small star is called a white dwarf. A white dwarf has no fuel, so it cannot produce any energy. It has only leftover heat from when it was a red giant. Over millions of years it will cool down and become a cold object called a black dwarf.

Very large stars do not become black dwarves. They shrink very rapidly, until they can shrink no further. They stop suddenly, causing a huge explosion called a supernova. A supernova can be billions of times brighter than the star ever was. All that is left is a ball of neutrons, about twenty kilometers across, called a neutron star.

If a very large star collapses, its gravity can cause it to keep shrinking until it becomes a black hole. A black hole is a point in space with so much gravity that nothing can escape being pulled into it, not even light.

Stars' Lives

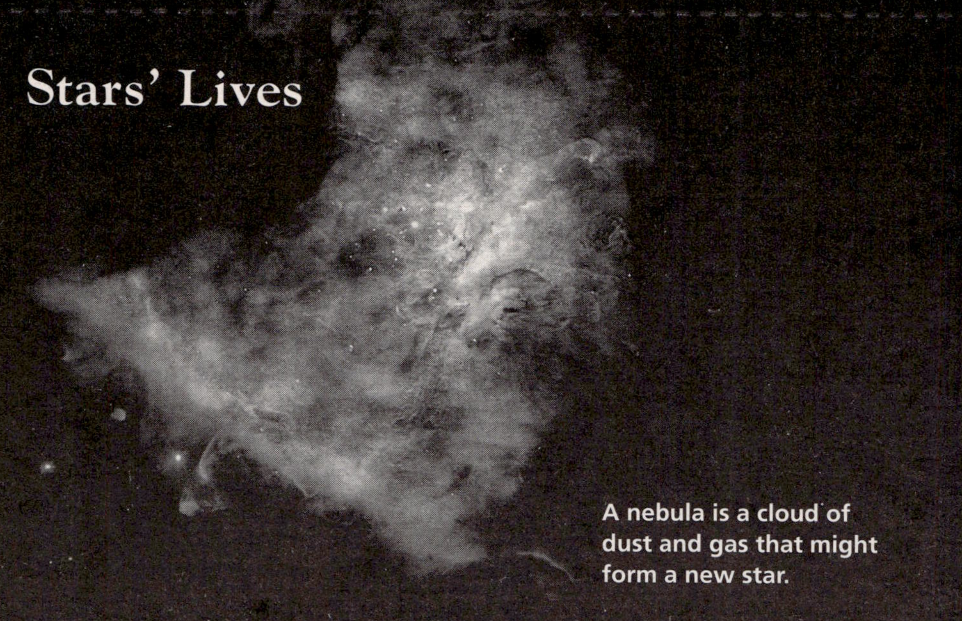

A nebula is a cloud of dust and gas that might form a new star.

Stars do not last forever. They go through a life cycle in which they are born and eventually die. A nebula is a cloud of dust and gas in which new stars may form. This cloud rotates and churns. Gravity makes some particles move into a tight ball in the nebula's center. The particles move together with great force as gravity pulls them in. This raises the temperature within this ball of particles. If the temperature gets high enough, the gases change. Hydrogen converts to helium, releasing huge amounts of energy. Eventually, this ball of gas will become a star.

The life cycle of stars can be very long. The Sun, which is the star closest to Earth, is already about 4.6 billion years old! Scientists estimate that the Sun will shine for about another 7 billion years. As it ages it will use up all the hydrogen in its core. It will become thousands of times brighter than it is today. It will become so large that it will extend as far as the orbit of Mars.

Parkes Radio Telescope in New South Wales, Australia

Radio Telescopes

Take a look at the huge instrument pictured above. It probably doesn't look much like a telescope to you. But it is! This is a radio telescope. Instead of mirrors or lenses, it has a large, bowl-shaped dish. It collects radio waves given off by objects far away in space.

Radio telescopes are located around the world. Some are huge single dishes, while others are networks of dishes. One famous radio telescope is the Arecibo in Puerto Rico. It's the world's largest single-dish radio telescope. In Australia there is a large network of radio telescopes called the Australia Telescope National Facility. Another network is called Atacama Large Millimeter Array. It is under construction in the Andes mountains in Chile. When finished, it will have sixty-four antennas.

Stars

Earth is not really this close to the Sun. Compared to the size of the Sun in the photo, Earth should be about 20 meters away.

The Sun

The Sun is the closest star to Earth. But what is a star? Stars are huge balls of gas that give off electromagnetic radiation. The Sun is an average-sized star. Some stars, known as supergiants, can be up to three hundred times the size of the Sun! Other stars are as small as Earth. You might not think of Earth as being small, but it is only about one-millionth the size of the Sun!

Deep within the Sun enormous heat and pressure press hydrogen atoms together. These atoms combine to form helium. When this happens, a huge amount of heat, light, and radiation is released. This is what makes the Sun shine.

Eruptions on the Sun

Fiery gases often leap off the Sun's surface in huge loops and fountains. These are called prominences. They may last for a few minutes or several months, and they may be more than a million kilometers high.

Sometimes a part of the Sun's chromosphere will erupt like a volcano. This is called a solar flare. Solar flares last from a few minutes to several hours, and they release huge amounts of energy. Protons, electrons, and electromagnetic waves from a solar flare may disturb radio signals and damage electrical systems on Earth.

Solar prominences may rise at a speed of one thousand kilometers per second.

Features of the Sun

You may think of the Sun as a smooth ball of light, quietly glowing in the sky. But the Sun is actually very active. It is made up of several different layers. The photosphere is the Sun's surface layer. It gives off the light we see. The layer above the photosphere is called the chromosphere. The outermost layer is called the corona.

Scientists have discovered lots of activity on the Sun. Remember, you should never look directly at the Sun! Scientists must use special protective equipment when observing the Sun, to keep its rays from hurting their eyes. By using this equipment they have found dark spots on the photosphere, called sunspots. Galileo saw these spots moving across the surface and concluded that the Sun was rotating. Their movement shows us that the Sun rotates more slowly at its poles than at its equator. Sometimes there are more sunspots than at other times. The number of sunspots changes in cycles of about eleven years.

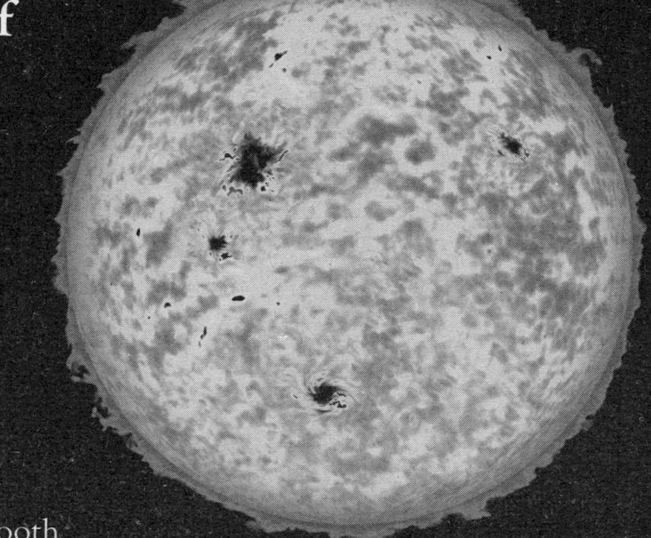

Dark places on the Sun are called sunspots.

The Sun is so large that more than one million Earths could fit inside of it.

Brightness, Color, and Temperature

Only the Sun appears brighter than the star Sirius.

The Sun is the brightest object in space that we can see. In fact, it is so bright that during the day it is usually the only object in space that we can see. But being close to Earth is not the only thing that controls how bright an object appears. Sirius is the next-brightest star in the sky after the Sun. It is about nine light-years away from Earth. A **light-year** is the distance light travels in one year, or about nine trillion kilometers. The closest star to Earth other than the Sun is only about half as far away. But this star can't even be seen without a telescope! So what makes Sirius so much brighter?

Sirius looks brighter because it is very large and gives off a huge amount of energy. If you were to travel close to Sirius, you would find that it is twenty times brighter than the Sun. But because it is so far away, it doesn't look as bright as the Sun.

Stars come in different colors. These colors tell astronomers how hot each star is. There are red, orange, yellow, white, and blue-white stars. Red stars are the coolest. Yellow stars, such as the Sun, are hotter than red stars. The hottest stars, such as Sirius, are blue-white. Even though we talk about red stars as being "cool," they are still amazingly hot. At 2,250°C, they are hot enough to melt iron instantly!

THE EARTH
and Its Neighbors

by Donna Latham

Genre	Comprehension Skill	Text Features	Science Content
Nonfiction	Make Inferences	• Diagrams • Captions • Maps • Glossary	Earth and Space

Scott Foresman Science 5.17

PEARSON
Scott Foresman

scottforesman.com

ISBN 0-328-13965-3

What did you learn?

1. How does the movement of Earth in space create cycles we all experience?

2. Why does the Moon seem to change in appearance as it goes through different phases each month?

3. Why is a year on Earth different from a year on Pluto?

4. **Writing** in Science The Sun's extreme heat and power cause actions to take place in the solar system. Write about the Sun's effects on the solar system. Include examples and details from the book to support your answer.

5. **Make Inferences** Other than Earth, the Moon is the only object in the solar system that has been visited by humans. Why do you think that is?

Picture Credits
Every effort has been made to secure permission and provide appropriate credit for photographic material. The publisher deeply regrets any omission and pledges to correct errors called to its attention in subsequent editions.

Photo locators denoted as follows: Top (T), Center (C), Bottom (B), Left (L), Right (R), Background (Bkgd).

14 (B, BR) NASA, (C) Science Museum, London/DK Images; 17 (BR) Getty Images; 18 (CR) Tina Chambers/National Maritime Museum, London/DK Images; 21 (BL, C, BCL) NASA Image Exchange; 23 NASA.

Scott Foresman/Dorling Kindersley would also like to thank: 1 (BL, BR) NASA/DK Images; 2 (Bkgd) NASA/DK Images; 5 (C, TR) NASA/DK Images; 8 (BL) NASA/DK Images; 10 (CR) NASA/DK Images, (BL) NASA/Finley Holiday Films/DK Images; 11 (B) NASA/DK Images, (C) Jet Propulsion Lab (JPL)/DK Images; 12 (C) NASA/DK Images; 13 (CLA) NASA/DK Images, (CL) Jet Propulsion Lab (JPL)/DK Images; 15 (TL) NASA/DK Images, (CR) Jet Propulsion Lab (JPL)/DK Images; 18 (CL) NASA/DK Images.

Unless otherwise acknowledged, all photographs are the copyright © of Dorling Kindersley, a division of Pearson.

ISBN: 0-328-13965-3

Glossary

asteroid   a rocky object that orbits the Sun in the asteroid belt and is less than one thousand kilometers across

axis   the imaginary line on which Earth rotates, or spins

comet   an object made of ice and dirt that travels around the Sun in a long orbit

Moon phase   the shape of the lighted part of the Moon at a particular time

revolution   one orbit

rotation   one complete spin of an object on its axis

satellite   an object that orbits another object

solar system   the Sun and its satellites

space probe   a spacecraft that gathers data without having any people on board

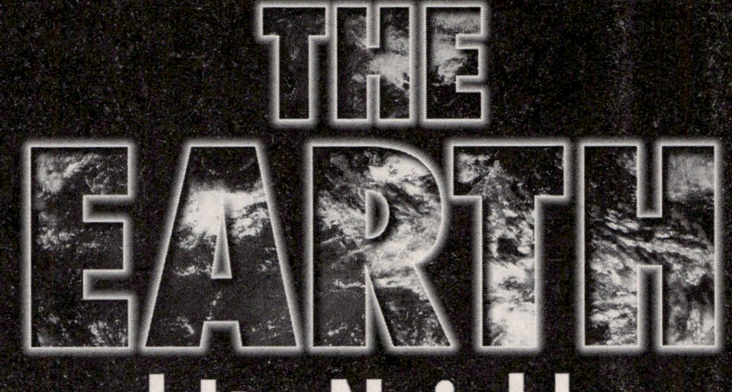

Galileo was the first scientist to study the planets with a telescope.

Close-up of Saturn's rings

Think about all you know about the solar system. You know that it is made up of the Sun and its satellites. You know that the Moon and other objects, such as meteors, comets, and asteroids, are part of the solar system too.

You are aware of the many changes that occur in your world, from the switch between day and night, to the seasons, to the phases of the Moon and the daily tides. You know that the movement of Earth through the solar system causes those changes. You've learned quite a bit. Galileo would be impressed!

The Moon and the Tides

Have you ever spent a day at the ocean? You may have noticed that the tide, or rise and fall of the water, changes throughout the day. Most places on Earth have two high tides and two low tides each day. Why?

The Moon is the main reason the tides change. Its gravity causes Earth's land, water, and atmosphere to bulge out toward the Moon. The water moves more easily than the land, so it bulges more. The water forms a tidal bulge, or big wave, which lags about an hour behind the movement of the Moon. In places where the water is bulging out, water levels rise, causing high tide. On other parts of Earth, water flows away, toward the bulge, causing low tide.

While the difference between high and low tide is only about two feet in the middle of the ocean, it can reach fifty feet at some places on the coast!

Into Orbit

In 1610, a scientist named Galileo first discovered Saturn's rings. He had built his own small telescope and became the first person to use one to observe the nighttime sky. Galileo didn't know what the rings were. His telescope was too weak to make them out clearly.

Through his observations of the Moon, he announced that its surface was pitted. Others had claimed that it was smooth. Galileo also discovered the four largest moons of the planet Jupiter.

Now, centuries later, we know a lot more about the Sun, Moon, and planets than Galileo did. Scientists have discovered that there are nine planets traveling around the Sun. They have taken close-up pictures of these planets and mapped their paths around the Sun. We have even sent people to walk on the Moon! What other discoveries have we made about the objects that are our neighbors in space? Let's find out!

How does the Earth move?

The Orbit of the Earth

You can't feel it, but right now, Earth is traveling through space. It's one of nine ball-shaped planets circling the Sun. Vital to our lives, the Sun is a star at the center of our solar system. The solar system is made up of the Sun and the nine planets that revolve around it.

Each of the planets travels around the Sun in its own path, at its own pace. An orbit is the path that a planet follows around the Sun. The planets share the same type of orbit. Each has an elliptical orbit. That means the orbit is shaped like an oval.

The planets don't travel around the Sun alone. They take their own orbiting moons with them. Many other smaller objects travel around the Sun too.

It takes Earth a year to complete a revolution around the Sun. It takes the Moon about twenty-eight days, or a month, to revolve around the Earth.

The Moon from Earth

Compare Galileo's drawings to these photos of the monthly phases of the Moon. How accurate were his drawings?

1. New Moon
When the Moon is new, you can hardly see it. At this phase, the Moon is passing between Earth and the Sun. The side hit by the Sun faces away from Earth. So we see the side that is in shadow.

2. Crescent Moon
A few days after the New Moon, a Crescent Moon appears. A crescent moon is shaped like a thin slice of watermelon.

3. First Quarter Moon
Around a week after the New Moon, you can spot a First Quarter Moon. Lit by the Sun, half of the Moon is visible.

4. Full Moon
About a week after the First Quarter and two weeks after the New Moon, the Full Moon makes its appearance. The Moon looks like a big, glowing ball.

You know that a year on Earth is 365 days, or twelve months, long. That's the time it takes Earth to travel around the Sun. The Earth's orbit is huge, so it takes a long time for Earth to get all the way around it. A **revolution** is one complete orbit. So Earth's revolution around the Sun takes a year.

What causes Earth and the other planets to orbit the Sun? It's the pull of gravity between the Sun and the planets. Gravity is a force that draws objects together, and larger objects have more gravity than small ones. The Sun is massive, so the pull of its gravity is very strong. In fact, the pull of the Sun's gravity is so strong that it controls the orbits of all nine planets, even though they are millions and millions of miles away.

People of the past tried to explain why the Moon looks different over the course of a month. Today, we understand that **moon phases,** or different shapes the Moon seems to have, are caused by the Sun. The Moon, Earth, and other bodies in the solar system get light only on the sides that face the Sun. So each seems to be lit on only one side. The lighted side of the Moon doesn't always face us, so at different times of the month we see different amounts of its lit surface. When we see the whole lit side, we call it a full moon. When the lit side is completely turned away, we call it a new moon. There are also many phases when we can see part of the lit side of the Moon.

Galileo made these drawings of the phases of the Moon in 1610.

Night and Day

What causes the change between day and night? It happens because as Earth travels around the Sun, it also spins like a top. As the planet spins, only part of it faces the Sun at a time. It is day on this part of Earth. As the planet spins and this part is turned away from the Sun, it becomes night.

Earth always spins in the same direction, around an imaginary line called an **axis.** This line runs right through the center of Earth. Earth's axis tilts sideways a bit, just as a top's sometimes does.

As the top spins on its axis, it tilts, or slants to the side.

Rise and shine! During your twenty-four-hour day, you probably experience some hours of daylight and some of darkness.

Footprint left behind by Neil Armstrong

Did you know that the Moon is the only place in the solar system, other than Earth, on which people have stood? On July 20, 1969, Neil Armstrong became the first person to actually set foot on the Moon. Because there is no air on the Moon to blow it away, his footprint is still there.

As the Moon orbits Earth, we can see only one side. This is called the "near side." This same side faces Earth at all times because of the Moon's rotation. Only astronauts have seen the other side of the Moon, called the "far side" or "dark side."

Some people once believed there was a man in the Moon. Without the telescopes we now use, they could only see the Moon with their eyes. Shadows and craters made it seem as if a "face" was looking back at them!

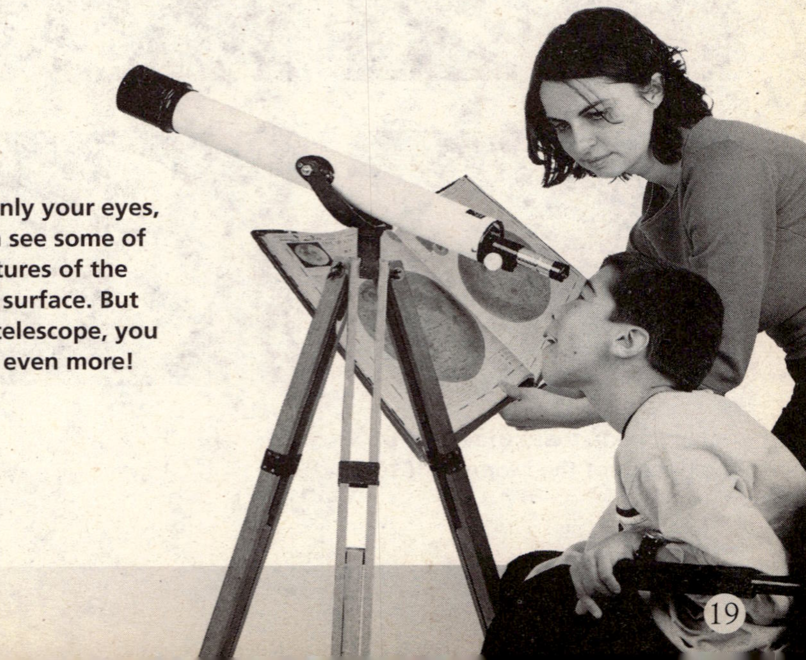

Using only your eyes, you can see some of the features of the Moon's surface. But with a telescope, you can see even more!

What do we know about the Moon?

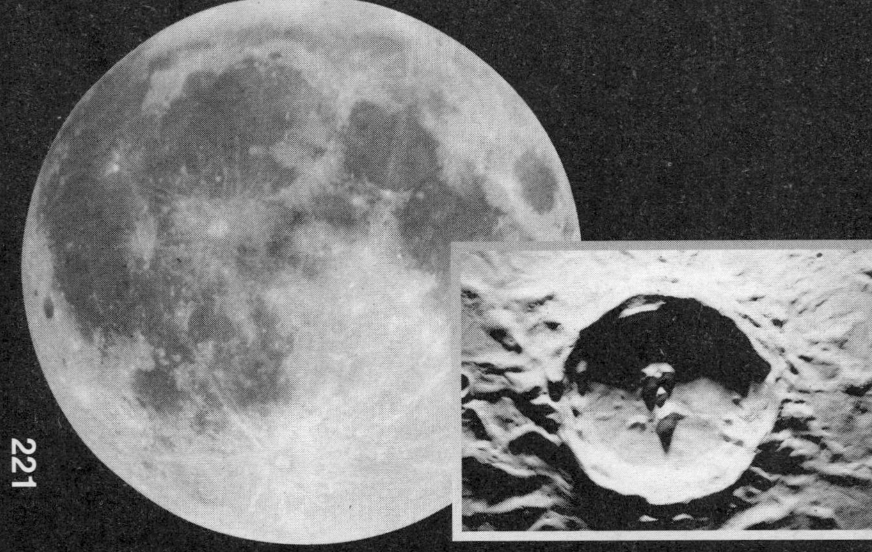

Like Earth and the planets, the Moon is ball-shaped.

Many rocks or comets from space have struck the Moon, leaving pits called craters.

Moving with Earth

At about 384,000 km away, the Moon is Earth's closest neighbor in the solar system. The Moon is Earth's only natural satellite. It is about one-fourth the size of Earth, and it has no air or water. The Moon does have some ice, which may have come from comets crashing into it.

One Day on Earth

A **rotation** is one whole spin of an object on its axis. It takes the Earth twenty-four hours to complete one rotation, so a day is twenty-four hours long. Earth's tilt causes the length of day and night to change. It changes all year long. Places closer to the poles experience more of a change than places near the equator.

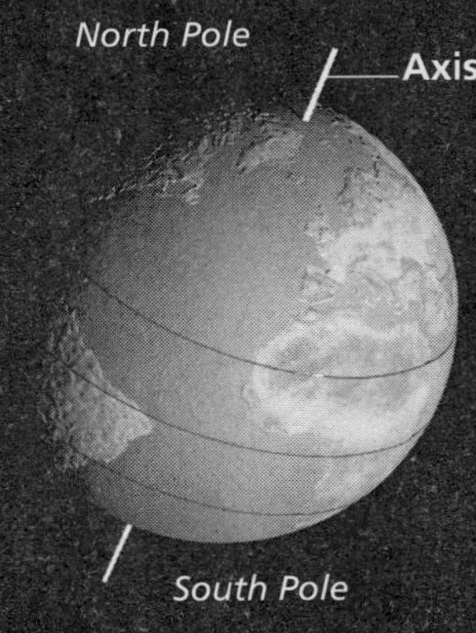

During some parts of the year, the Sun shines twenty-four hours a day at one pole, while the other has twenty-four hours of darkness.

The Temperature on Earth

When the Sun sets at night, temperatures drop. Since Earth spins swiftly on its axis, day follows night fairly quickly. So temperatures are mild enough for all life to exist. If the Earth spun more slowly, the long days would get very hot, and the long nights would get very cold.

Unlike some planets, Earth has a thick atmosphere. This blanket of air keeps Earth from getting too hot in the Sun's rays. It holds warmth near the Earth's surface. Some planets have no atmosphere. Their temperatures are too extreme for life. For example, the temperature on the sunny side of the Moon reaches hundreds of degrees, while the dark side is colder than any place on Earth.

The Pattern of the Seasons

Do you live in a place where there are four separate seasons? In some places, you might bundle up in a heavy coat during the winter, but wear shorts and flip-flops during the summer. What causes this pattern of changing temperatures?

As Earth moves around the Sun on its tilted axis, the tilt never changes. This means that sometimes the North Pole is tilted toward the Sun, and at other times the South Pole is. This makes the number of daylight hours change through the seasons, with more in the summer and fewer in the winter. It also changes the angle at which the Sun's rays hit Earth. Places that are tilted toward the Sun get more concentrated rays, which make temperatures warmer. Places tilted away from the Sun get more spread-out rays, which don't raise temperatures as much.

Asteroids and Meteoroids

Asteroids also revolve around the Sun. An asteroid is a rocky mass that can range from the size of a tiny pebble to a width of several hundred kilometers. Some large asteroids even have smaller asteroids orbiting them.

Most asteroids in our solar system travel in a belt between Mars and Jupiter. Asteroids sometimes hit the inner planets, but this is very rare. Jupiter's powerful gravity usually holds asteroids in the asteroid belt.

A meteoroid is a small asteroid. A meteor is a meteoroid that hits Earth's atmosphere. Meteors usually burn up in the atmosphere, but sometimes they make it through to strike the ground. These are called meteorites. One hit this site in Arizona thousands of years ago. The crater, or large, bowl-shaped hole, is 1,275 meters wide and 175 meters deep. Have you ever heard of a meteor shower? They happen when Earth passes through the orbit of a comet.

Many asteroids have unusual shapes. Some look like potatoes, noses, and even dogs.

Arizona's Meteor Crater

Comets and Asteroids

Only the largest comets can be seen without a telescope. Notice the comet's fuzzy tail.

Comets

Planets are not the only things orbiting the Sun! Comets orbit it too. A **comet** is a frozen mass of different types of ice and dust. The hard center of a comet is called the nucleus. Around the nucleus is a coma, or giant cloud of dust and gases. A comet may also have one or more tails. Tails and comas form only when the comet gets close to the Sun. There, the Sun melts the nucleus, which turns into gas. Then the comet gets the fuzzy look that we often associate with it.

Much smaller than planets, most comets come from areas beyond Pluto. You know that Pluto is the planet farthest from the Sun in our solar system, so comets travel a long distance. They travel in very stretched out, elliptical paths. Most comets are too small to be seen without a telescope.

Seasons on Earth

As Earth travels in its elliptical orbit, its distance from the Sun changes. You might think that this has something to do with the change in seasons, but it does not. Actually, Earth is closest to the Sun in January, when the Northern Hemisphere experiences winter. Earth's tilt is the real cause of the changing seasons.

This diagram shows the seasons in the northern half of the world. The southern half has the opposite seasons. For example, in June, July, and August, when it is summer in the United States, it is winter in Australia. Find the axis in each image of Earth. Notice that each is exactly the same.

The Solar System

The Paths That Planets Follow

A **satellite** is an object in orbit around another object. As you know, our solar system is made up of the Sun and its satellites. All the planets are huge. They are extremely far away from one another, so scientists measure their distances in astronomical units, or AUs. One AU equals the distance from Earth to the Sun, about 150 million kilometers.

The four planets closest to the Sun are Mercury, Venus, Earth, and Mars. They are made up mostly of rock and iron. Some of these planets have gases around them.

Venus has a thick layer of poisonous gases that make it impossible for you to breathe there.

Voyager 2

In 1986, *Voyager 2* visited Uranus, and in 1989 it visited Neptune. Through photos it sent back to Earth, we have discovered rings around all the gas giants, as well as several new moons. In addition, strong lightning storms were discovered on Jupiter.

The many spacecraft that have visited Mars have helped us learn that it has polar ice caps made of frozen water and frozen carbon dioxide. They have also sent back information about Mars' huge volcanoes.

224

Visiting the Planets

If you could visit any planet in the solar system, which one would you choose? Although people may not be able to travel to all the planets, **space probes** have allowed us to explore them. Space probes are spacecraft that gather data without any people on board. They are equipped with special instruments and cameras. Since the 1970s, the United States has sent space probes to collect data from the planets. Here are some observations the probes have made.

Mariner 10 **first photographed Mercury in 1974.**

In 2004, two rovers, *Spirit* and *Opportunity*, landed on two separate areas of Mars.

Opportunity

Farthest from the Sun are Jupiter, Saturn, Uranus, Neptune, and Pluto. Jupiter is the largest planet in the solar system, and Pluto is the smallest. Except for Pluto, these planets are all gas giants. Gas giants are huge planets that are made up of layers of gas. A gas giant does not have a solid surface as Earth does. Scientists think that they may have solid cores. As you can see, gas giants are much larger than Earth. All of the gas giants have rings. Most of the rings are very faint and cannot be seen in this illustration.

Did you know that planets do not give off their own light? When we see them in the sky, it is because of the light they reflect from the Sun.

The length of a year is different on each planet. The farther away from the Sun, the greater the time a planet takes to complete an orbit. So planets farther from the Sun have longer years.

Time taken to orbit the Sun

Planet	Year
Mercury	88 Earth days
Venus	225 Earth days
Earth	365.26 Earth days (1 Earth year)
Mars	687 Earth days
Jupiter	12 Earth years
Saturn	29.5 Earth years
Uranus	84 Earth years
Neptune	164.5 Earth years
Pluto	248.5 Earth years

Planet Fact File

Let's compare the planets. Some are solid and rocky, and others are huge balls of gas. Below is a fact file of the planets, starting with Mercury, which is the planet closest to the Sun.

Mercury
With its craters and rocky surface, Mercury is much like Earth's moon. This hot, dry, and airless planet moves very quickly around the Sun.

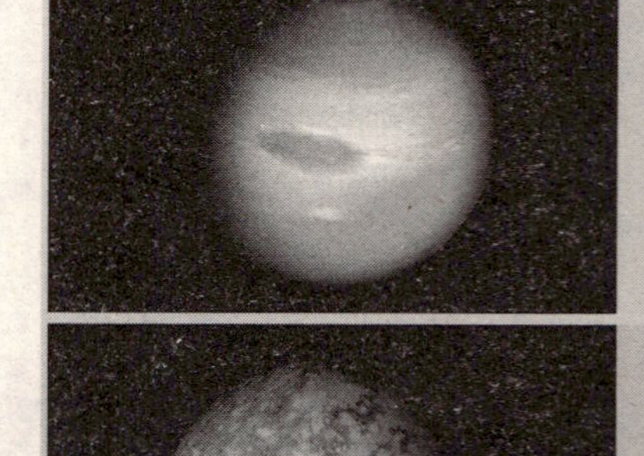

Venus
Venus is so close to Earth in size that it's often called Earth's twin. Covered by a thick layer of clouds that trap the Sun's heat, Venus is the brightest planet in the sky.

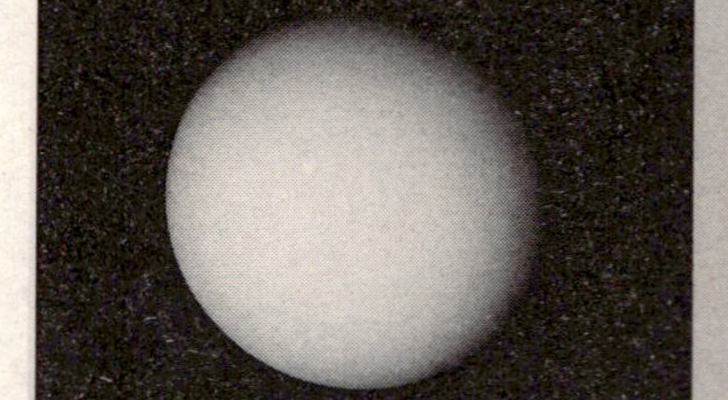

Earth
Solid and rocky, Earth has a surface that is nearly three-fourths water and ice. A thin blanket of air surrounds the entire planet.

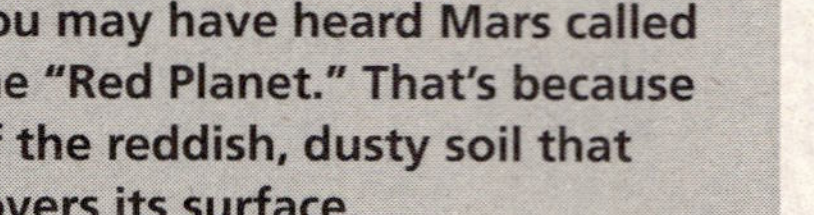

Mars
You may have heard Mars called the "Red Planet." That's because of the reddish, dusty soil that covers its surface.

Jupiter
The largest planet, Jupiter is a huge ball of gas and liquid. Scientists think Jupiter may also have a rocky core. Jupiter has faint rings.

Saturn
Saturn is a gas planet that is best known for its rings. Although all gas planets have rings made of dust, chunks of rock, and ice, Saturn has the most.

Uranus
Methane gas creates the blue-green color of this planet. Its winds give it bands of clouds. Uranus also has rings. The rings are not as bright as Saturn's.

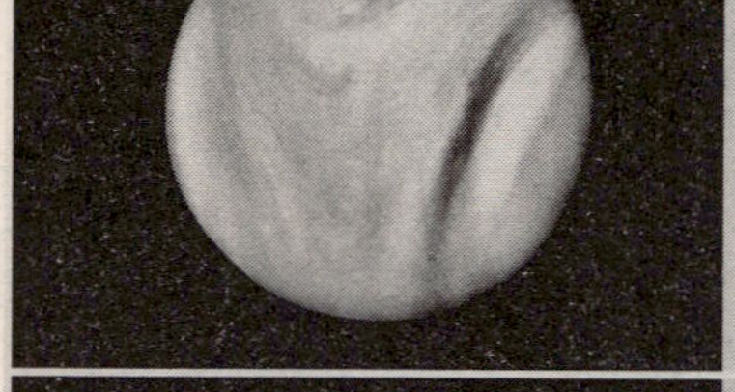

Neptune
Neptune's atmosphere has huge storms. They look like dark spots when viewed through a telescope. Neptune also has rings. They are not easy to see.

Pluto
Pluto is the smallest and coldest planet in the solar system. It is usually the farthest planet from the Sun, but for part of its orbit it comes closer to the Sun than Neptune.

Technology Today

by Colin Kong

227

Genre	Comprehension Skill	Text Features	Science Content
Nonfiction	Sequence	• Captions • Labels • Diagrams • Glossary	Technology

Scott Foresman Science 5.18

PEARSON
Scott Foresman

scottforesman.com

ISBN 0-328-13968-8

90000

9 780328 139682

What did you learn?

1. How did the invention of the power loom change how people lived and worked?

2. How have advances in transportation technology helped people?

3. How is computer technology used in science?

4. **Writing** in Science The gasoline engine has brought many positive changes to society, but it can also cause many problems. Write to explain some ways the gasoline engine has brought positive changes to society and some ways that it has caused problems. Include details from the book to support your answer.

5. **Sequence** What was the sequence of events in space exploration that led up to the first Moon landing in 1969?

Picture Credits
Every effort has been made to secure permission and provide appropriate credit for photographic material. The publisher deeply regrets any omission and pledges to correct errors called to its attention in subsequent editions.

Photo locators denoted as follows: Top (T), Center (C), Bottom (B), Left (L), Right (R), Background (Bkgd).

2 Corbis; 3 (T) Schenectady Museum/Hall of Electrical History Foundation/Corbis; 4 (BR) Science Museum, London/DK Images; 6 Science Museum, London/DK Images; 9 Paul A. Souders/Corbis; 10 Science Museum, London/DK Images; 11 Bettmann/Corbis; 12 Getty Images; 13 David Sailors/Corbis; 14 Bettmann/Corbis; 18 SciMAT/Photo Researchers, Inc.; 19 NASA; 20 (TL) ITAR-TASS/Sovfoto/Eastfoto, (BR) NASA; 21 NASA Image Exchange; 23 Marshall Space Flight Center/NASA.

Scott Foresman/Dorling Kindersley would also like to thank: 7 (TR) Booth Cotton Mills Museum/DK Images; 8 National Motor Museum, Beaulieu/DK Images.

Unless otherwise acknowledged, all photographs are the copyright © of Dorling Kindersley, a division of Pearson.

ISBN: 0-328-13968-8

Technology Today

by Colin Kong

Glossary

assembly line	a row of workers or machines that a product moves along as parts are added
inventor	a person who uses technology to develop a new device, process, or solution to a problem
manufacturing	the production of goods on a large scale
microchip	a small part of a computer that contains microscopic circuits
space station	a place where people can live and work in space for long periods of time
technology	the use of scientific knowledge for a purpose
World Wide Web	a system for finding information through a network of computers

Technology

Technology is the use of scientific knowledge for a purpose. Technology helps people do things more easily, quickly, and efficiently. When we think of technology we often picture new inventions or tools. But there is much more to technology!

George Washington Carver discovered or improved many products, including bleach, buttermilk, chili sauce, ink, instant coffee, mayonnaise, shaving cream, and shoe polish.

Solar panels supply power for all the equipment on the station. The panels turn energy from sunlight into electrical energy. Batteries store the power for use when the station is in Earth's shadow.

The ISS crew lives in the service module.

The control module contains computers to control the station. It also has rockets to keep the station in orbit.

The Space Station

Beginning in 1981, NASA concentrated on sending astronauts to space in the space shuttle. But space shuttle trips are usually too short for many experiments and research. A space station was needed so that people could stay in space for long periods of time. A space station is a place where people can live and work in space. With a space station, people can now run experiments for months or even years!

Sixteen countries have agreed to build the International Space Station (ISS). The ISS is currently being put together piece by piece in space. New sections, or modules, continue to be added to the station all the time. The first component was the control module called *Zarya.* It was built by Russia. Next was the U.S. module called *Unity.* Once finished, the space station will be about the size of a football field. It will have a mass of more than 450,000 kilograms.

Space shuttles can dock at this end of the station.

This photo was taken in 2002, before the station was completed. The ISS will eventually have six modules to hold laboratories where astronauts can work and do research.

Thomas Edison had a team to help him work on new ideas.

An **inventor** is a person who uses technology to develop a new device, process, or solution to a problem. George Washington Carver was a famous inventor who found more than three hundred uses for peanuts and hundreds more uses for soybeans, pecans, and sweet potatoes. Carver worked alone, but other inventors, such as Thomas Edison, had teams of people to help them develop new inventions.

Technology can be beneficial in many ways. For example, the discovery of penicillin and invention of antibiotics have helped heal many people from diseases. But technology can also have some negative effects. Many machines and processes pollute our air, water, and soil. People must think about possible negative effects of new inventions.

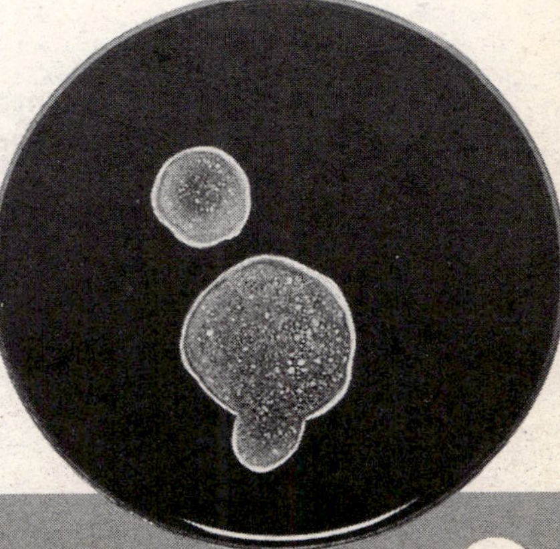

Penicillin was discovered by a British doctor named Alexander Fleming in 1929.

Technology at Home

If you look around your house, you will see how technology has completely changed the way we live. Not all technology in the home is new. The light bulb is an invention that is more than one hundred years old. Thousands of years ago, houses themselves were new technology!

We use technology for almost everything around the house. Light and electricity are important in our everyday lives. Talking on the telephone to communicate with others is also a common use of technology.

Technology makes it easy and more convenient to do many things at home. When we want to cook food, we can simply turn a knob on the stove or push a button on the microwave. In the past, cooking involved gathering wood and starting a fire. We no longer need to wash our clothes by hand and then let them dry. Washers and dryers do it for us.

The light bulb was invented more than one hundred years ago.

The Soviets landed a space probe on the Moon's surface in 1959. It was named *Luna 2*. In 1961 Soviet cosmonaut Yuri Gagarin became the first person in space. American astronaut Alan Shepard, Jr., followed soon after. A major goal in the Space Race was to send people to the Moon. This was accomplished in 1969 when American astronauts Neil Armstrong and Buzz Aldrin landed on the Moon.

During the Space Race, scientists and government leaders from both countries were under great pressure to meet some tough deadlines. They developed and used many new space technologies in a very short period of time. Today the Soviet Union no longer exists. It was divided up into several smaller countries in 1991.

The space shuttle, launched in 1981, was the first reusable spaceship.

Technology in Space
The Space Race

Yuri Gagarin was the first human in space.

We have always been curious about what is in space, beyond our planet. This curiosity has led to our desire for space exploration. Humans first traveled into space in the 1960s.

After World War II, there were strong political differences between the United States and the Soviet Union. The two countries competed to make discoveries in space.

This heated competition was called the Space Race. It began in 1957 when the Soviet Union launched *Sputnik 1*, the first satellite to orbit Earth. Later that year, the Soviet Union also sent a dog named Laika into space. In 1958 the United States successfully launched their own satellite called *Explorer 1*. The National Aeronautics and Space Administration, known as NASA, was also formed in the United States that year.

In 1969 Neil Armstrong became the first person to set foot on the Moon.

What modern technology can you see in this photo?

How we store food has been improved by technology. At one time, there was no way to keep food fresh. It had to be eaten right away, or it would spoil. Today, refrigerators and freezers allow us to keep food for long periods of time. Even plastic storage containers and plastic wrap help us store our food. They are inexpensive technologies.

Technology is also used for entertainment purposes. Before the late 1800s, if you wanted to hear music, you had to go to a concert or play an instrument yourself. The same was true for other forms of entertainment, such as plays or sporting events. Today, we listen to music on the radio and on compact discs. We can watch performances and sports from all over the world on TV.

Technology in Our Jobs

Technology does not only change the way we live, but it also changes the way we work. When this happens, an entire society can change!

An example of how technology has completely changed society is through manufacturing. **Manufacturing** is the production of goods on a very large scale. Think about the clothes you wear. How were they made?

Until the early 1800s most people made their own clothes. Making clothes involved gathering cotton or wool, spinning it into threads, and weaving the threads into cloth. The cloth was then sewn together to make clothes. The process was very slow because it was done almost entirely by hand.

Robots are used to perform tasks that humans cannot do, such as exploring the harsh surface of Mars.

Today many devices such as cellular phones and digital cameras use computers. People in business can talk on their phones wherever they go. Digital cameras use microchips to capture and store images. There is no need for film anymore.

Computers are also used to control different machines. These machines are useful when very precise movements are needed. They are also important when a task is too dangerous for a person to do. That is why scientists sent a robot to collect samples from the planet Mars. The environment on Mars is so harsh that humans cannot survive there, but a robot can.

Computers for Science and Business

Many tasks that took weeks or months on early computers now take only a few seconds. However, some tasks still take computers a long time to accomplish. For these tasks, people may use powerful supercomputers or computer networks.

The invention of the computer has led to the development of other new technologies. Different types of microscopes, telescopes, telephones, and cameras use computers. Scientists use a scanning electron microscope to magnify objects up to 200,000 times. This would not be possible without computers. Some new telescopes use computers to help them focus with great accuracy on objects in the sky.

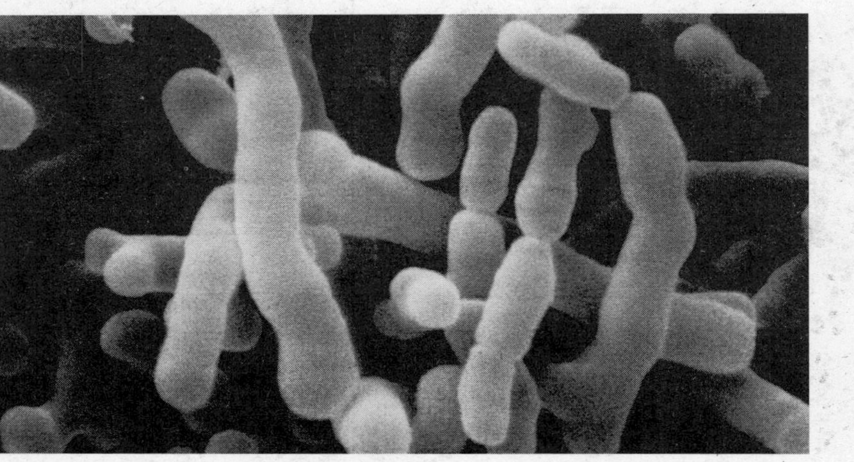

This image was made with a scanning electron microscope. These microscopes use a beam of electrons to study the surface of an object.

In 1785 Edmund Cartwright invented a machine called the power loom. It could weave cloth automatically. Power looms were set up in factories and powered by moving water from rivers. The factories produced cloth that was cheap enough for most people to buy, so they no longer had to weave it themselves. Soon, young women were moving away from their homes in the country to work in factory towns. The power loom transformed society, changing the way people lived and worked.

The invention of the power loom changed the way people lived and worked.

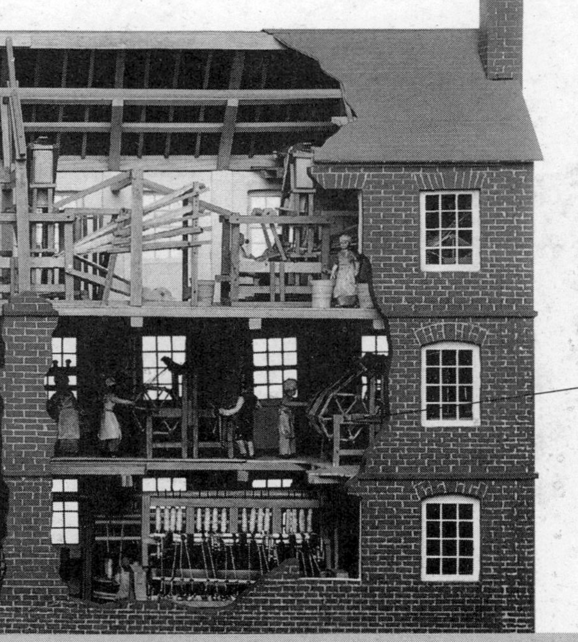

Factories such as this one used power looms to produce large amounts of cloth.

The car is the most common form of transportation in the United States. But one hundred years ago, cars were so expensive that only the very rich could afford them. In the early 1900s, cars were built one at a time. A group of workers would build just one car until it was finished. The process was slow and expensive.

Henry Ford solved the problem by perfecting the assembly line. In an **assembly line,** a product moves through the factory while workers add parts to it. Each worker has only one job, which can be performed very quickly. Ford's assembly line used a moving conveyor belt to bring the car from one group of workers to the next.

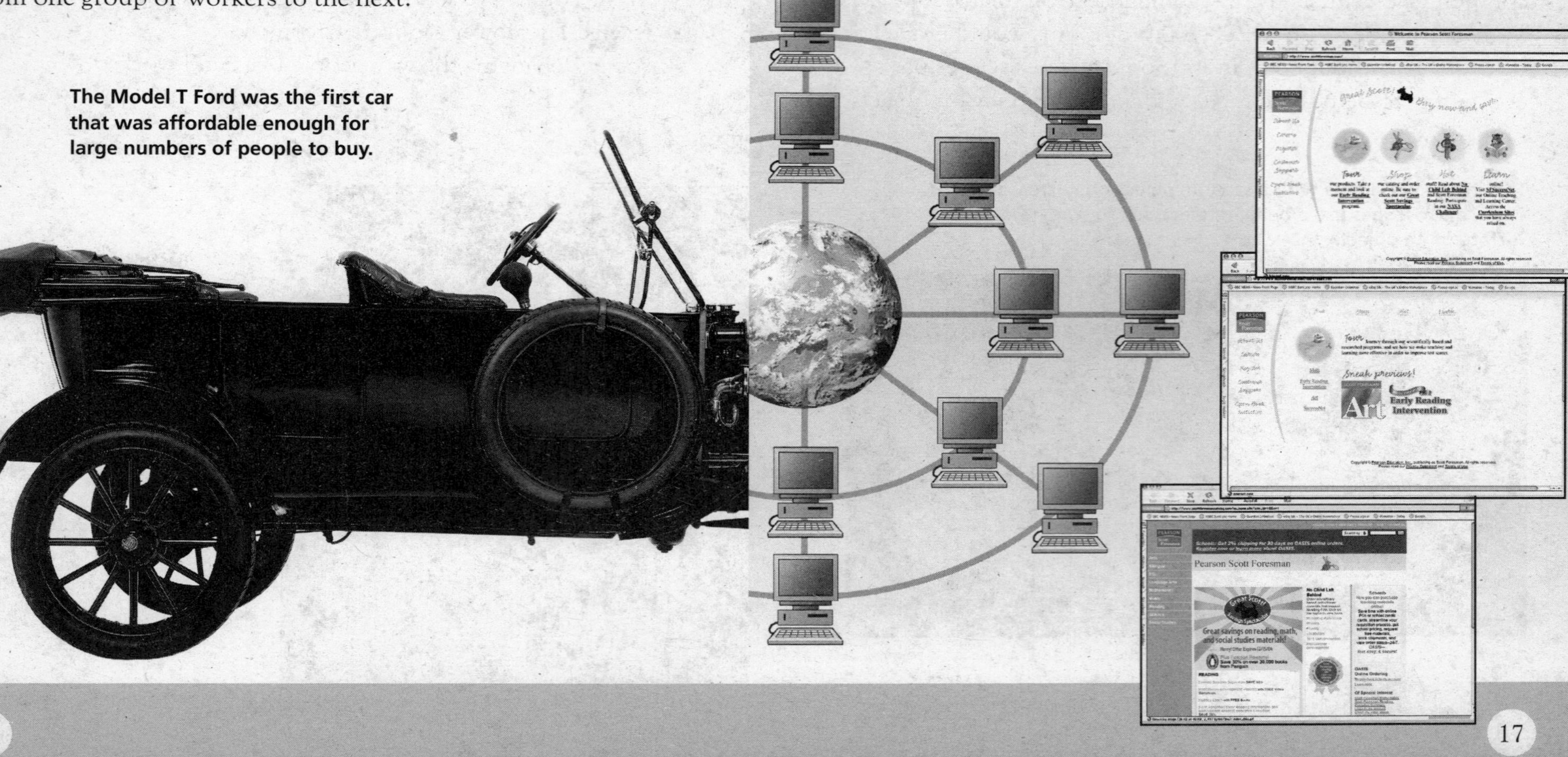

The Model T Ford was the first car that was affordable enough for large numbers of people to buy.

Although the World Wide Web is a valuable tool for learning and communicating, it can cause some problems. For example, incorrect information can spread very quickly over the Web. The Web also makes it easy to collect information about other people. Criminals have found out how to commit identity theft using information from the Web. Identity theft is when somebody uses another person's personal information.

236

In the 1980s computer technology went through another great change. A British computer scientist wanted to make it easy to communicate with other scientists who were far away. The result was the World Wide Web. The **World Wide Web** is a network of computers. This network was developed for the European Organization for Nuclear Research. The first version of the Web was finished in 1990. The Web can be used to communicate with people all over the world. It can also be used to share and get information on almost any topic.

People can use the Web to communicate with others all around the world.

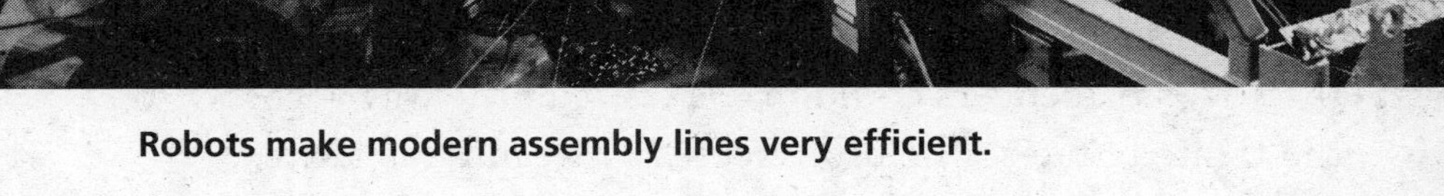

Robots make modern assembly lines very efficient.

This new process was much faster and less expensive than the old way of building cars. This made it affordable for more people to buy cars, changing the way Americans lived. For the first time, millions of people could go wherever they wanted, whenever they wanted.

Many modern assembly lines don't need a lot of people to operate them. Robots and machines are often used to build cars because it is cheaper. Machines do their tasks quickly and accurately. A negative result of using robots and machines on an assembly line is that it eliminates many people's jobs.

Technology and Transportation

Before the 1700s, there were only a few ways for people to get around. They could walk or ride an animal on land, or they could sail or row on water. Then things began to change.

A man named James Watt perfected the first practical steam engine in 1769. A steam engine turns the energy from burning fuel into movement that can be used to do work. Watt's engine was first used to pump water, but soon people were using steam engines for transportation. In 1804 a steam-powered train carried seventy people and a load of iron. By the 1870s passengers could take a train all the way across the United States. The first successful steamboat started carrying passengers in 1807. By the late 1800s steamships were carrying passengers and cargo around the world.

Although this computer is small enough to fit on a desk, it is many times more powerful than UNIVAC.

A model of Watt's steam engine

The biggest problem with these early computers was that they were impractical. They were too large and too expensive. Only big companies could afford them. Manufacturers knew they had to make a smaller, faster, and cheaper computer that more people could use.

One of the most important advances in computer technology was the invention of the microchip. A **microchip** is a small part of a computer that contains microscopic circuits. Microchip technology made it possible for computers to process information very quickly. It also made the computer much smaller and less expensive.

Computers and Society

History of Electronic Computers

For hundreds of years, people tried to build mechanical calculating machines. Electronic computer technology first began in the 1930s and 1940s. Early computers were so large that one computer filled up an entire room. Each one weighed thousands of pounds. Despite their huge size, these computers weren't nearly as powerful as one of today's common desktop computers. Even though early computers were very different from what we see today, they still used the same basic steps as modern computers to solve mathematical problems. The steps are input, processing, output, and feedback.

UNIVAC (Universal Automatic Computer) was built in 1951. It weighed eight tons!

Orville and Wilbur Wright designed, built, and flew the first successful airplane in 1903.

The next major advance in technology was the use of the gasoline engine. Gas engines provided reliable power for cars. In 1903 the first airplane was flown. The flight was made possible by the gas engine, which was the first engine light enough for use on a plane. Eventually, large commercial airplanes were developed to carry hundreds of people. Voyages that used to take weeks on ships now take only hours in airplanes.

Electric motors propel our subway trains and some cars. Electric motors have an advantage over gas engines, because they do not produce pollution. Magnetic force technology may be the next advance in transportation. Scientists have developed high-speed trains that can travel more than 250 miles per hour. These trains are powered by magnetic and electric energy.

Problems from Technology

The automobile has given people the freedom to travel almost anywhere, whenever they want. However, gasoline-powered vehicles have also created new problems for society. In busy cities today there are many cars on the road. This means there are many traffic jams and more car accidents. People can spend a lot of time in a car traveling from one location to another. With so many cars in use, towns are pressured to build even more roads and highways. In the end, this takes away the natural habitats of animals. Some ways to decrease overcrowded roads are to walk or ride a bicycle instead of driving a car. You can also carpool or take public transportation, such as the bus or subway.

Gasoline engines in cars cause air pollution and smog.

Traffic jams are a common problem in busy cities.

Pollution from gasoline engines is also a problem. When gasoline is burned, carbon monoxide gas is released into the air, which can cause smog to form over cities. Besides air pollution, planes and cars also create a lot of noise pollution. Some cars are now designed to run on electricity or other fuels in order to decrease pollution. Both planes and cars are also being designed to run more quietly.

Most modern cars, buses, trains, and airplanes run on fuels made from oil. Oil will eventually run out. Society will run into great problems when this happens. Also, the process of transporting crude oil is complicated. Sometimes there are accidents in transporting the material, which leads to major oil spills in the ocean. These oil spills can kill a lot of fish and other marine life. Having more cars run on electricity or a different fuel may reduce these problems.